AN INTRODUCTION
TO THE
LEGAL SYSTEM

JAY A. SIGLER

Associate Professor of Political Science
Rutgers · The State University

1968

THE DORSEY PRESS, Homewood, Illinois

IRWIN-DORSEY LIMITED, Nobleton, Ontario

Library of Congress Catalog Card No. 68–30857
Printed in the United States of America

THE DORSEY SERIES IN POLITICAL SCIENCE

EDITOR NORTON E. LONG *Brandeis University*

A prefatory statement

IN MANY RESPECTS this book represents the fruit of a misspent youth. When I was in law school, although fascinated by that challenging subject, I felt something was missing. In graduate school I thought that the public law courses were somehow unreal. Both were worthy enterprises, but both were unsatisfying. This book is intended to satisfy myself and help others to do the same for themselves.

The public law area is one which is in deep academic trouble. It is misunderstood by many sociologists, who haven't the time to delve into its mysteries. Political scientists have begun to desert the field from which that discipline began. Clearly, a rescue operation is in order, because an understanding of legal processes is central to the problems of social control and of authoritative decision making, to which both sociologists and political scientists are profoundly committed.

A number of fine books already exist which describe some aspects of the legal system. These books have been influential in the thinking that led to this latest effort. However, the scope of this work in reference to the American system is probably broader than that of any other book, and its underlying methodology is distinctly different.

The pursuit of methodology is interesting in itself, for it is concerned with the discovery of the best way to examine a topic. Indeed, there are exciting new methods of studying the legal system which advanced students will want to explore. The author is indebted to pioneers like Glendon Schubert, Vic Rosenblum, C. Herman Pritchett, John Schmidhauser, Stuart Nagel, Fred Kort, and numerous others, whose writings illuminate the field. They have

v

labored to forge new methods by which we may all see the law more plainly.

However, this work is not primarily methodological in outlook. The problem was to construct a plan by which the numerous pieces of the puzzle could be made to fall into place. Thus, a fairly fresh perspective was adopted. It is not contended that this is the only or the best way to perceive the legal system, but it is clear, direct, and palpable. The construction of mathematical formulas, flow charts, probability tables, and the like are quite consistent with the approach adopted here, but they are largely avoided, whenever possible, for reasons of clarity.

If in the course of writing some errors appear, one can only admit them and remind the perceptive of the nature of our temporal life. These errors are not the fault of the good people who lent their assistance. They are not the fault of my helpful wife, Margaret; my assistant, Miss Janet Williams; my other assistant, Mrs. Eve Henry; my chairman, Dr. Harry H. Shapiro; Assistant Dean Berjooey Haigazian; Pat Coyle; nor of all those critical students who raised their hands in incredulity and disbelief at strategic moments. I cast about for objects of blame and find none.

This book is only a preliminary word on the subject. It is frankly exploratory. It is intended as a guide to the uninitiated and a stimulant to the old veterans. If it is successful at all, it will make the curious wish to pursue further research in order to fill in the gaps and test the concepts presented.

June, 1968   JAY A. SIGLER

Table of contents

Introduction

IT IS HOPED that this text will enable the reader to perceive the judicial process as just one variety of social experience, though surely among the most formal known to men. Beneath the trappings, the robes, the technical papers, and the elaborate terminology is another human procedure for building order out of a welter of facts and conflicting values. Emphasis will be placed upon the special aspects of legal problem resolution which make that behavior different from most human activities. Nonetheless, the essential situations are the same as those found whenever men come together in a disagreeing frame of mind, except that institutions replace force and tradition supplants naked selfish demands.

For the purposes of easy comprehension and ready appreciation of the complex factors involved in the judicial process, a cybernetic analogy has been adopted. Although not entirely original, this technique allows for a comprehensive overview of the problems of legal behavior. The definitions used here and the scope of the survey are unusual and, though arbitrary, will be found useful throughout the text. In employing a cybernetic analogy, it is not intended that judges or courts be perceived as mere machines. Instead, the analogy serves to relate judges and courts to the total social process of which they are a part and in which they play unique and personalized roles.

As a first cybernetic assumption, the term "system" will be found useful. By using this term, what is meant is "a system of communication . . . that has dynamics in which circular processes of a feedback nature play an important part."[1] Originally, the term was applied to the study of a

---

[1] Norbert Wiener, *Cybernetics* (2d ed.; New York: John Wiley & Sons, Inc., 1961), p. 24

1

mechanical-electrical device, but it has been extended to many social phenomena. A "system," then, is a self-contained unit of analysis, whose components are linked by interconnecting processes of communications. Law may be perceived as a system including litigants, courts, lawyers, judges, juries, and law professors. All of these elements and more contribute to the total law process by communicating with each other. The law system is part of the larger political system, but it has an internal communication process which differs from the practices of the political system in many distinctive ways. Law is not just part of the total process of politics. It is an internally developed system which is best analyzed by temporarily removing it from other aspects of social life.[2]

The family is one type of social system, the church another, and the political party a third. Each system is linked in the system called society, which is the largest system in human experience. The boundaries of the social system usually coincide with the political boundaries of the political system.

The terms "input" and "output," which will be used with great frequency, may seem self-explanatory. They are the motive forces of the regulating process. Input and output refer to data or information transferred from outside the system, as well as that generated from within the system. By using the concepts of input and output we may deal more directly with the problem of relating the environment to the system, discriminating among the enormous number of possible influences, and isolate those few which are definitely related to the system. Because of this we need not consider the climate, temperature, geography, topography,

---

[2] Glendon Schubert, *Judicial Policy-Making* (Chicago: Scott, Foresman & Co., 1965), pp. 3–4, adopts a different definition of "system," as a "structure or pattern of interaction among the actors." This approach, while consistent with the systems analysis approach sometimes found in other fields of political science, suffers from vagueness which makes the boundaries of the legal system very difficult to draw. Indeed, the number of variables introduced by Schubert is greater than those required by a stricter definition.

biology, or chemistry of the environment of the legal system. They are not sufficiently relevant to be considered "inputs."

The "outputs" of one system may become the "inputs" of another. In this way, two or more systems are often linked together. The legal and social systems are certainly joined in this way. If a court decides that Mr. Jones owes Mr. Brown one thousand dollars, that decision may force a change in the relationship between the two men. A lifelong enmity may ensue. In our terms, the legal output became a social input with a limited social effect.

There are different qualities and intensities of inputs and outputs. Some are more significant than others, and segregating the more from the less important ones is the task of a careful analyst. More than that, one type of input may be more significant in a single situation than it may be in a later situation. Consequently, the input and output factors isolated here will be generalized in order to cover the normal or typical situation. The relative importance of various inputs and outputs will be indicated, but they are not intended to be absolute or final.

Another valuable concept is "feedback." This is the use of a portion of a machine or a system to control the input. The fresh input may add to or subtract from the total input. Negative feedback is the type which is of greatest relevance to politics. This is a variety of feedback which causes a self-correction of the system, like a thermostat. The American Supreme Court, it will be suggested, operates as a system which is self-regulating and receives, as an input, the feedback elements of a society which had been affected by the outputs of its efforts.

The "conversion process" is a vital part of the analysis of a system. The way in which inputs are turned into outputs must be understood or else the decision-making methods will remain a mystery. Conversion of inputs into outputs takes place in all systems, although not in the same way. By examining the conversion process we can see the living core of a system. In the legal system the conversion process is more obvious and more readily seen than in many other systems. The trial and the appeal are largely public events and are highly suitable for systems analysis.

One final essential concept is that of "homeostasis." This process, which is a variety of feedback, is devoted to the self-preservation of an organism. Within an organism the inner thermostats provide adequate blood pressure and body temperature to maintain the delicate balance which supports life. Homeostasis, then, is an unconscious, essential, life-sustaining process which protects the organism from destruction. Of course, the legal system is not an organism, but it can be perceived as a homeostatic factor in American society, encouraging social balance and helping to settle socially disruptive problems. The legal system is not ordinarily progressive, but tends to be conservative, in the sense that its main purpose is to preserve order in the social system.

Finally, what is proposed here is a logical framework for analysis of legal policy making.[3] It is a way of ordering experience, not a final version of legal reality. Used with care, good analysis should both enlighten and clarify.

---

[3] A somewhat similar logical analysis to that adopted here is Layman E. Allen and Mary Ellen Caldwell, "Modern Logic and Judicial Decision-Making: A Sketch of One View," *Law and Contemporary Problems*, Vol. 28 (Winter, 1963), p. 213. Those interested in the methodological problems involved in this approach should read A. Smitis, "The Problem of Legal Logic," *Ratio*, Vol. 3 (1960), p. 60, and current issues of the journal: *Modern Uses of Logic in Law* /M.U.L.L./, especially Vol. 3 (1960), pp. 60–66. The Allen-Caldwell analysis is more restricted than that used in this text. A more philosophical study of considerable heuristic value is Charles D. Raab, "Suggestions for a Cybernetic Approach to Sociological Jurisprudence," *Journal of Legal Education*, Vol. 17 (1965), pp. 397–411. For a treatment of the concepts of "support" and "demand" as variant types of input, see David Easton, *A Systems Analysis of Political Life* (New York: John Wiley & Sons, Inc., 1965). It should be noted that the name of the journal M.U.L.L. has been changed to *Jurimetrics Journal*.

I

Law as a social process

LAW MAY BE regarded as one type of social authority, perhaps the most refined and formal type. All social relations are marked by conditions of influence and control. In the family the child often models himself after the parental example. The parents are regarded by the child and by outsiders as possessed of the legitimate authority to influence and control the child. However, since families are integrated into larger social units such as the church and the school, differing authority situations are experienced by the child. Sometimes these new demands and commands may run counter to the authority pattern previously learned by the child. In fact, it is inevitable that conflicting lines of authority will arise, because of the competing values of various social institutions.

Within the bosom of the family, rules of behavior of a lawlike kind may be easily seen. The command that the child wash his face may be enforced by disciplinary sanctions, such as a spanking following noncompliance with the rule. If the rules are enforced with consistency and without special exceptions, the similarity to law expands. The absence of a court or a jury does not detract from the serious aspects of the proceeding.

However, the extremely personalized processes found in the family lack the qualities of generality and persistence. The rules of Mr. Jones's family are not applicable in the Brown household, a fact rapidly known to the children of both houses. Besides, the rules will change as all of the participants in the system grow older, marry, depart, or die. Although this system cannot be called law because of its casual features, its flux, and informality, it is the source of much of the psychological predisposition toward law found later among adults. It is also a prime source of deviant, law-breaking behavior.

Primitive society

Considerable debate rages among anthropologists as to the point at which "law" may be said to exist within a society. As will be indicated later, it is the view of this text that law, seen as a "system" in the cybernetic sense, cannot be discovered within a social system until it has rather completely articulated its internal, formal characteristics. It is these characteristics which allow a process to be defined, within the scope of this book, as law.

The advantage of a sharp definition of law is that it permits a distinction to be drawn between laws, social rules, and customs. Too broad a definition might require consideration of societies in which courts and police are not present,[1] or a confusion of law and custom which makes them indistinguishable.[2] It is tempting to find in a binding rule an obligation to obey similar to that created by modern law. These rules usually treat subjects such as marriage, religion, house building, and certain economic activities found in primitive societies. Despite the fact that the content of the rules may resemble law, certain central elements are lacking in primitive societies which deny the possibility of law. Therefore, it

---

[1] T. O. Elias, *The Nature of African Customary Law* (Manchester: Manchester University Press, 1956).

[2] William Seagle, *Quest for Law* (New York: Alfred A. Knopf, Inc., 1941).

is misguided to find in primitive rules the origins of modern legal systems.[3]

Among the elements missing in the creation of primitive rules, but found in a legal "system," are the formal institutions of government: a legislature, courts, or legal officials. Without these there can be no final, authoritative, legitimate, and collective source of authority. The rules will not form a coherent body of standards but will rest upon individual or group memory.[4] Doubts as to the existence or meaning of a rule will be impossible to settle without resort to some sort of force or social power.

Law, as we are acquainted with it, involves a "systematic and formal application of force by the state in support of explicit rules of conduct."[5] The structure of the law is found in its formal, coherent statement of rules and its process of rule enforcement. Simple societies, lacking full political organization and specific juridical institutions, can present us with little more than situations which are "incipiently legal."[6] It is, then, interesting to know what the sources of our legal ideas may be, but not informative so far as the character of any modern legal system is concerned. Some primitive societies exist without any formal means of resolving disputes among individuals.[7] Others have a highly complicated sliding scale of social penalties.[8] But until some rudimentary state organizations concerned with law enforcement can be discerned, the beginnings of the legal system are not present.

---

[3] Geoffrey Sawer, *Law in Society* (Oxford: Clarendon Press, 1965), pp. 27–47.

[4] This is also the view of A. S. Diamond, *Primitive Law* (New York: Longmans, Green & Co., Inc., 1935).

[5] Robert Redfield, "Primitive Law," *University of Cincinnati Law Review*, Vol. 33 (1964), pp. 3–22.

[6] William Seagle, "Primitive Law and Professor Malinowski," *American Anthropologist*, Vol. 39 (1937), p. 275, note 4 at p. 280.

[7] A. R. Radcliffe-Brown, *The Andaman Islanders* (Glencoe, Ill.: Free Press, 1948), p. 48.

[8] A. Barton, "Ifugao Law," *University of California Publications in American Archeology and Ethnology*, Vol. 15 (1958), pp. 1–186.

The mere presence of a court, or something resembling it, does not, in itself, announce the existence of a legal system. A council of elders exercising tribal authority was found among the North American Indians, but no rules of procedure or of evidence were available.[9] In certain African tribes, decisions of courts were left to the individual parties and their kinsmen to enforce.[10] These examples show that modern legal systems differ in the degree to which their components are integrated into each other. A modern legal system has interrelated segments.

The homeostatic character of primitive law and customs is quite pronounced. The small, tightly knit community tends to promote social balance and to preserve order through its social rules.[11] The distinction between law, custom, and rule is not easy to make at this cultural level, but it may be unimportant to insist upon a distinction, because the purpose of attaining homeostasis is secured by any of these techniques. Homeostasis may be found, then, even in prelegal systems.

Origins of our legal system

With the gradual emergence of the apparatus of law and government, the objects of law can be discerned. The legal system slowly replaces the informal justice of individual and social rule enforcement. Rules begin to disappear or become absorbed into official law, supported by government. At this point the legal system has its beginning.

In England, the origin of the legal system can be found in the early stages of the regularization of government administration. As late as the reign of Henry I (1100–1135), the sheriffs locally administered the law according to vari-

---

[9] Redfield, *op. cit.*, p. 18.

[10] Gerhard Lindblom, *The Akamba in British East Africa* (2d ed.; Uppsala, Sweden, 1920).

[11] Norbert Wiener, *Cybernetics* (2d ed.; New York: John Wiley & Sons, Inc., 1961), p. 160.

able local custom. But the centralization of legal administration in the hands of the king was begun in the reign of
Henry II (1154–1189). During that period the system of itin-
erant justices was started, the courts of law gradually
emerged, the jury came into common use, and criminal procedure was becoming organized.[12]

The first great outburst of national legislation occurred
during Henry II's rule. Some legislation established new
forms of trial and new forms of legal action, as in the law
of real property. What was purported to be local custom of
ancient vintage was ascertained and declared in the remarkable Constitutions of Clarendon (1164).[13] The pretense
that new law was not being created by these royal declarations was retained for a century.

The necessary state force to support the legal system at
the lowest levels was supplied by 13th-century statutes. In
1252, constables were to be appointed, and in 1253, necessary weapons were to be locally provided at the level of the
"vill," the smallest unit of government.[14]

Informal inquiry in the form of the early "hundred" preceded the establishment of formal courts under royal control. However, procedure in these tribunals became regularized by royal order in 946, when King Edgar insisted that
they meet every four weeks, pursue and punish criminals,
issue fines, and decree outlawry. These hundreds could not
be considered courts, though, because they were in private
hands, and even at times subject to private ownership by
purchase.[15]

Gradually and deliberately the kings of 12th-century
England sought to gather together under royal control the
informal and private tribunals of justice. In the 13th and

---

12 Theodore F. T. Plunckett, *A Concise History of the Common Law*
(Boston: Little, Brown & Co., 1956), p. 19.

13 Sir Frederick Maitland, *History of English Law* (2d ed.; Washington,
D.C.: Lawyer's Literary Club, 1959), Vol. I, pp. 151–52.

14 Plunckett, *op. cit.*, p. 86.

15 *Ibid.*, p. 89.

14th centuries, the crown's traveling legal officials had an impressive civil, criminal, and administrative jurisdiction called the General Gyre.[16]

The formation of national courts was made permanent by Magna Charta itself in 1215, when the Court of Common Pleas was fixed in its location at Westminster.[17] The judges ceased to travel without the monarch and stayed at the place of the king's residence.

For the characteristic structure of modern legal systems, the legal profession is a major element. Parties appeared in person to represent themselves even after the development of centralized royal courts. By the time of Henry III (1216–1272), a professional lawyer class had evolved. A narrator who could tell the plaintiff's story better than he himself might was available to the more wealthy.[18]

The office of the judge was only slowly separated from the role of royal courtier or suitor. The king's courts were, at first, literally his possession. The ancient *curia regis* gradually extended its prerogatives until it emerged as the House of Lords, the English high court, and later their parliament. But at first the king met with his court in his council in the parliament and controlled its deliberations. In the 12th century, the judges were drawn from the small group of royal clerks, but in the 13th, William de Raleigh and Martin de Pateshull asserted some judicial independence of the throne, earning them the designation of modern judges in a formal sense.[19]

The English legal system did not arise full blown from the conscious creation of a single king. Its origin was somewhat unplanned and incidental to the struggle to centralize royal authority. At the close of the 14th century its

---

[16] *Ibid.*, pp. 147–48.

[17] The requirement was that the court sit in "some certain place" but in practice that meant Westminster.

[18] Herman Cohen, *History of the Bar* (London: Sweet & Maxwell, Ltd., 1929), p. 172 ff.

[19] Plunckett, *op. cit.*, p. 235.

main structural features had begun to complete their formation. Changes in structure continue to the present day, but they are not as fundamental as the separation of legal authority from the immemorial customary authority of local bodies.

In the United States, the legislature was perceived by most citizens as the prime agency for legal development from 1750 until the 1820's. After 1875, the courts came to appear, in the popular view, as the embodiment of the law.[20] However, the basic outline of the legal system had existed, in developed form, since colonial days. Americans adopted English law and did not need to create a legal system from the point at which independence began. Although English and American practice and procedure differ widely, the latter has clearly built upon the experience of the former. The current contours of the American legal system are the product of national and local experimentation, but the newer structure was built upon an already highly sophisticated legal system.

The common law

In Western civilization two basic types of legal systems are in existence, the civil law and the common law. Common law was brought to the New World by the English settlers, and its spread was fostered by the destruction of French influence incident upon their defeat in the French and Indian War.

The common law in the United States is derived from the English, although now separated from that system because of the American Revolution and the development of a native version of common law. English common law was, at first, that body of principles defined and pronounced in the king's courts or discovered by his royal judges riding

---

[20] James W. Hurst, *The Growth of American Law* (Boston: Little, Brown & Co., 1950), p. 85.

circuit. These judges incorporated local customs into an official national legal system, but the fiction was retained, and continues to this day, that basic common-law principles are not written down. By means of this fiction royal judges were able to evolve a single national system of judge-made law which appeared to represent local customary practices.

The English common-law system demonstrates the transformation of community rules into an authorized, official national legal system. The cementing factor in this process is the principle of *stare decisis*, the legal rule that past precedents determine the outcome of contemporary legal disputes. This doctrine supplies the sanction of custom which mere naked legal decrees would not possess. However, the judicial practice of "distinguishing" precedents allows the modification of past decisions by the simple device of discovering dissimilarities of fact between the earlier case and the instant dispute.

Common law became a reasonably flexible mode of settling social disputes, but it created a prejudice in favor of very gradual change by the slow accretion of precedent. Of course, the overruling of precedent is always a possibility, but judges prefer to maintain the sense of legal continuity and certainty which *stare decisis* provides. In any event, statutes may be, and are, increasingly employed to change the old precedents. The effect has been to reduce the range and scope of common-law rules as they become replaced by new statutory standards. Even so, the spirit of the common law prevails in most English and American courtrooms, as the judges establish new precedents to form interpretations of the statutes themselves.[21] Though the common law is disappearing, the process of the common law continues.

---

[21] See Roscoe Pound, *The Spirit of the Common Law* (Boston: Marshall Jones Co., 1921).

In the United States, it is said that there is no body of federal common law. Nevertheless, the federal courts, in certain classes of cases, must apply the common-law rules of the states.[22] Many states, and the federal government, have abolished the old common-law crimes, replacing them by entirely statutory policies. The zone of the common law is now limited to civil (noncriminal) suits for the most part, especially to the areas of real property, torts, and contracts.

The English common law was first incorporated into American law by the royal colony of Virginia in 1660. In 1665, a New York assembly made local modifications in the English common law, but elements of Dutch law crept in as well. Colonial law was generally a mixture of local customs and theological and political demands.[23] In 1776, despite the spirit of revolution, Virginia expressly adopted as much of the English common law as was not repugnant to its Constitution and Bill of Rights.[24] This became the model for similar statutes in other new states and, eventually, for newly added territories as they attained statehood. However, a few elements of Spanish law have been adopted in southwestern states, and French civil law prevails in Louisiana.

The civil law

The earliest Western legal system of significance was the Roman law, from which most of the continental systems of law derive their origin. Roman law was restated and codified in the famous Justinian Code of the sixth century A.D. Roman law spread, after the Renaissance, into Germany and northern Italy. It was carried into the New World by the French, the Spanish, the Portugese, and the Dutch.

---

[22] *Erie R.R.* v. *Tompkins*, 304 U.S. 64 (1938).

[23] F. W. Hall, "Common Law: Account of its Reception in the United States," *Vanderbilt Law Review*, Vol. 4 (June, 1951), pp. 791–825.

[24] *Virginia Code*, 1–10.

Emperor Napoleon Bonaparte encouraged a comprehensive modernization of the continental legal system. As part of his plan for a reunited Europe, Napoleon provided for the drafting of his *Code Civil*, which restated the ancient principles in more modern terms. Most modern continental legal systems are based on the Napoleonic model.

The differences between common law and civil law are not as sharp as their historical development might suggest. Usually, civil-law systems are based upon a series of codes so that the primary character of law is statutory. The judge merely applies the statutory policy, but in so doing a body of precedents may evolve to serve as a guide. Procedural differences are marked, especially the more frequent use of the jury in common-law jurisdictions. Yet it has been suggested that in the United States, where *stare decisis* is not applied too rigidly, especially in the Supreme Court, some features similar to the civil approach are becoming apparent.[25]

The language of law

The technical language of law at times appears to mystify the layman, but much of its apparent complexity is due to the same historical factors which helped shape the legal system from the beginning. Legal language may be regarded as an impartial means of communication within the system, with only an indirect effect, as an output, upon the society which may not grasp its intricacies and professional meanings. As the craft of the lawyer became a necessary part of the operation of the legal system, the professionalization of language became inevitable. In addition, the judge shares the lawyer's special knowledge of language, even though the jurors do not. This gap may cause confusion in the application of legal rules to specific fact situations.

-----

[25] Denis Lloyd, *Introduction to Jurisprudence* (New York: Frederick A. Praeger, Inc., 1965), p. 371.

The language of the common law is uncommon. Frequently, ordinary words are employed in a nondictionary sense. Latin words and phrases, now vulgarized, are still employed. Formal words and methods of phrasing are often used in legal documents. Special "terms of art" are found in legal usage (lessor, laches, felon, plaintiff) which are shorthand expressions for more complicated ideas. At times, law language may be deliberately vague or deliberately more precise than common language, depending upon the purpose.[26]

Since the use of legal language is largely in impartial communication within the system, it should be observed that it does not always serve that purpose. Overly vague language may help prevent a client from realizing his personal intentions. Many wills have been effectively attacked for this reason. On the other hand, a good lawyer attempts to foresee all possible contingencies which might affect the eventual satisfaction of his client's desires. This may require resort to highly refined language. Basically, then, the language of law should not be different from common language without a reason. Otherwise, it serves only to obscure, mystify, or to retard the effective operation of the legal system. A communications medium must be used to convey information if a system is to properly respond to its inputs. Distortion in communication can cause a breakdown in the system. To some extent, this is the explanation for a certain variety of "injustice" found in all legal systems.

A few basic legal words should be part of the equipment of any layman. The word *trial* denotes an initial tribunal to consider (usually for the first time) the legal effects of a disputed situation. Often the dispute centers around specific events, called *facts*, and the determination of their probable occurrence is often made—in the United States—by a jury. The *plaintiff* is the individual who first institutes the pro-

---

26 David Mellinkoff, *The Language of the Law* (Boston: Little, Brown & Co., 1963), pp. 11–23.

ceeding by the process of filing certain papers with a court clerk. These papers, and others which pass between the parties, constitute the *pleadings*. The *defendant* is the individual against whom trial is first instituted, although, by issuing a *counterclaim*—another pleading—a defendant could become, in some respects, a plaintiff, insofar as he is making a new complaint. A *case* itself is the normal context of a legal dispute within the common-law system. The case as a unit could contain many plaintiffs and many defendants, if all of them have joined together to resolve a dispute held in common.

Types of law

Basic descriptions of the varieties of law found within the American legal system will identify the substructure of that system. The legal system is composed of separate elements which, though often administered by the same officials, differ in their properties in some fundamental respect. Each subsystem of law serves a different social purpose, but the differences between them have important procedural effects.

Private law is that variety which governs the relationship between private citizens or persons.[27] Its primary characteristic is the resolution and regulation of disputes involving the relationship of individuals within the society. The subject matter of a dispute may consist of property, a contract, negligence, wills, or similar matters. Sometimes private disputes may indirectly involve the state, as in marriage and divorce, but since the state is not itself a litigant (or a party) it remains a matter of private law.

Public law disputes involve the state or its agencies in a more direct manner. Normally, the state is a litigant, often a plaintiff, in a public law matter. The interest of the state,

---

[27] *Black's Law Dictionary* (4th ed.; St. Paul, Minn.: West Publishing Co., 1951) provides a source of basic legal definitions used here. It is not an official volume, but there are no standard legal definitions of these terms.

in such cases, embraces a larger public concern, so that the legal resolution of the dispute will commonly affect the society at large, as well as the parties directly involved. Obvious examples are provided by constitutional and administrative law. The definition and enforcement of larger social matters are involved in the public law system.

In a sense, the entire political system generates public law. The Congress enacts public legislation, the President issues executive orders, and the administrative agencies issue regulations. However, the generation of public law provides an input for the legal system of which the courts are the major portion. Not all public law matters reach the court as an input, but those which produce resistance and disputation will be fed into the legal system at some time. The overlap of the legal and political systems is often apparent, but nowhere more evident than in the area of public law.

In *constitutional law* the subject of dispute may be the organization of the state itself, of the structure of the federal system, the extent of the powers of government or the character of individual rights under the basic constitutional document. In America, the Constitution of the national government is supreme over all other types of law. It is at the apex of the legal system and superior to all public and private law. Even the President himself is subject to its restrictions.[28]

The Constitution is subject to formal change only by means of a complicated amendment process.[29] Yet, each major judicial interpretation represents a shift in its current significance. Within the field of public law, this is the most striking zone of confluence between the legal and political systems. Constitutional law is the most public—hence the most political—variety of law. The outputs of constitutional law, in the form of Supreme Court decisions, serve as inputs into the political system. Sometimes these outputs

---

[28] *Youngstown Sheet and Tube Co.* v. *Sawyer*, 343 U.S. 579 (1952).
[29] Article V.

profoundly alter the structure and dimensions of the political system.[30]

Another vital area of public law is the *criminal law.* In criminal law matters the state, or its agencies, brings the suit as plaintiff before a legal tribunal. The decision to prosecute is usually made by a public official charged with that duty. This input is made after it is determined that an infraction of a publicly determined standard of conduct has occurred (almost always a statute). Supporting that standard is a special criminal sanction of fine or imprisonment which serves as a penalty for this antisocial behavior. The major categories of criminal law are homicide, burglary, larceny, fraud, rape, and assault.

Since it is possible that the same act may constitute a basis for both public and private legal treatment, two trials in two separate tribunals might result. The party bringing the criminal action will be the state, but the noncriminal action might be brought on behalf of the alleged victim. Since the victim wishes to be repaid for his injuries, his suit to remedy his wrong is known as a civil action. The purpose of a civil suit is the resolution of a personal, not a public, dispute. The nature of the legal award, as well as the method of legal procedure will differ greatly from the criminal suit, and different legal conclusions may be produced. The civil suit *does not* serve as an input for the criminal suit, nor may it work in reverse fashion. They are, then, two different subsystems of law.

The test to determine the existence of a subsystem of law is whether the output of one may serve as the input of another. In all the types mentioned above, with the exception of constitutional law, the test is met. Constitutional law,

---

[30] *Baker* v. *Carr*, 364 U.S. 898 (1960) began a reformation of the apportionment of the state legislatures. The political ramifications of the new interpretation of the Fourteenth Amendment will be felt for years to come, as the structure of political power in the states is drastically altered to meet the standards of "one man—one vote."

being the supreme variety of public law, necessarily embraces all other types of public law.

Equity is not a subsystem of law in states where, as in the federal system, the same court might administer equity law while treating other varieties of law. The merger of equity with other types of law is a rapidly developing process in the United States. The historical character of equity law is rapidly declining in importance.

At the moment, in most states, equity techniques provide unusual and personal remedies for legal disputes of a civil nature. The most familiar equity decree is the *injunction*, which restrains further activity by the party enjoined which would tend to cause irreparable harm if the injunction were not issued. *Specific performance* is another kind of equitable writ which requires the performance of a duty created by contract or other agreement. A man who buys a thoroughbred racing horse of proven abilities might prefer the horse to any other legal award he could receive. Equity procedure would satisfy this desire if the plaintiff could show a breach of an agreement and the uniqueness of the horse.

Law in the social system

Law is just a part of the society's system of social control. It is part of the culture, habits, and attitudes of a people. It is organized into special institutions, but these are not independent of the influence of other social organizations. Law does not exist independent of economic, family, political, or other concerns.

It has been maintained that law provides a reflection of the values or norms of the society in which it functions.[31] Evidence exists to show that civil law is an index of social differentiation, while criminal law reflects social similarity,

---

[31] Max M. Laserson, "Rights, Righthandedness, and Uprightness," *American Sociological Review*, Vol. 4 (August, 1939), pp. 534–42.

or generally accepted values.[32] In any event, the law is rarely far from the society's general moral precepts, its contemporary ideas of right and wrong, or at least those of an earlier day. It may be said to provide an "ethical minimum" for social behavior.[33]

The extent to which legal norms will be realized is not determined in the courts, administrative tribunals, or legislatures. It is determined by the society itself, as its members agree to support the legal rules in their ordinary conduct. Those legal norms which are in accordance with ordinary morality are most likely to be supported in actual behavior. To contradict by law the values established by religion and morality is to invite lawbreaking.[34]

Law cannot guarantee social conformity, but it can supply the element of socially legitimate force to bring social deviants into line. Law becomes the "cornerstone of the edifice of order."[35] Although families, schools, and other social groups help maintain order, it is the primary function only of these legal agencies which are a part of the government. When other groups fail to ensure unity, the law may supply the necessary element to represent the collective view of society on a matter of social control.

The law is usually dependent upon other social institutions for its effective implementation. Legal rules concerning business and marriage are not, in themselves, adequate to shape the contours of those significant institutions. At times, the legal machinery may fall under the domination of particular groups or classes. When this occurs, the danger that the law may become an instrument of oppression arises. In democratic societies it is hoped that the conflicting in-

---

[32] Frank G. Harting, "Common and Discrete Group Values," *Journal of Social Psychology*, Vol. 28 (1953), pp. 3–22.

[33] C. A. Ellwood, *The Psychology of Human Society* (New York: Appleton-Century-Crofts, 1925), pp. 396–401.

[34] Yehezekel Dror, "Values and the Law," *Antioch Review*, Vol. 17 (Winter, 1957–58), p. 446.

[35] E. A. Ross, *Social Control: A Survey of the Foundations of Order* (New York: Macmillan Co., 1901), p. 125.

terests of competing groups will prevent the law from being captured by any one group or coalition of groups. It is the avowed purpose of law to serve the public interest and to satisfy the private demands of individual justice.

II

Legal reasoning and feedback

SEEN FROM the vantage point of the layman, the law is a body of abstract doctrine, of a semipermanent nature, which is both mysterious and powerful. It is guarded by the professional caste of lawyers and shrouded in a technical jargon too obscure for ordinary men to penetrate. The judges are even more remote figures who discover the law in the course of their presumed search for justice, though justice itself is supposed to be the common property of all.

Most lawyers and judges do not maintain the pretense of the automatic, unambiguous character of the law. But a few still prefer to convey to the lay public the impression that the judge merely applies the facts of the given case to a known principle of law in order to render his decision.[1] It is also convenient to pretend that statutes and constitutions do not contain a great deal of ambiguous language. The purpose of these disguises is clear. It is to maintain popular respect for law by advancing the genial fiction that the law is known, definite, and precise in all cases. Of course, sophisticated laymen know that the law is not so

---

[1] See Jerome Frank, *Courts on Trial* (New York: Atheneum Publishers, 1963), pp. 14–16.

simple, and that words cannot be so determinative of the events of a real world of experience.

In order to give to the law some semblance of order and a quality of connectedness, the legal system depends upon a special means of communication which is called "legal reasoning." From the perspective of cybernetics, the problem may be perceived as one of receiving message impulses as free from disturbance or "noise" as possible, in a coded form in order to recombine these impressions so as to produce a response which helps to preserve the whole system.[2]

The source of these principles might be either the legislature or the judiciary. Much of the common law, as applied in the United States, is judge-made law. In effect, the common law is an internal communication medium among judges, presented to them by lawyers representing opposing parties, which permits the judge to select among competing rules that version of the law which he wishes to apply to the given case. Of course, the desire for certainty in the law is supported by the doctrine of *stare decisis*, which requires the application of precedents to contemporary cases. The desire for legal stability is the major reason for following the principle of *stare decisis*.

Stare decisis can be avoided if judges can reason their way around the earlier, and possibly undesirable, precedent. The technique of "distinguishing" the precedent allows its force to be narrowed to the "precise question" involved. In making that distinction, the effect of the precedent may be negated. Another way to avoid an old precedent is to make verbal changes in the category, thus obscuring the change or transformation taking place. Finally, the value of the precedent can be extinguished by rejecting the decision itself as a significant factor, and penetrating to some deeper layer of meaning—an ultimate meaning called the *ratio decidendi* of that case. This shift in meanings can effectively expand

---

2 Norbert Wiener, *Cybernetics* (2d ed.; New York: John Wiley & Sons, Inc., 1961), pp. 42–43, suggests this approach.

or alter the original meaning of the precedent.[3] Although *stare decisis* is the most fundamental of all legal principles, there are other principles which allow deviation from it.

The legal analogy

Most legal reasoning depends upon analogy, rather than upon purely logical or empirical processes. There is no "science" of law in the natural science sense because the subject matter of law contains innumerable variables and also because questions of a value-laden, ethical, or moral nature pervade the legal method.

The ordinary principles of logic, though useful, will not always help solve legal problems. Even the more advanced systems of logical analysis will not fit the categories which the law employs.[4] Basically, all logical systems must start with an agreement upon the existence of facts, and their concern is with the relationship among true statements, or the detection of false statements. But the problem in law is first to discover the most probable version of an actual past event and to apply to it an official policy which serves the interests of the community and the internal consistency of the system of law. Merely testing formal statements for their truth value is of little assistance. Of course, obvious logical fallacies should be avoided by any person, layman or lawyer, who seeks to deal rationally with others.[5]

As defined by one expert: "A working legal system must therefore be willing to pick out key similarities and to reason from them to the justice of applying a common classification."[6] This manner of reasoning lacks the closed quality

---

[3] Frank, *op. cit.*, pp. 275–85.

[4] Williard van Orman Quine, *Methods of Logic* (New York: Holt, Rinehart & Winston, Inc., 1959) provides a valuable contemporary analysis.

[5] Irving Copi, *Introduction to Logic* (2d ed.; New York: Macmillan Co., 1961).

[6] Edward H. Levi, *An Introduction to Legal Reasoning* (Chicago: University of Chicago Press, 1965), p. 3.

of a logical system. The interplay of fact and rule is too intimate to ascribe to the rule any fixed or universal character.

In a court of law two or more competing analogies are suggested to the tribunal. The judge decides which fact-law situation is most similar to the one at hand and, making the choice, chooses a "law." Even in administrative agencies the same choice of precedents on an analogical basis is frequently used.

If the factual context of legal disputes remained the same from one year to the next, and if the values and demands of the society became fixed and static, the method of analogy could be replaced by a deductive logical method, proceeding from principles of law which were predetermined and certain. But no two identical factual situations are likely to occur. The current societal attitudes will shift. In order to reflect these changes, the law must be flexible. The method of analogy is convenient to this purpose.

Reasoning by example is a low grade of rational behavior. It requires a competition among examples in order to ascertain the preferred example, which becomes the law when the examples are clear and definite. When the examples are remote from the current controversy, the analogy must be extended to cover a dissimilar situation. The method of analogy is quite suitable for poetry because of the aesthetic advantages of ambiguity and a blurring of imagery. In law, where precision is required, it doesn't work as well.

Manufactured analogy

When the method of analogy is abandoned, another method must be adopted, which many will consider to be "nonlegal," because of its novelty. In *Baker* v. *Carr*,[7] the very important reapportionment decision, the United States Supreme Court was faced with a problem not previously treated by them. No precedents were available directly on the issue of the meaning of the Fourteenth Amendment in

---

[7] 369 U.S. 186 (1962).

the area of popular representation. Earlier cases had demonstrated the court's unwillingness to enter the reapportionment controversy.[8] But in 1962, the Supreme Court was ready to announce that it possessed jurisdiction of the subject matter, under the Fourteenth Amendment, but not yet ready to conclude what, in law, should be done to give meaning to the Fourteenth Amendment. With bated breath the public and the legal community awaited the answer. Gradually, the court evolved its standards.

After *Baker* v. *Carr*, the Supreme Court was faced with a flood of state and federal reapportionment suits. It was forced to announce novel general standards as a guide to the federal district courts, which had no other measure of constitutionality. The Supreme Court discovered in the Constitution an intention (despite the existence of the electoral college and the malapportioned Senate) "of making equal representation for equal numbers of people the fundamental goal."[9] Ultimately, in a vain search for a justification in constitutional history, the court fell back upon its own prescribed version of the political theory of representation:

Legislators represent people, not trees, or acres. Legislators are elected by voters, not farms or cities or economic interests . . . overweighting and undervaluation of the votes of those living here has the certain effect of dilution and undervaluation of the votes of those living there.[10]

Replying to its critics at the same time the Court (through Chief Justice Warren) replied that:

We are admonished not to restrict the power of the state to impose differing views as to political philosophy on their citizens. We are cautioned about the dangers of entering into political thickets and mathematical quagmires. Our answer is this: a denial of constitutionally protected rights demands judicial protection; our oath and our office require no less of us.[11]

---

8 Especially *Colegrove* v. *Green*, 328 U.S. 549 (1946).

9 *Wesbury* v. *Sanders*, 376 U.S. 1 (1964).

10 *Reynolds* v. *Sims*, 377 U.S. 533 (1964), at 562.

11 *Ibid.*, p. 566.

Ever since 1962, the Supreme Court has been pursuing its self-created task of establishing a method to secure substantial equality of representation. This new and unprecedented activity will, in time, generate its own precedents. The degrees of acceptable malapportionment will become more definite. The legislatures will receive specific guidelines, but until then a period of trial and error must be endured. In the absence of alternative courses of action found in past practices, only a crude experimentalism will suffice.

As this example should illustrate, when reasoning by analogy fails, a resort to abstract theory may be needed. Since political theory is often beyond the realm of factual verification, rebuttal of a theory can only be made by resorting to another theory. At that point the language of discourse becomes so dissimilar that logical analysis or rational discourse becomes impossible. One must simply accept the terms of the theory and attempt to criticize its internal weaknesses, contradictions, or improper application. We must learn to live with the reapportionment cases because they are "law" regardless of the reasoning process which supports them.

In essence, the reapportionment cases are excellent examples of legal rationalization. The court discerned a political evil—unequal representation—and forged a weapon to meet it. The political and social effects are sure to be profound, but the motive was to right a "wrong" and to bring the Constitution to bear against an undesired condition. Though no analogy could be found, one could be gradually created.

Historical analogy

The case method of the common law rests largely on the analogy of past cases. These are historical only in the sense that they occurred at earlier points in time, but the historical context of a case is usually ignored. The precedent stands apart from time and is considered to be almost eternal.

With the interpretation of documents, different problems arise. The court is faced with a written text which had, pre-

sumably, a definite meaning when it was passed by the legislature or by a constitutional convention. The application
of a document by a court requires, in the main, little more
than a literal enforcement of the provisions of the document, if that is possible.

When the document is not extremely clear and definite,
a court must attempt to give it meaning. The same thing is
true of that extraordinary document known as a constitution. When documents are vague, a court may be forced to
resort to the test of history. The question then becomes one
of recreating the state of mind of the original drafters and
the approving body itself. The "founding fathers" of the
American Constitution or the congressional committee
which reported the bill must be invoked to give legitimacy
to the judicial interpretation of vague documentary language.

Legislative history is one source of legislative intent.
Upon discovery, the original draft of a statute may often
be profitably compared with its final version, in order to
determine the meaning of ambiguous language.[12] Sometimes this information may cast doubt on long-held judicial
interpretations.[13] The voting down of an amendment or its
acceptance and explanation by a proponent may help disclose evidence of intent, as may acquiescence in a known
administrative interpretation.[14]

The attempt to recreate a historical event can never
be completely successful. Even if one could discover some
historical events, others, perhaps unrecorded, might be
overlooked. The task presented to the lawyers and judges
may involve the professional skills of a historian, and historians are not always in agreement on the occurrence of
past events, especially in the absence of reliable source
materials.

---

[12] See also *United States* v. *Pfitsch*, 256 U.S. 547 (1921); *Hood Rubber Co.*
v. *Commissioner of Corporations*, 268 Mass. 355 (1929).

[13] Charles Warren, "New Light on the History of the Federal Judiciary
Act of 1789," *Harvard Law Review*, Vol. 37 (1923), pp. 49, 85.

[14] *Patterson* v. *Louisville & Nashville R.R.*, 269 U.S. 1 (1925).

The drawing of a historical analogy requires a set of assumptions regarding the meaning of an ambiguous phrase in a document. It must be assumed that the document once had a definite meaning; that the meaning was once known to a legislative body; that it was accepted as a common meaning; and finally, that the meaning can be discovered by a fair-minded judge. Unfortunately, it can happen that sharp differences of opinion might arise where the policy was complex and the struggle for passage was protracted.[15]

Ultimately, the determination of the weight to be accorded legislative history is left in the hands of the judge. It is he who decides the force of the historical analogy. Many writers have suggested that history could be treated as irrelevant to the meaning of the document. Since the legislature which passed a statute had adjourned, "Why bother about what they intended or what they would have done?"[16] Perhaps the court should attempt to give the document a future meaning rather than make an attempt to reconstruct the past.

Contextual analysis

If history fails to provide a guide to the interpretation of ambiguous language in a document, it may be possible for a court to examine the text itself for a clue to the meaning of the document. Those judges who rely upon this approach presume that the placement of words in a sentence or paragraph provides an objective test for meaning. Grammatical construction may be internal evidence of the real meaning of a statute.

In the pursuit of contextual analysis, courts have constructed some "canons" of interpretation as rough guides. One such is the rule of *ejusdem generis*, which is "that where

---

[15] See Frank Horack, "In the Name of Legislative Intention," *West Virginia Law Review*, Vol. 38 (1932), pp. 119–38.

[16] Charles Curtis, "A Better Theory of Legal Interpretation," *Vanderbilt Law Review*, Vol. 3 (1950), pp. 407–37.

in a statute a general word follows particular and specific words of the same nature as itself, it takes its meaning from them and is presumed to be restricted to the same genus as those words."[17] According to this rule, a statute naming as criminal the shipment of obscene books, pamphlets, pictures, motion picture films, papers, "or other matter of indecent character" was held to include phonograph records.[18] A different but not quite contrary rule is denoted as *expressio unius est exclusio alterius* in which a statute "which appears upon its face to confine or limit the operation of its provisions to particular persons or things" will not be held to include other meanings beyond those contained in the specific language preceding a general word or phrase.[19]

Both inferences might be applicable to the same language. The relationship between specific language and general language is, in itself, rarely apparent from the face of the document. Such "canons" allow wide discretion to the judge interpreting the statute.

Whenever a court departs, in legislative interpretation, from the commonsense, "plain" meaning of documentary language, it is open to a charge of usurpation of authority. In a democracy the legislatures, not the courts, are supposed to devise new policy. It is up to the legislature to use exact and precise language if that function is not to be frustrated. Courts normally assume that a legislature uses common words in their popular meaning. If any other meaning is intended, the legislature should indicate it by providing technical definitions.[20] Otherwise, the courts are left to draw inferences which may be completely without foundation.

At times, the contextual analysis of documentary language assumes unusual significance. Two clauses of the United States Constitution contain general language: "necessary

---

17 *McNamara* v. *State*, 203 Ind. 596, 605, 181 N.E. 513, 515 (1932).

18 *United States* v. *Alpers*, 338 U.S. 680 (1950).

19 *Blevins* v. *Mullally*, 22 Cal. App. 159, 135 Pac. 307 (1913).

20 Felix Frankfurter, "Some Reflections on the Reading of Statutes," *Columbia Law Review*, Vol. 47 (1947), pp. 527–46.

and proper" (Art. I, sec. 8, cl. 18) and "the general welfare"
(Art. I, sec. 8, cl. 1). The determination of the meaning of
these phrases was essential to the constitutional development of the United States. Both phrases were interpreted
by the Supreme Court in a generous manner.[21] Another contextual reading would have sharply confined the ambit of
national power and prevented the emergence of the current
federal relationship between the national and state governments. The effects of contextual analysis have rarely been
so profound or pervasive. This expansion of the legislative
power of Congress was supported by the Supreme Court
of the United States.

The argument of John Marshall in *McCulloch* v. *Maryland* serves as a classic model of contextual analysis. The
problem at hand was the meaning of the "necessary and
proper" clause in Art. I, sec. 8 of the Constitution, which is
to be found after an extensive list of expressed powers of
Congress. In determining whether Congress could establish
a national bank despite the absence of specific language empowering that measure, the Chief Justice turned to the language of the document itself. He found that the word
"necessary" was capable of many meanings, but that from its
associated language in the clause, from its placement among
the powers of Congress, from the absence of the limiting
word "absolutely," and from the ordinary meaning of the
word, it was not intended to serve as a limitation upon the
powers of Congress. It was intended instead to permit congressional choice as to the means by which best to accomplish a specifically enumerated constitutional end. The argument is not without flaws, but it has been a rationale
which has settled a major dilemma of American federalism,

---

[21] The "loose construction" theory of the meaning of "necessary and
proper" prevailed in *McCulloch* v. *Maryland*, 4 Wheat. 316 (1819). *United
States* v. *Butler*, 297 U.S. (1936) settled the issue of the breadth of the power
of the federal government to tax for other than specifically enumerated
purposes in the constitution.

the basic relationship between national and state government flowing from the existence of a strong national government.

Legal fictions

It is, at times, necessary to fill the gaps in the allegedly logical fabric of the law by resorting to the use of nonfacts, called legal fictions. The use of legal fictions is a deliberate and conscious practice of courts which has developed as a way of producing desired (i.e. "just") results even when strict logic would forbid. The function of these fictions appears to be both extralogical and counterlogical, because they are employed both to supply missing factual elements or to contradict known factual elements in a legal situation.

For a long period of time American judges and lawyers "implied" conditions into a contract of employment which were, in fact, not agreed to by the parties. Early English common law did not imply this second agreement, but by the 19th-century American and English judges were ready to declare that an injury caused to one worker by a co-worker was part of the assumed risk incident to the contract of employment itself.[22] By 1875, Wisconsin modified the effect of the fellow-servant rule by legislative action,[23] beginning a trend which led to eventual legislative abolition of the fiction by the creation of employer's liability legislation.

Some legal fictions have been created by statutes, as is the case in deed recording. Under most state statutes the effect of recording a deed is to give "constructive notice" of its existence to any later purchaser, even though he did not

---

[22] *Farwell* v. *The Boston and Worcester Railroad Corp.*, 4 Metc. 49 (Mass., 1842); *Priestly* v. *Fowler*, 3 Mees. & Wols. 1 (Exchequer, 1837, England).

[23] Laws, 1875, Chapter 173. This was limited to railway companies and their employees.

really know of the existence of the deed. Another example is provided by the fictional citizenship of corporations which permits them to sue and be sued in federal courts.[24]

Perhaps the greatest of all legal fictions is the presumption of the knowledge of the existence of the law, which is the basis of the claim that ignorance of the law is no excuse. Under this fiction every citizen and resident is held to know about the existence of legal rules, even in the absence of personal knowledge or ability to find and understand the law. The maxim that "ignorance of law is no excuse" is a rule of necessity, for without it a defendant might be immune from the effects of criminal and civil law which the society requires for its good order and protection.[25]

It should be obvious that the purpose of legal fictions is to provide exceptions to the ordinary operation of legal rules, without disturbing the fundamental order or symmetry of the law. Since considerable benefit arises from the regular operation of legal rules, it is typical for these legal fictions to become settled and regularized into a body of predictable exceptions. The fictions become a nonfactual body of exceptional law. Lawyers and judges have learned that "justice" may require a distortion of the true facts and have agreed upon the exceptions.

In terms of cybernetics, the legal fiction may be regarded as an input derived from within the legal system and internal to it, while ordinary facts are inputs from the outside world of ordinary experience. Both kinds of inputs provide the primary raw material which law must treat by a conversion process to transform it into an output as a legal decision.[26]

---

[24] See Lon Fuller, "Legal Fictions," *Illinois Law Review*, Vol. 25 (1930–31), pp. 363, 513, 877.

[25] *Barlow* v. *United States*, 32 U.S. 404 (1833); *Utermehle* v. *Norment*, 197 U.S. 40 (1904).

[26] Jerome Frank, *Law and the Modern Mind* (New York: Tudor Publishing Co., 1930) lays emphasis upon the importance of the fact input. Although easily exaggerated, the fact input must be considered as of greater significance than the law itself.

Internal feedback phenomena: professional reasoning

The legal communication system is largely internal, and serves primarily to inform the bench, the bar, and the law schools. The legal audience is, in most situations, limited to the professionals. To a lesser extent the public lawmaking bodies (the legislatures and executives) are a part of the participating audience. At the furthest remove are the law "consumers" who constitute the lay public and are held to possess legal awareness and responsibility, despite their generally passive role as members of the legal audience.[27]

The communications matrix, then, permits more possibilities of feedback from within the profession than from the outside. This factor may explain the gap observed to exist between the legal rules and the commonly accepted standards of the community. Judges, lawyers, and law professors are not average members of society, and their perception of social needs is frequently dulled by professional activity, as well as by limited social contact.[28]

The feedback response of law school professors and their students is an increasingly significant aspect of the legal system. Today, periodical writing plays a central part in the shaping of the law. Every major law school in the country, and most lesser institutions, support the publication of law reviews whose primary purpose is to explicate and criticize the decisions of judges, legislators, and executives. In form, this is usually represented by several lead articles addressed to some general problems of law, and case notes, which are examinations of single case decisions at the state or federal level. The law reviews may be regarded as a virtual journalistic "fourth estate" within the profession, bent upon im-

---

[27] Edmond Cahn, "The Consumers of Injustice," *Social Research*, Vol. 26 (Summer, 1959), pp. 175–91.

[28] Geoffrey Sawer, *Law in Society* (Oxford: Clarendon Press, 1965), pp. 88–125.

proving and clarifying the principles and procedures of the legal system.[29]

The citation of journal articles in legal opinions is still rather rare, yet "legal periodicals and related sources have generally been relied upon as sources of facts—the sort of expert knowledge on which Mr. Justice Brandeis believed that the Court must base its opinions."[30] Different courts may have different policies regarding the utilization of journal articles, but judges and their clerks are often curious to know what legal scholars have to say, because judges are rarely scholars.

The feedback effect of journal articles is rarely immediate and only infrequently apparent in a given judicial decision. Probably the greatest impact of this source of data is in the long-term development of the legal system. Reform of established rules is usually a gradual process, so the effects of scholarly writing may be evolutionary.

In addition, the feedback phenomena of law reviews are reduced by the diffusion of the information flow resulting from the sheer number of these publications, as well as by their propensity to contain a reflection of particular editorial or scholarly biases. Excellent indices to legal writing make the retrieval problem rather minimal, but judges must become aware of the partisanships among legal writers if they are to respond reasonably to their articles.

Sometimes comments on cases are made while appeal is still pending, which raises delicate ethical problems. At other times, articles reflect official government policies, as when written at the behest of government agencies. Finally, articles may have a substantial effect on the character of legislation, especially when written by prominent people or

---

[29] Chester Newland, "Legal Periodicals and The United States Supreme Court," *Midwest Journal of Political Science*, Vol. 3 (February, 1959), pp. 58-74.

[30] Chester Newland, "The Supreme Court and Legal Writing: Learned Journals as a Vehicle of an Anti-Trust Lobby," *Georgetown Law Journal*, Vol. 48 (Fall, 1959), pp. 105, 142.

published by prominent journals (*Harvard Law Review, Columbia Law Review, Yale Law Journal, University of Michigan Law Review*, as examples).[31]

The American Bar Association and its affiliated state bar associations form a significant part of the legal audience. In at least 28 states, membership in the bar association is required for practice before the state courts.[32] Although the primary concerns of bar associations are the ethical and professional standards of the legal profession, they are frequently influential in other ways. Since 1878, when it was organized, the American Bar Association has expressed the most conservative ideas of the time, but it also served as a major supporter of the United States Supreme Court.[33] In the past eight years, the A.B.A. has been friendly to the Court, although it must be noted that Chief Justice Warren resigned his membership in 1959.

Another agency of internal feedback within the legal system is the American Law Institute. This organization, founded in 1923, has a limited membership of approximately 1,700, but most of the members occupy influential legal positions as lawyers, judges, and law school professors.[34] This group promotes the clarification and simplification of legal concepts in most of the areas of private and public law, especially torts, real property, and contracts. Its most recent project has been the construction of the Model Penal Code, which embodies many advanced concepts of modern criminal law and criminology. The American Law Institute usually takes definite positions on controversial matters of law, which it publishes as monographs called "Restatements." These are frequently referred to by judges and lawyers, al-

---

31 Noted by Newland, *op. cit.*, supra., note 29, p. 62.

32 Dayton McKean, *The Integrated Bar* (Boston: Houghton Mifflin Co., 1963), p. 21. Georgia must be added to the list.

33 Benjamin Twiss, *Lawyers and the Constitution* (Princeton, N.J.: Princeton University Press, 1941).

34 Herbert Goodrich, *The Story of the American Law Institute* (St. Paul, Minn.: American Law Institute, 1961).

though they are not in any sense official documents. Frequently, the American Law Institute views, which are often progressive, become adopted by more venturesome courts. In this way, the Institute serves as a major reformative body within the legal system. Its feedback role is clearly evident in the heavily footnoted references to statutes and judicial decisions appearing with the text of legal rules in the Restatements. These references represent a scholarly attempt to criticize and evaluate established legal doctrines.

As indicated earlier, the best illustration within the legal system of feedback is provided by the legal doctrine of *stare decisis*. Of course, it can happen that a novel case may arise for which there is no applicable statute or case, but the tendency to treat law as a body of rules all rationally related to each other discourages deliberate and conscious judicial policy making.[35] This tendency has been less noticeable in recent years because of the impress of modern legal philosophies, such as sociological jurisprudence, which emphasize extrajudicial factors in the society. Even so, the doctrine of *stare decisis* is still at the heart of the Anglo-American legal systems, and it has hardened as the systems matured.[36]

The basic purpose of the *stare decisis* rule is essentially homeostatic, that is, to preserve the stability and order of the system. Accordingly, a precedent serves as negative feedback into the current dispute to prevent a runaway, random result. The total result is to supply considerable certainty to the social system of which the legal system is a part. Yet, since the social system changes, the legal system must sometimes ignore the effect of the *stare decisis* rule, or else its output cannot serve as a relevant (self-correcting)

---

[35] John Dickinson, "The Problem of the Unprovided Case," *University of Pennsylvania Law Review*, Vol. 81 (December, 1932), pp. 115–29.

[36] T. Ellis Lewis, "The History of Stare Decisis," *Law Quarterly Review*, Vol. 47 (July, 1931), p. 411. The doctrine was firmly established in England in the second half of the 19th century (*Attorney Gen.* v. *Windsor*, 8 H.L. Cases 389; 11 Eng. Rep. 481 (1860).

input into the social system. This prevents the *stare decisis* rule from being consistently applied. Only if the legal system were self-contained and unrelated to any other system could it apply the rule universally.

In England the rule is much more rigidly applied than in the United States, because only an act of Parliament can change a well-established rule. This means that English judges would apply a precedent even if they did not approve it.[37] The American rule is *usually* applied because, as Justice Brandeis put it:

Stare decisis is usually the wise policy because in most matters it is more important that the applicable rule of law be settled than that it be settled right. This is commonly true, even where the error is a matter of serious concern, provided correction can be had by legislation.[38]

Questions of constitutional law have been those in which the force of precedent has been least felt in the American legal system. Even in that class of cases, the percentage of overruling decisions is always very low.[39] The explanation for the lesser effect of *stare decisis* might be that the outputs of the Supreme Court serve as major inputs into the political system, so that the needs of the legal system for internal consistency and homeostasis must be sacrificed for the greater needs of the political and social system for homeostasis. Consequently, the decisions of the Supreme Court may cause considerable disequilibrium in the legal system, a virtual positive feedback situation. In no other field of law is the effect of not following precedent so unsettling, but the Supreme Court is both a political and a legal body, holding responsibilities to both systems, but a primary responsibility to the society-at-large.

---

[37] *Beamish* v. *Beamish*, 9 H.L. Cases 274; 11 Eng. Rep. 481 (1861).

[38] *Burnett* v. *Coronado Oil & Gas Co.*, 285 U.S. 405 (1931).

[39] See S. Sidney Ulmer, "An Empirical Analysis of Selected Aspects of Lawmaking of the United States Supreme Court," *Journal of Public Law*, Vol. 8 (1959), pp. 414, 432.

III

External inputs

Mr. Dooley, eminent social critic of the last century, once accused the Supreme Court of following the election returns. Neighborhood humorists sometimes say that Judge X is the best judge that money can buy. Another popular joke tells of the poor Italian immigrant who, after many years, seeks American citizenship but fears that the judge may deny it to him because he can't speak the language clearly. "You no-a worry," says the judge, "you spikka justa fine, an you gonna make a real good 'Merican."

Behind these jokes and barbs is a strong public awareness of the existence of external inputs. By word of mouth, stories circulate among members of the public about the partisanship, biases, and payoffs of members of the legal establishment. Most of these stories are mere gossip, but a few show shrewd insight. Lawyers are even more aware of these factors, often sharing stories about judges and other lawyers in private sessions over coffee or a drink.

Most of these stories rest upon pure surmise. Many of them are a tangle of fact and fable. Bribes and payoffs have been extremely rare in American legal history, but still form a popular topic of discussion. For technical purposes it is best to separate the categories of influence into external and

internal inputs, and then to analyze each category inten-
sively. This approach will show that outside forces must
have some influence upon the legal process, and are not
necessarily "evil" or "good."

Outside the legal system itself, the political system continues to operate in response to social demands and pressures, as well as to the policies of political leaders. A few
people in legal and political circles still regard the separation of law and politics to be both necessary and complete.[1]
But seen from the vantage point of our analysis, the two systems are bound together inextricably, although their inner
processes are clearly different and distinguishable. It is true
that democratic states do not generally resort to the political
trial, nor do they seek to enlist the judiciary in the effort to
enforce political ideas. On the other hand, even democratic
judges have a limited part to play in the formulation of public policy.

The political scientist usually views the political system
as an arena of conflicting groups and elites in which, by the
processes of compromise and mediation, social policy is set.
The focus is upon the policy as a prize, and the concern is
primarily with the "authoritative allocation of values."[2]
However, between the point at which the policy is made
legislatively and the point of the social impact of the policy,
the political scientist in the public law area makes his studies. He makes no sharp separation between the enactment of
a statute and rendering of a judicial opinion concerning that
statute. Both are perceivable as political acts, although one
is treated according to the internal processes of the legal
system. The statute itself may be regarded as an input ex-

---

[1] As Judith Shklar points out, the presentation of law as an apolitical technique for attaining justice is a serious legalistic fallacy; *Legalism* (Cambridge, Mass.: Harvard University Press, 1964), pp. 111–23. Justice is merely
one policy among other competing social policies which affect law.

[2] David Easton, *The Political System* (New York: Alfred A. Knopf, Inc.,
1963), p. 129. Another formulation emphasizes "a working union of interests,
ideas, institutions and individuals" (Pendleton Herring, *The Politics of Democracy* [New York: Holt, Rinehart & Winston, Inc., 1940], p. 421).

ternal to the legal system; constitutions and rules are other inputs. In a broad sense the activity of outside groups and the influence of the environment and public opinion are also external inputs. This perspective allows for analysis of the process from the perspective of its actual operation, but the varieties of input should be sharply distinguished.

Statutes as input

The connection between legislation and adjudication is so intimate that some people cannot properly tell them apart. Certainly, in cases of statutory ambiguity, delegation, or conflict judges must shape an otherwise inchoate policy. This could not be called legislation but "legisputation," since it purports to supply a missing legislative meaning.[3] In any case involving a statute, judges must "interpret" its meaning. They are bound to do so as a duty which cannot be avoided.

The legal system could operate without statutes, but increasingly legal decisions are made in terms of statutes and administrative rulings which may come to the attention of courts. There is a history of strong judicial resistance to legislation and of preference for the common (judge-made) law, although this is more true in America and England than elsewhere.[4] In many fields of public concern the judges have restricted the implementation of new social policy by narrowly interpreting statutes.[5] Despite such resistance the common law has begun to recede in the states and has dis-

---

[3] Julius Cohen, "Judicial 'Legisputation' and the Dimensions of Legislative Meaning," *Indiana Law Journal*, Vol. 36 (Summer, 1961), pp. 414–23.

[4] The old maxim is that "statutes in derogation of the common law are strictly construed." It has less force in nations employing the Napoleonic Code, or some variation of it. See D. Lloyd, *Public Policy* (London: Athlone Press, 1953), pp. 149–50.

[5] W. I. Jennings, "Judicial Process at Its Worst," *Modern Law Review* (September, 1937), pp. 111–31, describes a remarkable instance of judicial resistance to public health legislation. Jennings also describes the resistance to administrative rulings in "The Courts and Administrative Law," *Harvard Law Review*, Vol. 49 (January, 1936), pp. 426–54.

appeared at the national level in the United States.[6] A tide of statutes has begun to sweep into the legal system.

If statutes now form the primary input of the legal system, it must be recalled that they are the output of the legislative and executive parts of the political system. Statutes enter the legal system in a peculiar fashion, however. They are not treated in a general fashion, but according to the techniques of the legal system, which requires attention to the particular rather than the general. The statute becomes merely one input ingredient in the combination of variables which comprise a "case." In any "case" there may be several available statutes, and only portions applicable to the "facts" may be presented. In theory the statutes are the most important guides to the legal decision (output), but the practice is far more complicated.

To take a simple and dramatic example, the national government may embark upon a program of restraining revolutionary activity. The Smith Act of 1940 attempted to do this. The act made it unlawful "to knowingly or willfully advocate, abet, advise, or teach the duty, necessity, desirability, or propriety of overthrowing or destroying any government in the United States by force or violence."[7] The language seems clear and relatively unambiguous, but the act has given rise to innumerable problems of enforcement and interpretation.

First the Supreme Court had to decide that Congress had acted within its constitutional power, which it did.[8] Later that Court proceeded to narrowly construe the words "teach" and "advocate" to avoid other constitutional problems.[9] Then the Court had to distinguish factually between be-

---

[6] It appears that *Erie R.R.* v. *Tompkins*, 304 U.S. 64 (1938), by overruling *Swift* v. *Tyson*, 16 Pet. 1 (1842) has eliminated the area of general federal common law.

[7] 54 Stat. 670, 18 U.S.C. 10, Sec. 2(a) (1940).

[8] *Dennis* v. *United States*, 341 U.S. 494 (1951).

[9] *Yates* v. *United States*, 354 U.S. 298 (1957).

longing to an organization which advocates forceful over-
throw of the government and personally advocating such a
deed.[10] These decisions, while preserving the essential policy
of Congress, have required the government to allege and
prove more specific facts regarding an individual's participation in revoultionary activity.

On a less dramatic level of public policy, a state court
may have to interpret an ambiguous highway statute. If the
statute is clear, descriptive, and comprehensive, the interpretation may involve a simple discovery that the facts alleged fall within the ambit of the statutory language. This is
generally simple. However, if the facts alleged do not clearly
fall within the definitions or contours of a statute, a court
may have to conclude that, for example, to condemn county
park commission lands the legislature would have to so provide "in plain and explicit language," in the absence of
which the condemnation would be deemed improper.[11] As
indicated earlier, though, the court has greater responsibility to supply a meaning to a policy when the legislative intent does not appear from a fair-reading of the text itself.
In any event, the court cannot find that the statute has no
meaning, but must, in applying it, draw inferences from
ambiguity.

Sometimes the court is faced with an apparent conflict
of statutes. When the input information is completely confused, we should expect the output to be unpredictable, and
this appears to be so. One solution is to resort to the fiction
of the "implied repeal." When a new law contains provisions
contrary to an earlier law, but does not expressly repeal it,
the court may choose to take the view that the legislature
would have repealed the earlier offending statute if they

---

[10] Compare *Scales* v. *United States,* 367 U.S. 203 (1961) with *Noto* v.
United States, 367 U.S. 290 (1961).

[11] *State Highway Commissioner* v. *Union County Park Commission,* 89
N.J. Super. 202, 214 A. 2d 446 (1965), interpreting N.J.S.A. 27:7–36 (New
Jersey).

had recognized the conflict (which is clearly an artificial inference).[12] Otherwise the court must select carefully among the statutes to apply in order to ignore the statutory conflict. In conflict-of-statute situations outputs are not predictable because courts are not equipped to process divergent policy information flowing from the legislature. They must invent a policy while pretending to respond to the statutory inputs.

A final demonstration of the significance of statutory input is provided by the statute which is improperly or irregularly passed. To have a proper statutory input the supposed "law" must have been duly passed by a properly constituted legislature according to the procedures constitutionally required.[13] A statute which does not conform to these requirements cannot be considered by a court. It is not a proper input and cannot effect a legal outcome.

Statutes: feedback

Over the course of time, a pattern of judicial interpretations of a statute may result in the development of a feedback policy loop in order to correct a policy direction of which a legislature disapproves. The feedback may be simple, as an immediate legislative response to a court interpretation, or it may be complex, passing through the social system and back into the political system in the form of public pressures. In either event, the effect is to serve as a fresh input to correct an undesired policy drift.

---

[12] The formidable power created by this fiction is discussed in *Hudson Motor Car* v. *Hertz*, 121 F. 2d 326 (C.C.A.Mich., 1941) and *Federal Trade Commission* v. *A.P.W. Paper Co.*, 328 U.S. 193 (1945). There is a "presumption" against implied repeal, but it is difficult to understand what that signifies.

[13] *Dawson* v. *Bomar*, 322 F. 2d 445 (C.A. Tenn., 1963). The fact that the Tennessee legislature was malapportioned was held not to make its statutes automatically invalid. The chaos and confusion which the reapportionment requirements would otherwise create is sufficient to discourage judicial refusal to enforce such laws.

Several illustrations will serve. In the area of subversive activity control Congress was so displeased with Supreme Court decisions concerning the Smith Act and other cases concerning legislative investigations into communism that seven bills were introduced in direct reaction to them. One went so far as to remove Supreme Court jurisdiction completely from the areas involved. All were rejected, but the Supreme Court reacted to the threat by moderating its decisions.[14]

Another example, but one in which new legislation was produced, is provided by the policy of antitrust regulation. Congress initiated the policy in 1887, only to find the Supreme Court reading the act so restrictively as to cripple the regulatory agency (ICC); the Court nearly destroyed federal control over trusts and monopolies in 1895 but breathed new life into the policy in a 1904 decision. Congress regained control over antitrust policy by passing the Clayton Act and the Federal Trade Commission Act in 1914.[15] More recent Courts have been less prone to narrowly confine antitrust policy.

At times the feedback reaction is rather long delayed. It took 14 years for Congress, in 1967, to respond to a 1950 Court decision regarding lobbying. The original Lobbying Act was passed in 1946 and was directed at persons or organizations attempting "to influence, directly or indirectly" the passage or defeat of any federal legislation. The Supreme Court felt that general lobbying activities intended to persuade the public were not included within the statutory language, leaving unregulated, as a result, virtually 90 percent of all lobbying activities at the federal level.[16] Only

---

[14] C. Herman Pritchett, *Congress versus the Supreme Court* (Minneapolis: University of Minnesota Press, 1961), pp. 59–69, 119–21.

[15] The first case was *United States* v. *E. C. Knight Company,* 156 U.S. 1 (1895). The second was *Northern Securities Co.* v. *United States,* 193 U.S. 197 (1904). The story is traced by Robert Carr, in *The Supreme Court and Judicial Review* (New York: Holt, Rinehart & Winston, Inc., 1942), pp. 99–138.

[16] *United States* v. *Rumley,* 345 U.S. 41 (1953).

in 1967 did Congress find enough agreement on a new
policy to substitute the words "substantial effect" for "directly or indirectly" in an effort to cover all federal lobbying.

It will take further research to illuminate the workings of
of the legislative-judicial feedback loop. At this moment it
is not easy to explain why certain decisions produce feedback response and others do not. It is not easy to explain
the time lag or to predict likely legislature behavior. Nonetheless, the problem is fascinating and awaits careful study,
since it is at the heart of long-range public policy formulation.

Constitutional inputs

A constitution is, formally, the highest quality of legal
input. It is "superior" to ordinary statutes, rules, and treaties. The superiority is normative in character because it
supplies the fundamental principles which support the political and legal systems. If pleaded in an issue in a case,
the constitutionality of a law must be demonstrated as a
condition prior to its interpretation and application. Yet,
because constitutional inputs are much less common than
statutory ones, a balanced view of the legal system requires
that they be treated after consideration of statutes. Students
of public law should realize that although constitutional interpretation is very important, it is only one variety of public law.

American political practice has historically differed from
that of most nations in its high regard for constitutional principles. In addition, the American judiciary has developed
extraordinary potential power to apply the norms of the
Constitution. More than anything else, the power of "judicial review" distinguishes the American legal system from
that of most other nations. Despite the existence of the
power to strike down the constitutionality of all federal and
state laws, federal treaties, administrative rules, and local
ordinances, it is rarely used.

It is true that the German Federal Constitutional Court had broader review powers than the American Supreme Court. The German Court can declare parties to be unconstitutional and cause "forfeiture" of constitutional rights to those who violate the rights of others.[17] But despite the German practice (which was based on American example) very few nations employ judicial review, and very few judges possess the power to declare national policies unconstitutional.

In expressing a judgment that a statute is "unconstitutional," a court is rejecting part of the input on normative grounds, derived from its individual interpretation of constitutional norms which are generally known to the source of the input. The justification must be that judges are in a better position to interpret constitutional inputs than anyone else. In fact, that is the premise upon which the doctrine rests in the United States.[18]

If this claim were pressed, the flow of policy would be reversed, and the judges would provide the largest output of policy in the political system. Realizing the unsuitability and impropriety of an active policy-making role, the United States Supreme Court has chosen to retreat in most areas to the safe sanctuary of legislative interpretation rather than use its assumed power of judicial review. This retreat is evidence of the fact that the normal flow of public policy making will not be interrupted by the courts except in extreme situations. This attitude is expressed in the judicial ideology of self-restraint with regard to economic issues. Activism prevails, however, in some other areas upon which Supreme Court members have deep policy conflicts with other agencies of the national government or the states.

---

[17] The law on the Federal Constitutional Court (*Bundesverfassungsgericht*) of March 12, 1951, even permits individuals to carry cases of deprivation of a civil right directly to the Supreme Court. Article 21 of the Constitution permits suppression of anticonstitutional parties, and Article 19 provides for loss of rights because of misuse.

[18] *Marbury* v. *Madison*, 1 Cranch 137 (1803).

The individual judges develop personal views of their proper roles in the legal system, which accounts for the prevalence of attitudes of self-restraint or activism in their use of the power of judicial review. Familiarity with these personal views will make it easier to anticipate, or even predict, policy shifts by the United States Supreme Court or, for that matter, state supreme courts. Activism, it should be clear, implies a conflict between the court and other public policy makers. Self-restraint implies agreement with the normal flow of the policy input stream.[19]

From 1925 until the present, the United States Supreme Court has lead national progress in the development of civil liberties. A conscious and deliberate attempt was made to develop the meanings of vague provisions in the Bill of Rights regarding freedom of speech, press, assembly, religion, due process, and equal protection of the laws. The most dramatic instances of judicial review occurred in the areas of racial discrimination and malapportionment of legislative bodies. It is submitted that Supreme Court activism in these fields is explained not only by a dynamic group of Supreme Court justices, but also by a general lack of policy initiative in other political bodies, which permitted the Court to play the unusual role of generating outputs in response to inputs from areas other than the usual political (legislative and executive) sources. The Court responded to inputs which it perceived in the society itself. In so doing, new constitutional norms—many unanticipated—were created.[20]

---

[19] An excellent discussion appears in Glendon Schubert, *Judicial Policy-Making* (Chicago: Scott, Foresman & Co., 1965), pp. 130–57. Schubert seems more concerned with the use of judicial review power than any other aspect of decision making, and relates these occasions to the social and political attitudes of the judges. In a broad sense this is a useful analysis, but it may neglect to consider the more typical public law situation.

[20] In *Griswold* v. *Connecticut*, 381 U.S. 479 (1965) the Court discovered a new "right of privacy" in the Ninth Amendment, combined with other amendments. *Baker* v. *Carr*, 369 U.S. 186 (1962) was even more startling in its effect by placing the Court in a novel position of reconsidering the adequacy of legislative districting, under the claim of the requirements of

Constitutional normative input can be suggested by many sources. It may be discussed in legal briefs, debated on public platforms, or spoken of in barrooms. But the mere suggestion of a constitutional interpretation is not meaningful until adopted by an authoritative decision maker, and ultimately the federal Supreme Court is likely to have the last word. Of course, most of the cases which reach the Court do not involve matters of great constitutional significance. Most of its decisions are not likely to affect many people or institutions.

Supreme Court justices, even more than other judges, are forced to develop a set of attitudes concerning a wide range of legal and social problems. These may be treated in terms of a "liberal" or "conservative" preference, or possibly in a variety of sets of preferences which may reflect the personal experience of each judge in varying fields. However shaped or conditioned, these preferences are a formative factor in constitutional input.

Constitutional feedback

When the United States Supreme Court, or other courts, assert constitutional norms to be superior inputs to statutory inputs, it is possible that reactions of a feedback character will be produced. Given the constitutional context of the situation, however, the effectiveness of the feedback reaction is severely limited.

The appellate jurisdiction of the Supreme Court is left by the Constitution for the Congress to describe. The Congress could deprive the Court of case inputs by reducing the area of jurisdiction in disputed zones of policy. A determined Congress could succeed in this attempt, but the at-

---

the Fourteenth Amendment "equal protection" clause. *Brown* v. *Board of Education of Topeka*, 347 U.S. 483 (1954), while of enormous significance in ending segregated public school facilities, was much less surprising to skilled observers of the Supreme Court, who could trace the gradual evolution of school desegregation in earlier opinions.

tempt has only rarely been pressed, although threats are repeatedly made.[21]

If Congress is sufficiently incensed, it may attempt to remove a single Justice by means of impeachment. This device was suggested for use against Chief Justice Earl Warren in congressional debate in 1962. But impeachment has been used only 12 times in history, 4 times against judges, and has never resulted in the removal of a Supreme Court Justice. The constitutional provision providing for life tenure during good behavior effectively limits impeachment to cases involving serious wrongdoing amounting to a crime.[22]

Congress could abolish federal courts other than the Supreme Court. It could increase or decrease the number of judges on the Supreme Court, or the Senate could resist the appointment of certain Presidential nominees for judgeships.

All of these methods are indirect varieties of feedback, aimed at the structure or the personnel of federal courts. More limitedly, the Congress can effect reversal of policy by adopting new legislation or by amending the Constitution itself. Three notable examples of the latter process are provided by the Eleventh, Fourteenth, and Sixteenth Amendments, each of which was directly intended to reverse Supreme Court opinions. Formerly, the process of amending the Constitution was considered arduous, but the prompt passage of the Twenty-Third, Twenty-Fourth, and Twenty-Fifth Amendments may signal a change in this condition.

In the broad view the process of constitutional feedback is most often a historic rather than an immediate process. Legislatures are usually indifferent to judicial policy making, or they are unable to muster a deliberate response. A co-

---

[21] In *Ex Parte McCardle*, 7 Wallace 506 (1869), the Congress succeeded in halting a case already argued before the Supreme Court before the Court rendered its decision. The Court dismissed the action for want of jurisdiction.

[22] Compare Art. III, Sec. 1 with Art. 1, Sec. 2 and Sec. 3 of the United States Constitution.

hesive political majority supported by a popular majority is likely to wear down judicial policies and interpretations. Most decisions will prevail against a passive response.[23]

Rules and orders

A great many legal decisions are made by agencies which are outside the usual legal apparatus in a deliberate attempt by legislatures to allow lawmaking by delegation to executive or independent groups. At first glance, it would seem that these groups are merely sublegislating, but to a considerable extent they may also prosecute and adjudicate disputes. In our terminology these agencies may be regarded as political subsystems which possess internal legal systems.

In some cases, Congress permits executive department heads to issue rules having legal effect, to hear complaints, and to decide disputes. In others, units within the executive departments, such as the Food and Drug Administration within the Department of Health, Education, and Welfare, possess these powers. Finally, independent regulatory commissions may be provided broad powers over particular sectors of the economy.

The mixture of legislative, executive, and judicial functions is intended to allow more rapid decision making than that provided by the normal channels of policy resolution. Administrative action is less encumbered by legalism, more flexible, and more expert than either legislative or judicial action. Each agency has the opportunity to develop a special competence and a special knowledge often required by the very nature of a modern industrial society.

Despite these apparent advantages, the legal input-output process still goes on internally. The quantity of adjudication in federal agencies is "probably many times the quantity of

---

[23] Robert Dahl, "Decision-Making in a Democracy," *Journal of Public Law*, Vol. 6 (Fall, 1957), pp. 279–95.

adjudication in federal courts."[24] Each agency has a peculiar machinery and a different set of rules. As a result, each subsystem requires a different set of legal experts to advise the agencies. An individual who deals with the agency will probably need the assistance of a lawyer acquainted with the jargon, expertise, and procedure of the particular agency. In sum, each is a separate system requiring separate law and separate lawyers.

A good deal of administrative action is unreviewable by ordinary courts. In such situations a closed system may be said to exist. The Federal Administrative Procedures Act makes unreviewable all actions defined as such by statute or committed to agency discretion.[25] The statute appears to create a general right of judicial review if the statute-creating agency is silent on the issue.

The Supreme Court is usually the final determiner of congressional intention on the issue of judicial review of administrative action. In sheer volume, "review of administrative action, mainly reflecting enforcement of federal regulatory statutes, constitutes the largest category of the court's work, comprising one-third of the total cases on the merits."[26] More dramatic cases may impress the public, but administrative actions are quantitatively the largest portion of the Supreme Court's business.

The internal operation, powers, and procedures of federal and state administrative agencies is part of the extremely complex area denoted as "administrative law." The substantive law produced by each agency forms a separate body of law called tax law, transportation law, labor law, public

---

[24] Kenneth Culp Davis, *Administrative Law and Government* (St. Paul, Minn.: West Publishing Co., 1960), p. 14. Exact comparisons are extremely difficult to make. In one year, though, the National Labor Relations Board may receive eight times as many cases as the Supreme Court and write opinions in nine times as many cases (cited by Davis, *ibid.*).

[25] Stat. 237 (1946); 5 U.S.C.A. 1001, Sec. 10.

[26] Felix Frankfurter, "The Supreme Court in the Mirror of Justices," *University of Pennsylvania Law Review*, Vol. 105 (April, 1957), pp. 781, 793.

utility law, and the like. Citizens need to be aware of the existence of these areas, but only highly skilled lawyers will be able to grasp the intricacies of these laws. In no other area is the law so removed from popular understanding and control. Because this area of law is only dimly understood, feedback response to administrative laws is minimal. Only the ordinary courts serve as a restraint, though sometimes a feeble one, due to their lack of expertise. Courts tend to confine the scope of their own inquiry into administrative decisions, rarely striking down administrative rules or actions on the ground that they are *ultra vires*—beyond the power delegated to the agency by statute.

Interest group inputs

Until this point, formal inputs have been considered. These have been tangible and documentary in character. A statute, constitution, or rule is printed, public, and available to examination. Other classes of inputs, less formal in character, may have profound impact upon the legal system, but by their nature will not be given credit or recognition by the system. Among these is the activity of the interest group.

One form of legitimate interest group activity is the institution of suit on behalf of injured members. At times, important trends are apparently influenced by group representation in the form of cases brought to a court. The NAACP (National Association for the Advancement of Colored People) is a leading example. Its treasury supported litigation which dramatically changed the course of race relations in America.[27] Indeed, its chief counsel, Thurgood Marshall, by becoming Soliciter-General in the Johnson ad-

---

[27] Clement E. Vose, "Litigation as a Form of Pressure Group Activity," *Annals of the American Academy of Political and Social Science*, Vol. 319 (September, 1958). Also, Vose, *Caucasians Only: The Supreme Court, the NAACP, and the Restrictive Covenant Cases* (Berkeley and Los Angeles: University of California Press, 1959).

ministration, indicated the newfound prestige and influence of this interest group. He has recently been appointed Supreme Court Justice.

The name or nature of the interest group which supports a case input may not be revealed upon the surface. The NAACP Legal Defense Fund does not always advertise its efforts, but it may supply legal defense to those requesting assistance, or, if the organization desires, it may convert an individual case into a class action. When this is done, as the Federal Rules of Civil Procedure permit, the group character of the case becomes obvious. In either event, the individual of little means may often require the assistance of an interest group in order to afford the price of a favorable outcome.

Sometimes the input takes the form of a "test case," a deliberate infraction of a law for the purpose of testing its validity or the propriety of its enforcement. The Planned Parenthood League of Connecticut attempted such a challenge of a state statute prohibiting the use of contraceptive devices. Twice the Supreme Court found that the group did not have a sufficient justiciable interest, but ultimately the right circumstances of violation were created to convince the Court that a definite individual injury had occurred, and the statute was stricken down.[28]

The interest group input may take the form of a legal "brief," a printed argument supporting a particular set of legal contentions. These briefs may be submitted by a group even if it or a supported client is not directly involved. If accepted by a court, the brief may serve as a guide to policy resolution. This form of communication is of particular importance in Supreme Court practice.[29]

An interest group will often pursue its views at various phases of the policy process. It may attempt to influence

---

[28] *Tileston* v. *Ullman*, 318 U.S. 44 (1943); *Poe* v. *Ullman*, 367 U.S. 497 (1961); *Griswold* v. *Connecticut*, 381 U.S. 479 (1965).

[29] Samuel Krislov, "The Amicus Curiae Brief: From Friendship to Advocacy," *Yale Law Journal*, Vol. 72 (March, 1963), pp. 694–721.

the courts and, finally, attempt to set up a feedback reaction by use of letter-writing campaigns, picketing, demonstrations, or "educational" campaigns directed at key sectors of the mass public. Judicial machinery is less responsive to such techniques than the other branches of government, but no doubt the judges and juries are not immune to impressions received from these external sources, although their connection with particular interest groups could be so obvious that it might produce a negative reaction.

Media input and feedback

The impact of the communication media upon the legal system, although of deep concern to jurists and civil libertarians, is very difficult to measure and evaluate. The input may take place at the trial level as an impression received by a juror, at the appellate level by a judge, or even prior to initiation of a case at the arrest, investigation, indictment, or grand jury phase.

In the remarkable television coverage of the Kennedy assassination and the Oswald killing, the enormous impact of the medium was demonstrated. The subsequent difficulties in obtaining a fair trial for Jack Ruby indicated the mass effect upon the legal system in Texas.

The media input tends to be generalized, selective, and diffuse. It is generalized because it is rarely directed at the legal system and influences it only as a side effect of the attempt to generate "news." It is selective because it emphasizes the sensational, usually the criminal case. Supreme Court reporting is quite scanty, while police court coverage is common. It is diffuse because, despite the rather emotional, even inflammatory tone, of some reportage, the effect upon the legal system is usually vague and unpredictable.

Particularly celebrated trials may require unusual precautions to be taken to protect the objectivity of the legal system. A defendant may seek to change the place of trial or seek a continuance to delay trial. The judge, if biased, can be removed; the jury will be shielded from receiving information from the media regarding the case. This legal insulation is intended primarily to protect the defendant, but it creates an artificial, sterilized, legal climate.

The commentary of the media at a point before initiation of a case or after conclusion of the trial is not considered as harmful. This is true because the prosecutors and appellate judges are considered less vulnerable to emotive media inputs than are jurors. This assumption awaits further proof. In any event, the public interest in the value of free speech and press must be balanced against the concern for neutral operation of the legal system, and at times, the latter must give way to the former.

The media input into the legal system is controlled, to some extent, by the procedural rules of the courts. The individual practices of judges also regulate the media impact. If a judge chooses to allow television cameras, photographers, and radio reporters into the courtroom, the atmosphere of a trial may be affected sufficiently to affect the outcome.[30]

Media feedback is exhibited by response to popular or unpopular court decisions. Media feedback may take the form of either reportage, commentary, or editorial writing. Television and radio feedback are much less significant than newspaper response because the high cost of time on the airwaves limits their use. Consequently, the coverage of legal processes is usually confined to the daily press. It is very unlikely that media feedback is influential upon the legal system itself, except in exposing the scandals or abuses which the media occasionally unearth.[31] The natural audi-

---

[30] Some states permit these practices if a judge agrees. See Warren Friedman, "News Coverage of Criminal Cases and the Right to a Fair Trial," *Nebraska Law Review*, Vol. 40 (June, 1961), pp. 391-412.

[31] The abuses of the Philadelphia magisterial system were exposed by several newspapers and television stations during 1965–66. Several magistrates were removed and tried for various types of malfeasance in office, and a general reform of the entire system has been actively considered. The matter became a campaign issue in the victory of Republican District Attorney Arlen Spector.

ence of the media is the general public, and it is through its public impact that the media produce an indirect feedback pattern.

Public feedback response

The mass public is usually uninformed about, and uninterested in, the legal system. Only specific groups, which often comprise members of interest groups, are likely to maintain a continuing focus upon the legal system. Members of the NAACP or the National Rifle Association are likely to have some familiarity with administrative decisions and court decisions affecting them. Members of these groups may respond to legal outputs individually.

On issues of particular sensitivity, the mass public may become aroused, in response to media coverage, with certain aspects of the legal system. The Supreme Court of the United States is better covered than any other court, and its decisions are more likely to bring forth response. At times, the Court's activities are misreported, producing an inaccurate, irrational response.[32]

An unusual outburst of public response may cause a noticeable feedback response by a court. The most obvious example is that of the flag-salute cases in which the United States Supreme Court reversed itself within three years from its initial decision which had required school children to salute the flag under certain state laws in spite of claims of religious beliefs.[33]

Public interest in criminal law policy has been excited by recent Supreme Court rulings regarding the use of con-

---

[32] Chester A. Newland, "Press Coverage of the United States Supreme Court," *Western Political Quarterly*, Vol. 17 (1964), pp. 16–23. Poor reportage of the school prayer decision (*Engel* v. *Vitale*) resulted in a great deal of public misapprehension regarding the practice of religion and the use of symbolism. (See William A. Hatchen, "Journalism and the Prayer Decision," *Columbia Journalism Review*, Vol. 1 [Fall, 1963], pp. 4–9.)

[33] *Minersville School District* v. *Gobitis*, 310 U.S. (1940); *West Virginia State Board of Education* v. *Barnette*, 319 U.S. 624 (1943). Recounted in David R. Manwaring, *Render unto Caesar* (Chicago: University of Chicago Press, 1962).

fessions, the right of counsel, and self-incrimination. Many police groups, in cooperation with the press, have caused a widespread pressure upon the Supreme Court. This is sometimes supported by internal feedback within the legal profession and the law reviews. It is likely that the Court will yield before this feedback reaction and retreat from some of its decisions in the criminal law area.

Public feedback response to the legal system is more likely to take the form of a pressure for new statutes than for better prosecution, trial procedure, or judicial decision making. It is more likely to be immediately reformist than innovative. Significant changes in structure, such as the major overhaul of the New Jersey court system in 1947, are likely to go unnoticed by the mass public, but are likely to be internally generated and supported by the attentive public (the informed, educated, and interested minority).[34]

Political parties as environmental input

The influence of political parties upon the course of decision making in the legal system is the subject of considerable debate among experts. No one would deny that parties are extremely influential in the selection of judicial personnel, in the choice of prosecutors, and in the administration of certain types of courts, especially probate courts. But the more difficult issue is whether the appellate courts, and particularly the Supreme Court, follow the election returns or instead pursue policies more internal to the legal system. In brief: To what extent do political parties affect the environment in which the legal system operates?

One scholar suggests that the power of judicial review, for example, has been most utilized by the federal Supreme Court in the period after the decline of sectionally powerful

---

[34] Bennett Rich, *The Government and Administration of New Jersey* (New York: Thomas Y. Crowell Co., 1957), pp. 24–36, shows that these vital changes were not the subject of public concern.

parties and before the rise of powerful urban parties (1865–1936).[35] This suggestive insight requires further refinement so that the relationship between party platforms and judicial decisions (or other responses) can be proven. Direct causal relationships are hard to establish.

The point at which the legal system is most prone to political influence is at the bottom. The magistrate, for example, "is almost unprotected so far as political influences are concerned and the political factors involved are very great."[36] At this level "string pulling," political debts, and favors may have considerable impact upon decision making. Adding to this impression the fact that in many states judgeships are elective posts makes clear the existence of a politicized climate within lower levels of the legal system.

Another point of political influence is in the initiation of suit by governmental units. The decision to prosecute antitrust violations, to sue for breach of contract on sewer construction, or to institute a civil rights prosecution are all likely to be the subject of political pressures. These events rarely reach the attention of the student of the legal system, but they do take place and are of some significance. The imponderable issue is the weight which they may supply, the degree of environmental input.

Community input

The community or groups within the community play a major role in shaping the general contours of law. This may

---

35 Wallace Mendelson, "The Politics of Judicial Supremacy," *Journal of Law and Economics*, Vol. 4 (October, 1961), pp. 175–85. This is supported statistically in Stuart Nagel's article, which also shows the weakness of the major (mostly Republican) party in Congress during these years: "Political Parties and Judicial Review in American History," *Journal of Public Law*, Vol. 11 (1962), pp. 328–40.

36 Raymond Moley, *Our Criminal Courts* (New York: Minton, Balch & Co., 1930), p. 29. This seminal work requires substantial empirical support, but it is difficult to obtain on so sensitive an area. No doubt, further research will soon fill in the lacunae in the administration of criminal justice.

take place in the form of group law input, pressure group demands, or normative input from the generally diffused sense of community-held values.

Group law input is best exhibited in the transmutation of private law system (internal to a particular group) into public law, as with the incorporation of the ideas of the private "law merchant" into common law and statutory law.[37] The code of ethics of a group such as a medical association or a bar association may also become adopted into the general body of the public law. When this happens, the group is transferring its authority to resolve internal disputes to state (public) organizations that have the power to authoritatively allocate values in the society at large. The purpose is to provide the sanctions of the entire society to resolve disputes which might otherwise be beyond solution by the group itself.

Interest group demands are, of course, well organized, and usually aim at initiating proposals to legislatures or countering proposed bills. Since this work is rather remote from the legal system itself, the only aspect of pressure group activity which is of significance at the community level is the propaganda activity of the groups. The hope of the interest group is to reach influential members of the public or the mass public to cause them to respond to undesirable outputs of the legal system. Such groups as the AFL–CIO and the American Medical Association provide typical examples.[38]

Many community norms serve as conscious or unconscious guides to decision makers in the legal system. Efficiency is an especially important American social value. In

---

[37] Louis L. Jaffee, "Law Making by Private Groups," *Harvard Law Review*, Vol. 51 (1937), p. 213.

[38] Gerald Pomper, "The Public Relations of Organized Labor," *Public Opinion Quarterly*, Vol. 23 (Winter, 1960), p. 487, and Harmon Ziegler, *Interest Groups in American Society* (Englewood Cliffs, N.J.: Prentice-Hall, Inc., 1964), pp. 236–40.

a great many legal situations courts ask themselves the "pragmatic" question, "What will be the impact of this decision upon the people who are to perform a function in society?" Without entering into the field of jurisprudence or legal philosophy, it should be obvious that the question itself assumes the relevancy of the value of efficiency; legislatures often adopt community values consciously in order to suit their sense of propriety, thus feeding into the legal systems contemporary—or antiquated—ideas about morality, censorship, the sanctity of the family, homosexual behavior, the use of narcotics, and the like. Other community values may be found in vague notions of freedom of expression, the right of privacy, and freedom of religion which could conflict with other community values. In such situations a court must choose, more or less consciously, between competing social values. This may lead a libertarian judge like Justice Hugo Black to emphasize the normative standards he discovers inherent in the Bill of Rights over other, presumably lesser, community values.[39]

In the realm of social values, while the social stakes are high, the standards of clarity are low. If the legal system is, in the long run, dependent upon the values of the community, which themselves often spring from community custom and habit, the task of the law decision maker is seen to be exceedingly complex. If the input information does not spell out the normative assumptions which support it, the law decision maker must infer the probable normative significance of the information. In the process his own personal norms, themselves societally conditioned, may intrude. The interplay of these conflicting values can provide fascinating analysis, but the dangers of the process must also be examined. It is possible that the legal system may develop goal conceptions inconsistent with those of the political system.

---

[39] Irving Dillard (ed.), *One Man's Stand for Freedom: Mr. Justice Black and the Bill of Rights* (New York: Alfred A. Knopf, Inc., 1963).

It is also possible that the legal system does not possess sufficient apparatus to become aware of the current social values of the community. In this event, the legal system could develop a runaway positive feedback reaction and lose the confidence of the community.[40]

---

[40] See Harry C. Briedemeir, "Law as an Integrative Mechanism," in William M. Evan (ed.), *Law and Sociology* (Glencoe, Ill.: Free Press, 1962), pp. 73–90.

IV

The machinery of justice

FROM THE processing of a lowly traffic ticket to the desperate manipulations of creditors in a bankruptcy proceeding, the legal system is committed to a complicated structure of decision making. This structure is often a variable in the process. If the wrong papers are filed, the wrong buttons pushed, the output will be distorted. An understanding of the legal machinery will not tell the whole tale, but it should provide a view of the environment of the legal system. The law in action is not merely an ancient skeleton. Instead, it is like those massive suspension bridges which span the Hudson River and San Francisco Bay, connecting bustling regions on either side, but constantly in need of a fresh coat of paint.

Separation of powers

As a starting point, mention must be made of the principle of separation of powers. By virtue of that principle the courts are placed in a passive condition in regard to most input and output matters. American courts depend upon the executive branch for the initiation of public suits and upon the legislative branch for the input of legislative policy.

Even so, the principle of separation of powers has had decreasing significance with the passage of time. Mingling of the three functions is commonplace in administrative agencies, and modern courts have begun to question the doctrine.

The separation of powers principle is implicit in the federal constitutional scheme of dividing functional authority. Article III provides the source of judicial power at the national level. Article I establishes legislative power, and Article II executive power. This scheme has been adopted by each American state and even by some city governments. The federal courts inferior to the Supreme Court are all of legislative creation. Their jurisdiction, from the first days of the United States was defined by the Congress.[1] The constitutional separation of powers did not signify equality or parity of power.

On the other hand, separation of powers has provided considerable independence for the American judiciary. Although this independence goes deeper in American traditions than the principle of separation of powers, it finds its rationalization there. This independence is often mistakenly assumed to mean independence of politics, but clearly, that is almost an impossibility, especially on the state and local levels.[2] Instead, independence signifies an ambit of authority which is relatively free from the intrusion of the other branches. It also permits judges to remain outside of political campaign activity once they have been elected or appointed. The security of the judge's position is usually so great that he may be immune to most temptations to venality or corruption.[3] In this sense, the judiciary is the most independent of the three branches of government. Judicial

----

[1] Act of September 24, 1789, 1 Stat. 73. This is the famous Judiciary Act of 1789.

[2] See Wallace Sayre and Herbert Kaufman, *Governing New York City* (New York: Russell Sage Foundation, 1964), pp. 530–34.

[3] Bernard Botein, *Trial Judge* (New York: Cornerstone Library, 1963), pp. 291–95.

tenure is long, usually for a lifetime, if not by constitutional provision, then at least by force of custom.[4] This practice makes separation of powers a meaningful source of judicial independence. Retaliation against a judge by a legislature or chief executive is extremely difficult to obtain.

Federalism and court structure

A second vital principle of judicial organization is that of federalism. The existence of a federal system is supplemented by dual judicial structures for the state and national levels. From this fact arise many of the weaknesses of American law enforcement and policy implementation. The dual structure is not found in all federal systems, but for historical reasons, America has 51 separate judicial structures.[5]

Fifty-one legislatures added to 51 judicial structures creates an enormous complexity in decision making within the American legal system. It creates the possibility of choice of forums for the plaintiff. The defendant also may be able to obtain a transfer from a state to a federal court. The possibility of different outcomes in different forums is strongest when state courts attempt to evade Supreme Court decisions,[6] but subtle differences in procedure between the court structures may also affect the outcomes.

---

[4] Art. III, Sec. 1 of the U.S. Constitution provides that federal judges "shall hold their offices during good behavior, and shall, at stated times, receive for their services, a compensation which shall not be diminished during their continuence in office." In any event, as Botein says, state judges "enjoy the practical equivalent of life tenure by political protocol." (*Ibid.*, p. 292).

[5] Glendon Schubert, *Judicial Policy-Making* (Chicago: Scott, Foresman & Co., 1965), pp. 21–33, emphasizes the role of municipal judiciaries, some of which are larger in size than court systems in small states. He also groups "metropolitan judicial systems" together in a blend of federal, state, and municipal court "systems." This analysis raises the count of legal "systems" to at least 100. However, there are only 51 formal legal structures.

[6] Note, "State Court Evasion of United States Supreme Court Mandates," *Yale Law Journal*, Vol. 56 (February, 1947), pp. 574–83.

Direct conflicts between the federal and state judicial systems are rare. However, when they occur, they are most dramatic. In 1815, when the Court of Appeals of Virginia refused to accept the mandate of the United States Supreme Court, which had decreed a particular disposition of a land title, a violent controversy developed. The Virginia court maintained that the Supreme Court was acting beyond the scope of its constitutional power. The Supreme Court reasserted its earlier decision in ringing language.[7]

The supremacy of the federal Supreme Court was established by this landmark decision. This means that the 50 state courts, their legislatures, governors, and constitutions are all inferior to the Constitution of the United States, as interpreted by the United States Supreme Court. At times, the court must remind the states of this fundamental fact of federalism.[8]

Through the powers of judicial review and statutory interpretation, the Supreme Court has become the arbiter of many federal-state disputes and the arbiter of disputes between states. Recent judicial decisions reveal an attitude which supports an expansion of federal power at the expense of the states, especially through the tax and commerce clause powers.[9] Relations between the states are often resolved in the name of the constitutional full faith and credit clause, interstate compact provision, the extradition clause, or the privileges and immunities clause.[10] Suits between

---

[7] *Martin* v. *Hunter's Lessee*, 1 Wheaton 304 (1816).

[8] In *Cooper* v. *Aaron*, 358 U.S. 1 (1958), the Court reminded the officials of Alabama that every state legislator, executive, and judicial officer takes an oath to uphold the Constitution. This meant that the Supreme Court view of the constitutional necessity of desegregation of public schools was binding upon those state officials.

[9] *United States* v. *Darby*, 312 U.S. 100 (1941), reduces the Tenth Amendment to its current scope and denies that it is a source of positive state power to limit national power. The power to regulate by the use of national authority to levy taxes was upheld in *Steward Machine Co.* v. *Davis*, 301 U.S. 548 (1937).

[10] Art. IV, Sec. 1; Art. I, Sec. 10; Art. IV, Sec. 2; Art. I, Sec. 2; and Amendment XIV, Sec. 1.

states regarding boundaries are also considered by the Supreme Court.[11]

Finally, the relations between federal and state courts may exhibit considerable cooperation or antagonism, depending on the subject and the personnel of the court. It is customary for federal courts to abstain from deciding controversies still unresolved by a state court, but the custom may be undergoing some modification of late.[12] Also, state courts may find themselves required to enforce federal statutes, and federal courts may be required to enforce federally adopted state law.[13]

The state judiciary

The judicial power of the states is principally limited, constitutionally, by two provisions. One requires that "full faith and credit be given in each state to the public acts, records and judicial proceedings of every other state,"[14] while the other commands that no state shall "deprive any person of life, liberty and property, without due process of law."[15] Within these restrictions, and those implicit in federalism, an extremely varied pattern of state judicial structures can be found.

A basic pyramidal structure of authority may be considered a model of a state judiciary. There are usually three levels of judicial power: the court of first instance (trial

----

[11] *Virginia* v. *West Virginia*, 11 Wallace 39 (1871). A state may choose to sue another state directly in the Supreme Court, as part of its original jurisdiction under Art. III.

[12] Compare *Spector Motor Service, Inc.* v. *McLaughlin*, 323 U.S. 101 (1944) with *Hotstetter* v. *Idlewild Bon Voyage Liquor Corp.*, 377 U.S. 324 (1964).

[13] The federal Congress conferred jurisdiction upon state courts under the Federal Employer's Liability Act, 53 Stat. 1404 (1939); 45 U.S.C.A. Sec. 51. The Assimilative Crimes Act of 1948, 18 U.S.C.A. Sec. 13 is an example of the latter.

[14] Art. IV, Sec. 1.

[15] Amendment XIV, Sec. 1.

court); the appellate court, to consider disputed matters of law; and the supreme court, which is nominally the chief agency of judicial policy making. There is also a further division between civil and criminal matters, which accounts for the existence of certain minor or petty courts. These inferior courts constitute, where they exist, a fourth level of the judicial structure. Their jurisdiction is frequently defined in terms of a maximum monetary figure. Criminal jurisdiction is defined in terms of the maximum sentence which might be imposed (usually six months). Geographical limitations may also control minor court jurisdiction.

These minor courts, which may be called Justice of the Peace Courts in rural areas,[16] and Magistrate Courts in urban areas, are major arenas of judicial action in terms of cases treated, yet they typically keep no detailed records, they proceed informally, and they utilize judges of limited or no legal training. Appeal to a higher trial court is usually available to the losing party.

Trial courts of general jurisdiction go by many names. Sometimes they are called Courts of Common Pleas, Superior Courts, Districts Courts, or Circuit Courts. Curiously, the state trial court of general jurisdiction in New York is known as the Supreme Court. Under whatever name, their distribution is geographic, and their jurisdiction takes up, includes, and surpasses the inferior courts. The largest trial court of general jurisdiction in the nation—perhaps the world—is the Superior Court of Los Angeles, which has 120 judges. In such large courts a division of function between civil, criminal, juvenile, probate, and domestic relations matters is common.

A trial court of intermediate jurisdiction, usually based upon the county, is also found in most states. Its jurisdiction is defined by pecuniary limitations and by specialized juris-

---

[16] Conviction rates are very high in J.P. courts. Since fees are often the J.P.'s prime source of judicial income, prejudice is possible in favor of conviction.

diction over areas such as the administration of the estates of dead persons, minors, and incompetents. Other specialized trial courts exist in some states whose jurisdiction may be limited to divorce actions, juvenile matters, the settlement and dispositions of wills, and the like.

Intermediate appellate courts exist in 15 states, although less populated states have omitted them from the structure (as in Idaho). The number of judges on these tribunals varies from 3 in Alabama to 33 in Texas. Their jurisdiction is very broad, excluding only certain classes of cases, such as cases involving the death penalty, in which direct appeal to the highest court is possible.

The highest court is usually called the Supreme Court, but is also known as the Court of Appeals in New York State and the Supreme Court of Errors in Connecticut. These courts receive appeals from all levels of the state judicial systems and also, in some states (as in New Jersey), exercise superintending control over lower courts. This is done by the issuance of rules of procedure, or more generally, by the issuance of writs directed to a lower court, such as habeas corpus. The New Jersey system, copied in 20 states, utilizes a chief administrative officer who assigns and transfers judges, according to supreme court direction.

The review power of appellate courts is confined to the record of the case which was made in the trial court. Review of facts, rather than law, is very rare. However, the distinction between "fact" and "law" may be extremely tenuous. The theory holds that trial courts discover facts, to which they apply the substantive rules of law. Appellate courts supposedly consider only the rules of law.[17]

Undoubtedly, the major defects of the state judicial structures are found in antiquated institutions and delay in judicial process caused by court congestion. At the trial court level, delay has become most notorious. Major surgery may

---

[17] For a criticism of this view, see Jerome Frank, *Courts on Trial* (New York: Atheneum Publishers, 1963).

be needed in some situations, including constitutional reform. The appointment of a judicial administrative office to develop efficiency may be a helpful reform. Improved judicial selection, shortening trials, compulsory arbitration of small claims, and pretrial conferences may also help solve the problems of the "law explosion" in the state courts. Delay of two or three years in processing trials may prevent a just or inexpensive resolution, yet these are common.[18]

The federal court system

In considering the structure of the American federal courts, account must be taken of the distinction between "constitutional" and "legislative" courts. The former are created pursuant to Article III and the latter Article I, the legislative article of the constitution. Legislative courts may be given broader functions than those assigned to the three original constitutional courts because the legislature courts exist to administer particular national statutes. Also, the legislative courts may issue advisory opinions, in advance of actual disputes, a power forbidden constitutional courts by the requirement in Article III that there exist an actual "case or controversy."[19] Different tenure safeguards exist for the two types of courts, so that, theoretically, legislative court judges could be completely subject to the whims of Congress.

The three constitutional courts are the best known federal courts: the United States District Courts, the United States Courts of Appeals, and the United States Supreme Court. Since only the Supreme Court was specifically mentioned in Article III, the other two were created by Congress, as the Constitution allows.

---

[18] Maurice Rosenberg, "Court Congestion: Status, Causes, and Proposed Remedies," in *The American Assembly, the Courts, the Public and the Law Explosion* (Englewood Cliffs, N.J.: Prentice-Hall, Inc., 1965), pp. 29–59. A. Leo Levin and Edward A. Wooley, *Dispatch and Delay* (Philadelphia: Institute of Legal Research, 1961).

[19] *Muskrat* v. *United States*, 219 U.S. 346 (1911).

The jurisdiction of these courts is carefully defined in Article III to include "all cases, in law and equity, arising under this Constitution, the laws of the United States, and treaties made . . . under their authority." This phrase is the basis of federal judicial authority and indicates that the existence of a valid dispute must hinge upon a disputed interpretation of the federal Constitution or statute or treaty. The subject matter of admirality and maritime law is also specifically assigned by Article III to the federal courts. Beyond this, the relationship between the parties to the case or the status of a party may create the basis for federal judicial jurisdiction. This is true in cases in which the United States is a party, or a state is a party (though not if the plaintiff is any individual or a foreign country[20]), or if citizens of different states are parties, or if foreign emissaries are parties. The federal jurisdiction may exist concurrently with that of the states, if Congress permits. Thus, in suits involving a contract claim between citizens of different states, the parties can choose to sue in either a federal or a state court, although the amount in controversy must, by statute, attain the value of $10,000 or else the case reverts exclusively to the states.

At the base of this federal structure are the 92 United States District Courts, whose 311 judges are the busiest in the structure, in terms of sheer volume.[21] These courts possess original jurisdiction only, and treat all crimes against the United States, cases involving diversity of citizenship, admirality and maritime cases, cases involving review and enforcement of orders of most federal administrative agencies, and civil cases arising under federal statutes, treaties, or the Constitution if the value of the controversy is in excess of $10,000.[22] This trial court level utilizes juries and is most active in heavily populated areas, such as the Southern Dis-

---

[20] Amendment XI.

[21] Two hundred and fifty thousand cases a year in all categories is the recent usual level.

[22] Except for the original jurisdiction of the Supreme Court.

trict of New York, whose 24 judges are among the most influential of federal district court judges.

The 11 United States Courts of Appeal have 78 judges who possess appellate jurisdiction authority only. They receive appeals only from other federal courts and from the national regulatory commissions and certain other administrative agencies and departments. Statutes sometimes permit a bypassing of the Courts of Appeals, and a direct appeal to the Supreme Court from the District Court, especially from special three-judge District Courts or in cases "of such imperative public importance as to require immediate settlement."[23] Appeals Court judges sit in groups, usually of three, to hear cases, but their number may vary upwards to nine, depending on the subject matter of the case.

The United States Supreme Court, of nine Justices, possesses both original and appellate jurisdiction authority. It may sit as a trial court in cases between the United States and a state; those between two or more states; in cases involving foreign ambassadors, ministers, and consuls; and in cases begun by a state against citizens of another state, aliens, or against another unrecognized country. Except for cases between states (which is exclusive to the Supreme Court), original jurisdiction trials are extremely rare. The Supreme Court is primarily an appellate body.

Appeal to the Supreme Court may come from the highest state court directly, if a "substantial federal question" is involved. Appeal may also come from all lower constitutional courts and from most legislative courts.

Technically, there are three writs which lawyers may obtain to secure their clients a hearing before the Supreme Court. The first, *appeal*, is theoretically a right in statutorily defined situations, but it is actually controlled by the court itself, which requires the existence of a self-defined "substantial" federal issue. A state statute which appeared to possibly conflict with a federal statute, treaty, or the Con-

---

[23] *Youngstown Sheet and Tube Co.* v. *Sawyer*, 343 U.S. 579 (1952).

stitution is most likely to be the subject of an acceptable appeal, especially if the highest state court upheld the state statute. The declaring of a federal law or treaty as unconstitutional will also enhance the chances of successful appeal. *Certiorari* is a discretionary writ issued when a minimum of four judges agree that the dispute merits the court's attention. Although in most years approximately 10 percent of these requests are granted (usually no explanation accompanies denials), the certiorari cases comprise a significant bulk of the court's business. *Certification*, a rarely used procedure, is also available internally to the lower federal courts. These courts may "certify" a question to the court's attention if they are in doubt as to a course of action which they have taken or might take.[24]

The work load of the Supreme Court is growing increasingly burdensome, even though the Court has substantial control over its own business. Recently, it has refused to review an average of 2,000 cases each term. A majority of cases arise from the court of appeals. A usual total of 200 cases are considered for review each term. Most of the denials of certiorari involve cases drawn from the Miscellaneous Docket, which consists largely of pleas from persons in penal institutions, seeking review of their convictions.[25]

The federal judicial apparatus has a simpler structure and a better administrative direction than that found in most states. The Judicial Conference of the United States, established in 1922, integrates the efforts of the Supreme Court with those of the lower federal courts, under the chairman-

---

[24] See *United States* v. *Barnett*, 375 U.S. 805 (1963) in which the Court of Appeals wished to determine whether the criminal contempt citation against the Mississippi governor and lieutenant governor required a trial by jury.

[25] Occasionally these are of great significance, as in the landmark *Gideon* v. *Wainwright*, 372 U.S. 335 (1963), which established the policy of requiring lawyers for the defense of indigent defendants, to be paid at public expense. The story is told in brilliant detail by Anthony Lewis, *Gideon's Trumpet* (New York: Random House, 1964).

ship of the Chief Justice. In its annual meeting the Conference attempts to make a comprehensive survey of the business of the federal courts. It also presents plans for rules, and other reforms.

The Administrative Office of the United States Courts, controlled by the Supreme Court, is a statistical clearinghouse and housekeeping agency for the federal courts. This admirable institution, which compiles budgets, examines dockets, and allocates supplies for the courts has been emulated in several states. However, neither the Judicial Conference nor the Administrative Office possesses the power to shift judicial personnel to meet the demands of increasing work loads, although some state chief justices (as in New Jersey) may do so.

The specialized federal courts include the United States Court of Military Appeals and the Tax Court, which are legislative courts, and the Customs Court, the United States Court of Claims, and the Court of Customs and Patent Appeals, which are all constitutional courts. The Territorial Courts, which were created to consider cases in outlying areas are usually thought of as legislative courts. One of the more important of these is probably the Court of Claims, which was established in 1855 to consider claims against the United States. In this court the government allows itself to be sued by private citizens, usually for contract disputes. The existence of this court relieves the Congress of pressure to pass private bills to resolve the claim. The largest specialized court is the Customs Court, whose nine members renew the decisions of collectors of customs regarding duties on imported goods. Decisions made by the Customs Court may be appealed from, thus calling on the Court of Customs and Patent Appeals.

The Department of Justice

The Department of Justice was created in 1870 to centralize most of the legal activities of national government.

Its chief purpose is to enforce federal laws by furnishing legal counsel in federal cases and by construing the laws under which other departments act. The Department conducts all suits in the Supreme Court which involve the United States, supervises the federal penal institutions and investigates, detects, and prosecutes violations against federal law.

The Attorney General of the United States, unlike his counterpart in the states, has the power to supervise and direct the activities of prosecuting attorneys, called United States attorneys, in the national structure. The United States Marshals are also subject to the control of the Attorney General, although neither the attorneys nor the Marshals are appointed by him, nor subject to removal by him.[26] There is a required training program for federal attorneys.

The burden of federal law enforcement falls primarily upon the shoulders of the district attorneys and the federal Marshals. These positions are filled on the basis of patronage and carry with them an obligation not to continue in private practice.

The United States attorney, unlike most county prosecutors, has both civil and criminal responsibilities. He is a virtual corporation counsel for the United States in his district, and a prosecuting officer. His jurisdiction runs across state boundaries to coincide with the judicial districts. The caseload is often subdivided into criminal and civil aspects, handled by assistant attorneys. Federal crimes within the district are investigated by other federal agencies, such as the FBI, the Federal Bureau of Narcotics, and the Internal Revenue Service, although the attorney's office may itself institute an investigation. Most criminal and civil matters are disposed of without trial, often by a pretrial settlement, or by a decision not to prosecute. Nonlitigation is a vital phase of a case and sometimes flows from cooperation

---

[26] The President, with Senate approval, appoints them. He may also remove them, which may give the Attorney General effective control in most situations.

of the private parties, a lack of evidence, or from the personal predilections of the United States attorney.[27] Information about this aspect of the legal process is scarce, and further research is needed.

Within the federal Attorney General's Department, other government lawyers may institute investigations, supervise or direct litigation in federal courts. The Antitrust Division, the Civil Division, the Civil Rights Division, the Criminal Division, the Internal Security Division, the Lands Division, the Tax Division, and the Administrative Division all perform these activities. In addition, the Antitrust Division considers business mergers and, in essence, approves or discourages them, although its decision may be the subject of litigation. The Civil Rights Division, assigned the dramatic functions of enforcing federal civil rights policies, has recently been deeply concerned with voter registration problems. The activity of each Division is determined by the degree of congressional support and the energy of the Assistant Attorney General in charge, although the Attorney General himself may intrude to set general policy, especially in sensitive political matters.

The Solicitor General has special charge of the business of the government in the Supreme Court. He may conduct and argue any case in which the United States is interested in any court in the nation, if so requested by the Attorney General. He must also give his approval to all appeals taken by the United States. The Solicitor General is both the most frequent and the most successful litigant to appear before the Supreme Court or to suggest cases for its review.[28]

Other agencies nominally falling under the Attorney Gen-

---

[27] Paul W. Williams, "Through the Looking Glass: The Office of the United States Attorney," *The Practical Lawyer*, Vol. 3 (November, 1957), pp. 49–58.

[28] Joseph Tanehaus, Marvin Schick, Matthew Muraskin, and Daniel Rosen, "The Supreme Court's Certiorari Jurisdiction: Cue Theory," in Chapter 5 of Glendon Schubert (ed.), *Judicial Decision-Making* (New York: Free Press of Glencoe, 1963).

eral's control within the Justice Department are the Federal Bureau of Investigation and the Immigration and Naturalization Service. The FBI enjoys considerable autonomy due to its wide basis of support in the Congress and from the press and the public.

State prosecuting attorneys

The prosecutor, also called the commonwealth attorney, the county solicitor, and the criminal district attorney, is a man in a highly political position, possessed of extraordinary power to investigate and enforce the criminal law. He is usually elected to countywide office (appointed in Connecticut, Delaware, Rhode Island, and New Jersey) and is especially sensitive to political considerations because of the delicacy of the criminal laws which he must frequently decide to enforce. The prosecutor must decide whether gambling laws, Sunday closing laws, prostitution laws, and housing codes should be vigorously or laxly enforced. Decisions regarding serious crimes such as rape and murder are much more easily made, and the defendants are usually much less powerful or influential. To the prosecutor falls much of the community's dirty work.

Often this position is a part-time, ill-paid post used as a springboard to higher political office. From 1930 through 1950, 35 public attorneys became governors.[29] The prosecutor usually practices law on the side and is subject to the pressures of groups and individuals whose support he may need to gather votes. Although the chief law enforcer in the United States, the public prosecutor is peculiarly vulnerable to political pressure, personal ambition, and conflict of interest. Being a part-time semiprofessional, his institutional independence is less than that of the police and the judiciary with whom he must work.

---

[29] Joseph A. Schlesinger, *How They Became Governor* (East Lansing: Michigan State University Press, 1957), p. 94.

The decision not to prosecute may take several technical forms, the most flexible tool being the *nolle prosequi*. This occurs after an arrest and indicates the prosecutor's feeling that adequate proof is lacking to proceed further. *Nolle prosequi* can be pleaded at any time before trial. The prosecutor may also greatly influence the grand jury or, in some states may indict through his own bill of information. The choice of offense category and the choice of type of penalty upon conviction are largely in the hands of the prosecutor. Legal obstacles exist in some states which restrict his absolute discretion. Individuals may rarely force him to institute prosecution, or even more rarely, the state attorney general may influence him. In 14 states he may dismiss a case only with court permission, which is usually automatically granted.

The state attorney general is largely unconcerned with criminal law enforcement. He usually has little authority over the county prosecutors and is most concerned with advising officers of state government as to their legal authority and with litigating civil suits on behalf of the state government, either as defendant or plaintiff. The constitutional weakness of this office and its lack of supervisory power make it much less important than its federal counterpart.[30]

The office of the public defender is still too new in most states to examine its actual impact and effectiveness. It is usually a career, salaried position, and the public defender works with criminal accused persons of limited economic means. New offices are springing up in cities and counties throughout the country, partly in response to United States Supreme Court rulings regarding the right to counsel.

---

[30] William A. Saxbe, "Functions of the office of Attorney General of Ohio," *Cleveland-Marshall Law Review*, Vol. 6 (May, 1957), pp. 331–35.

The President's Commission on Law Enforcement and Administration of Justice, in *The Challenge of Crime in a Free Society* (Washington, D.C.: U.S. Government Printing Office, 1967), pp. 148–49, recommends enhancement of the state attorney general's power, a general coordination of effort in criminal law administration, and conversion of the prosecutor's office into a full-time, well-paid, professional, nonpartisan position.

Private and public lawyers

The law profession is a highly segmented semipublic institution. Although overwhelmingly private in the structure of internal operations, most law firms and individual practitioners are usually involved in public matters to a considerable extent, regardless of the type of law specialty which is practiced. The best example is the direct participation of lawyers in politics, an important American phenomenon, which often results in lawyer dominance of key legislative committees, especially at the state and local levels. However, the fact that a legislator happens to be a lawyer does not necessarily make his behavior different from that of other legislators. Yet there is a clear natural affinity between the law profession and politics, partly explained by the time available to lawyers, and partly explained by personal characteristics of lawyers.[31]

The decision to practice alone or in a group is one of the most important career matters a lawyer may determine. Lawyers in individual practice are likely to be from minority religious backgrounds and from working-class homes, and they are likely to have had a poorer legal training. The better legal talent is more likely to be attracted into large firms, with the resulting creation of an elaborate proliferation of specialists and an increase in the expense of legal services.[32] Often only the largest clients—major corporations or state and local governments—can afford the best legal talent. The price paid for the lawyer may have a direct bearing, in our adversarial legal system, upon the legal outcome.

---

[31] Heinz Eulau and John D. Sprague, *Lawyers in Politics: A Study in Professional Convergence* (Indianapolis: Bobbs-Merrill Co., 1964).

[32] Jack Ladinsky, "Careers of Lawyers, Law Practice and Legal Institutions," *American Sociological Review*, Vol. 28 (February, 1963), pp. 47–54; Jerome Carlin, *Lawyers on Their Own* (New Brunswick, N.J.: Rutgers University Press, 1962).

Certain large private law firms have exceptional reputations for success in dealing with public agencies. These firms are likely to have the lion's share of the business involving government contract. One of the best known was the firm of Arnold, Fortas, and Porter, in which each of the main partners had served in government at high levels. Thurman Arnold had been a trustbuster and a federal judge under Franklin D. Roosevelt. Paul Porter had been Chairman of the Federal Communications Commission. Abe Fortas later became a member of the Supreme Court of the United States. When this firm entered a case for a client, his chances probably improved. Abe Fortas was assigned to serve as counsel for the petitioner in a vital case involving the constitutional right to counsel. The original legal petitioner, an untrained jail denizen, was aided by one of the most influential law firms in the country, but without cost, because Fortas was assigned by the Supreme Court Chief Justice. The outcome is history. The petitioner won.[33] Fortas had also represented the Lever Brothers Company, Federated Department Stores, Unilever, millionaire Cyrus Eaton, and the Commonwealth of Puerto Rico.

The legal profession has distinctive submechanisms and distinctively different patterns of interaction. The primary relationship is lawyer to client, but relationships with other lawyers and with judges may be of greater importance. The lawyer has a collectively oriented role as a member of a great profession with obligations as an officer of the court. He also has business relationships and client relationships which may not coincide with his collective role. In such situations ethical problems can arise, although they appear to be uncommon.[34]

---

[33] Anthony Lewis, *Gideon's Trumpet* (New York: Vintage Books, Inc., 1966), pp. 48–55.

[34] Jerome Carlin, *Lawyer's Ethics: A Survey of the New York City Bar* (New York: Russell Sage Foundation, 1966).

On the various roles played by lawyers, see B. O. Soni, "A Study of Mechanisms in Lawyer-Client Relationships," *Journal of the Social Sciences*, Vol. 1 (January, 1958), pp. 63–70.

Many public services of a political sort are performed by lawyers in addition to their roles as legislators. Lawyers are active researchers, assisting the Congress and some legislatures as legislative draftsmen or as legislative counsels. Lawyers are active in city halls, where they serve as municipal law officers, who may be called, variously, "city attorney," "city solicitor," or "corporation counsel." The lobbyist is frequently a lawyer, and performs legitimate representational functions on behalf of his private clients. Some major law firms are virtual lobbying agencies. In the service, many lawyers play an active role as military law officers in the Judge Advocate General's departments. Finally, many lawyers devote their efforts to part-time political or voluntary community work. In all these ways lawyers have become significant decision makers on many levels of American political and social life.

Direct links between law and politics are not hard to establish. The influence of the legal profession upon the society is surely profound. For this reason the major restraints upon deviant behavior among lawyers is less likely to come from government or the mass public than it is to come from within the legal profession itself. Higher status lawyers, the bar associations, and the professional community generally may help curb the occasional deviant.[35] Aside from these, the society and the government usually can do little.

New patterns

Recently, certain new patterns of legal practice have begun to emerge which may have profound effect upon the legal system and the society as well. Increasingly, certain groups, such as labor unions, have begun to provide legal service as an incident and benefit of membership. Free legal aid clinics are available for members of the New York City

---

[35] Kenneth J. Reichstein, "Ambulance-Chasing: A Study of Donation and Control within the Legal Profession," *Social Problems*, Vol. 13 (Summer, 1965), pp. 3–17.

Hotel Trades Council. Foundations, such as the Ford Foundation have also begun to spend money to support legal defense funds for the indigent.

The problem of poverty and its treatment has begun to interest national and state government. On the national level the Office of Economic Opportunity has entered the legal service field to an increasing extent. In 1966, the sum of $25 million was provided for separate legal staffing within the Anti-Poverty program. These moneys are distributed to cities in order to establish free or cheap legal service for low-income residents. Neighborhood law offices are located primarily in slum areas and are most concerned with safe and sanitary housing conditions. The poor themselves are sometimes members of boards of legal aid. At times, federal funds may be curtailed in an effort to secure the use of nonlawyers, as in the city of New York. By the end of 1966, about 125 communities were aided by various projects.

Going beyond this, the OEO sponsored a Judicare project in 1966 as a one-year experiment in which the poor of 26 Wisconsin counties could obtain private legal aid by direct federal payment to private lawyers, rather than by establishing the project's own legal staff. The program led to a rush of divorce actions, which provided the largest single class of business. The poor clients were issued "credit cards" good for free legal service from private lawyers.

The law profession has generally supported some changes in the traditional attorney-client relationship. The American Bar Association has grudgingly come to accept the idea of free legal aid for the poor, although the method of administration is in dispute.[36] In North Dakota the State Bar Association questioned Governor Guy's veto of two federally financed programs. The greatest professional resistance arises to proposals to use nonlawyers to provide legal

---

[36] The American Trial Lawyer's Association, a smaller group, still criticizes the OEO legal aid system. See Symposium, "Revolution in Law Practice?" *Cleveland-Marshall Law Review*, Vol. 15 (May, 1966).

services. Even a bill to permit senior law students to act as attorneys for the poor was defeated in the New York Assembly. The charge of "socialized law" is not so horrifying to most lawyers as is the possibility of nonprofessional practitioners. Other private groups seeking to offer legal services may run afoul of state laws created to protect the profession against lay "lawyers."

The borderline between the public and the private aspects of the legal profession is shifting. Increasingly, the retaining of legal counsel is a matter of the concern of interest groups, labor unions, the poverty-stricken, and the criminal accused. These groups and individuals, because of their lack of it, have sought legal assistance in unusual ways. It is clear that inputs from the social system in the form of new group demands are changing the characteristic lawyer-client pattern in ways which are bound to produce a legal output more responsive to subtle social shifts.

The best illustration of an important change in the character of the legal profession is provided by the growing numbers of lawyers for the federal and state governments. These are 13,000 lawyers working for the national government and a great many more working for the state and local governments. Not all of these lawyers are full-time employees, but there is a tendency toward the creation of a completely public group of attorneys. Although many return to private practice after a stint of government service, a professional corps of public lawyers definitely exists in the United States. Many of these individuals are elected to office at the state level, but most are appointed. Curiously, there is no separate professional legal training for public lawyers. The traditional law school curriculum is not devoted to many public law courses. The completion of the process of the professionalization of the public practice of law will require a separate type of training, or at least, a greater choice of courses in law schools for those individuals who choose to make a public career in the law. When this transpires, the connection between the legal and the political systems will become extremely close.[37]

The greatest technical change which could, conceivably, alter the complexion of the legal profession could flow from an increasing use of computers. Currently, many lawyers are suspicious of the computer, even for data retrieval purposes, so that computerization of legal materials is not yet a profitable venture. But the very existence of computer technology makes inevitable the eventual intrusion of new research techniques into the legal profession. Law schools generally have avoided the problem by failing to provide courses in the use of computers or encouraging the formal study of computer systems, or of the logic upon which they rest. Dually trained lawyers will have a substantial advantage over their conventionally trained colleagues. A new generation of computer-trained lawyers is bound to arise. The effects upon the legal system are hard to predict, but it is certain that the role of the lawyer's training, his lack of research skills, and the judges' lack of legal data will be reduced as applicable case law and statutory precedents become commonly agreed upon. It is possible today to obtain an accurate search of New York and Pennsylvania statutes from machine-programmed cards in a matter of minutes. The future awaits the competent computer-trained lawyer.[38]

---

[37] That even law professors may prove inept in the application of public law principles to practical affairs is admitted by Professor Bernard Schwartz, in *The Professor and the Commissions* (New York: Alfred A. Knopf, Inc., 1959). On legal education reforms for public law, see Arthur Selwyn Miller, "The Impact of Public Law on Legal Education," *Journal of Legal Education*, Vol. 12 (1960), pp. 483–502, and Richard E. Speidel, "What Should the Law Schools Do About Federal Government Contracts?" *Journal of Legal Education*, Vol. 18 (1966), pp. 371–94. In Germany, judges and prosecutors are trained in separate law schools with a greater public law curriculum.

[38] For a study of law retrieval and data processing and their influence upon the legal process, see "New Uses for the Computer: How ADP Helps Write New Laws," *Journal of Taxation*, Vol. 25 (September, 1966), pp. 178–79, and Note, "Computer Retrieval of Statutory Law and Decisional Law," *Vanderbilt Law Review*, Vol. 19 (June, 1966), pp. 905–18.

Appeals and clemency: homeostasis

At the peak of the structure of the legal system are found institutions of internal accommodation. If unacceptable results are produced by trial courts, the institutions of appellate tribunals and of executive clemency exist as correctives. In effect, these institutions provide a homeostatic control for the legal system, as well as a means of responding to social demands for new or different applications of law. Since the law may be applied by lower courts in a manner which fails to account for novel situations, novel demands, or individual peculiarities, the higher courts and the Chief Executive are in a position to make these adjustments. After the adjustments are made, the feedback may result in an individual solution, as in a reversal order remanding a case for a new trial, or it may result in a total reconstruction of an area of legal doctrine. The end product is a new balance within the legal system which keeps order while permitting change.

New trials can be ordered by trial courts on the ground of newly discovered evidence, either in a civil or a criminal case. On the other hand, the right of review by an appellate court, an essentially 19th-century development, is a more flexible technique in an expanding legal system. In some states the right of review embraces final judgments, and intermediate orders made in the course of the proceeding. In the latter situation the pending case is halted until the matter appealed is settled. This serves to unify and consolidate the methods of conducting a trial. In federal courts the right to appeal from intermediate orders is much more restricted. In place of appeal, the device of a trial *de novo* is often available from decisions rendered by petty courts, such as proceedings before justices of the peace; the new court may open any issue and retry all the facts, just as if there had never been a first trial. This technique reveals suspicion of the integrity of the petty court and serves as a useful corrective.

Generally, however, appellate courts do not have the power to retry the facts. The jury's supremacy in the field of questions of fact is left undisturbed, except in the cases of outrageous verdicts, or in situations in which the weight of the evidence was so one-sided that the jury should not have been given the opportunity to pass upon the facts (a directed verdict situation). Appellate courts may set verdicts aside on the grounds of excessiveness, inadequacy, or inconsistency.

Other grounds for setting aside the verdicts of trial courts are more significant in exemplifying homeostasis. If "errors" in procedure or in substantive law have been made, the first judgment may be set aside and a new trial ordered, or the judgment may be modified in other ways. The word "error" is probably a legal fiction. It allows for the departure from previous precedents or for the setting of novel precedents, as well as the correction of a trial judge's misreading of the rules, the law of evidence, or the substantive rules of law. The improper conduct of a judge may also be a basis of a modification of a lower court judgment.

Reversal of a judgment usually results in retrial of all the issues. If the "error" was one of substantive law, the new or proper interpretation of the appellate court will serve as the guide for the new trial. The result can be expected to be quite different from that of the first trial. If the "error" was procedural, the admission of a confession obtained without a lawyer to advise the defendant, for example, the new rule *may*, although it need not, result in an acquittal because of the omission of the now faulty evidence. In this fashion the legal system achieves some semblance of coherence and stability.

Executive clemency is a power available to Presidents and governors. It amounts to a quasi-judicial power which is assigned to these executives. A *pardon*, which is a release from the legal consequences of a crime, results in a remission of the penalties imposed. A *commutation of sentence* is a reduction of a penalty imposed, while a *parole* is a release from a confinement in prison, conditioned on the future good behavior of the parolee. All three devices involve the liberty of a person already convicted of a crime. They are almost always granted after the recommendation of a board (although the governor has sole responsibility in nine states). These forms of clemency are intended to permit a flexible and individual response to the reform and rehabilitation of convicted felons. This power to exempt individuals from the full legal effect of their misdeeds has been a part of Anglo-American law for centuries, and permits it to remain responsive to individual needs and conditions.

V

The decision makers

THE LEGAL SYSTEM processes inputs received from a variety
of sources, resolving them through formal decision making.
In criminal cases a key preliminary decision is made by
semiprofessional prosecutors who decide to introduce cases
into the courts and grand juries. In civil cases the introduction of disputes is a private decision made by a client and
a lawyer. In either event, the direct or primary input takes
the form of a "case." It is this "case" which is the basic unit
of legal decision making after the dispute has failed of settlement in some other way (by political or social influence,
for example). Thus, the "case" decision is the unit of study
in this section.

Decision makers need not be professionals. Jurors are
qualified on the basis of their amateur, generalized abilities.
Not all judges are lawyers, nor need they be lawyers to sit
on the highest courts in the land. Despite this, the backgrounds, personalities, partisanships, philosophies, and social identification of legal decision makers permit some generalization. There are certain common characteristics of
judges and juries which have effect upon legal outputs. The
precise measure of the effect is not easy to calculate, but the
existence of an effect can be demonstrated. It is these fac-

91

tors which, when taken together with other input variables, allow some prediction in legal decisions. The aggregate of all these variables accounts for all outcomes. However, the identification of the relative significance of each variable is a source of uncertainty. It is assumed here that the variables mentioned in this chapter: recruitment, social background, ethnic and religious orientation, economic status, political affiliation, value preferences, professional status, and intra-group dynamics are more significant in determining outcomes in a single case than are others treated earlier.

Selection of judges: the states

The answer to the question "Where do judges come from?" need not be shrouded in creation myths. It is a legitimate and important issue to raise, as vital a matter as how governors and Presidents are selected, and the process of selection is more systematic.

It appears that the selection process for the judiciary is different from that of most political decision makers. Judges are not usually organized into political parties nor represented directly in interest groups. This makes recruitment a more difficult process, especially in view of the special skills required.

The states follow five different legal methods of choosing judges. The most common is by partisan election, often with partisan nomination at primaries or convention. Slightly less common is the nonpartisan election, in which there are restrictions on the partisan designations of candidates. Election by the legislature is used in five states, gubernatorial appointment in seven, and the Missouri Plan in six others. The Missouri Plan permits the governor to select judges from among a list recommended by a special commission, but also requires the judges to be voted upon in a public referendum after having served a period of time. The voter is given the choice of yes or no on retention. The judge has no opponent.[1]

The variations in the style of selection would seem to have an effect upon the type of judge and the degree of the judge's dependence upon partisan allegiances. The Missouri Plan rests upon the belief that better educated and more qualified judges will be appointed and retained by its procedure. Although this has not been borne out in practice, it seems clear that elective judges have less political experience than appointed judges and that different methods of selection do produce judges with different social and political backgrounds.[2]

Whether a judge is appointed or elected, he is likely to be attached to one of the two major parties. His partisan activities will be helpful in obtaining his appointment, even if he is relieved of the necessity of engaging in a strenuous campaign. A governor or legislative committee—since some legislatures appoint judges—is likely to be influenced by political factors aside from competence or experience in approving a judicial appointment. Factional political issues are usually most significant, so that it is best that the prospective judge find some political ally in a favored party faction.[3]

Judicial elections are not always partisan matters. In fact, most are not hotly contested. Most judicial incumbents win reelection, and many are not opposed during their tenure. The issues which face the public are not clear-cut policy matters, and the record of the judge's performance is diffi-

---

[1] The source is *State Court Systems* (Chicago: Council of State Governments, 1962). The states using the Missouri Plan, or some variation, are Alaska, California, Iowa, Kansas, Missouri, and Nebraska.

[2] Herbert Jacob, "The Effect of Institutional Differences in the Recruitment Process: The Case of States Judges," *Journal of Public Law*, Vol. 13 (1964), pp. 104–19.

[3] John E. Crow, "Subterranean Politics: A Judge is Chosen," *Journal of Public Law*, Vol. 12 (1963), pp. 275–90.

cult for voters to evaluate, in the absence of extensive media coverage. Judges are not prominent public officials, and their low visibility helps insulate them from bitter political campaigns. Nonpartisan judicial elections are also held in some states, but political party endorsement is helpful even in these states.[4]

It is clear that the quality of a judge's performance is not dependent on whether he is elected or appointed. Even if a judge may have been appointed through the influence of a criminal he may, once on the bench, perform admirably. Judicial independence of politics at the selection level is very uncommon and may not even be necessary to secure competent personnel. However, if appointments are virtually purchased from political parties, obvious problems of party influence and judicial corruption arise.[5]

Other factors which may enhance the prospects for judicial appointment include prior legislative experience, experience as a district attorney, and the support of the state or local bar association. The relative importance of each of these factors varies from state to state, depending upon the formal system of selection and upon the political culture of each state. The techniques of judicial selection in Alabama might be unacceptable to the citizenry and the political leaders of Wisconsin.

Selection of judges: the federal level

The pattern of federal judicial selection is quite unhampered by legal restrictions. The President could, if he desired, appoint anyone to the federal judiciary, whether an

---

[4] Malcolm Moos, "Judicial Elections and Partisan Endorsements of Judicial Candidates in Minnesota," *American Political Science Review*, Vol. 35 (1941), pp. 69–75.

[5] Adolph Berle, "Elected Judges or Appointed," *New York Times Magazine*, December 11, 1955, pp. 26–40. In New York City, judicial nominees have been known to "contribute" $20,000 to the party's local campaign. See Wallace S. Sayre and Herbert Kaufmann, *Governing New York City* (New York: Russell Sage Foundation, 1960), p. 542.

alien, a child or a nonlawyer. Neither the Constitution nor federal statutes prescribe any particular qualifications for these posts. The selection process is guided by informal criteria, but these are better understood and more confining than those of most states.

In addition, unlike most state judicial appointments, federal judgeships carry life tenure. The appointments of one President may affect the judicial decisions of several decades. The number of vacancies at any one time will always be low (unless the total number of judges is increased). These facts mean that each Presidential judicial appointment is the subject of a great deal of political bargaining and haggling, although this does not usually extend to his Supreme Court appointments.

The Senate is empowered by the Constitution to withhold its consent from Presidential nominations. These nominations are sent to the Committee on the Judiciary, which turns the matter over to a subcommittee. This smaller group holds hearings and reports to the whole committee. The subcommittee recommendation is certain to be accepted by the Judiciary Committee and the Senate. So the fate of a Presidential nomination rests with the approval of a small group within the Senate.

In practice the Senate has rejected or obstructed many nominations, with an overall rejection percentage of about 20 percent. Supreme Court nominations are very rarely rejected. Even if a Supreme Court appointment were rejected, the President could not be forced to select a particular individual.[6]

The powerful custom of "senatorial courtesy" applies most certainly in the selection of judges to the lower federal courts. The practical effect of this custom is to remove much of the appointing power over these judges from the President, and to bestow it upon the senators from the states

---

[6] Joseph P. Harris, *The Advice and Consent of the Senate* (Berkeley: University of California Press, 1953), pp. 302–24.

involved, if they are of the President's own party. It is damaging to the senator's prestige to be disregarded by the President in making appointments within the senator's own state, especially if another faction of his party is so rewarded. As a consequence, senators will tend to support another individual senator of the President's party who opposes the President's nomination to an office within the senator's state. However, the senator must actively fight the unapproved nomination if he hopes to block it. Even senators not of the President's party may protest and receive senatorial sympathy and support.[7]

Ever since Washington's administration it has become the custom to consult an appropriate senator before making judicial nominations. A President could insist on his own choice of nominees, and may consult with other party leaders, national or state, before making his choice. But the President's choice is never a free one and, below the Supreme Court level, is safest if made in conjunction with the affected state's senator. The President can stall, delay, and haggle in order to bargain for a particular candidate, and he is held responsible for the quality of the nominees. In the last resort he may make recess appointments when the Senate is not in session. Beyond that, only public resistance to an obnoxious or clearly unqualified candidate can offset senatorial influence.[8]

Presidential appointments must meet a test of competence and qualification which will not reflect discredit upon the President. The actual negotiation with individual senators has been the assigned task of the Deputy Attorney Gen-

---

[7] *Ibid.*, p. 224.

[8] The 1965 incident involving Municipal Judge Francis X. Morrissey of Massachusetts shows the limit of senatorial power and influence. Judge Morrissey, a personal friend of the Kennedy family, seemed to the local bar associations to be clearly unqualified for a federal judgeship, and despite Senator Edward Kennedy's support and President Johnson's compliant nomination, his name was withdrawn, probably on the instructions of Senator Kennedy. The newspapers generally attacked the nomination, and this allowed the President to retreat from his commitment.

eral in recent administrations. He has assigned an assistant to aid him in this delicate work. Recent Deputy Attorneys General have been men of energy and ability, such as Byron P. White (now Justice White), Nicholas de B. Katzenbach, and Ramsey Clark. Each attempted to take the initiative in negotiating judicial nominations, but they could do no more than their Presidential support allowed.

Ultimately the Department of Justice, under the Attorney General, recommends judicial appointments to the President. If the President chooses, other members of his staff may supply additional advice. John Macy, Chairman of the Civil Service Commission, currently reviews Justice Department nominations to pass upon their quality.

Further screening of judicial nominations takes place in the Senate Judiciary Committee. Important independent advice is solicited, especially that of the American Bar Association. The Association maintains a Standing Committee on the Federal Judiciary, which passes upon the qualifications of federal judicial nominees. Its reports are considered in evidence by the Judiciary Committee. In addition, the ABA usually submits a general report on proposed nominees for the consideration of the Justice Department. In this report a rating scale is used denoting candidates as "exceptionally well qualified," "well qualified," "qualified," or "not qualified." The impact of these ratings is hard to measure, but there is no doubt that the ABA enjoys more influence and respect than any other private source of information, except that its preferences are known to be on the conservative side respecting judicial ideologies.[9]

No matter who makes or influences the nomination of a federal judge, it is a near certainty that the candidate's party affiliation and activity will be a vital factor in the process. In a Democratic administration, good Democrats will be preferred as judicial candidates and vice versa. The defini-

---

[9] Joel B. Grossman, *Lawyers and Judges* (New York: John Wiley & Sons, Inc., 1965), pp. 82–196.

tion of deserving "good Democrats" will depend upon the relative distribution of power within the affected judicial district. In Chicago, for example, a Democratic nominee must be at least acceptable to the Democratic mayor of the city, who is a powerful figure in the state and national party. If it were a Republican Presidency, a different constellation of party forces would be involved. Nonetheless, Presidents will reserve a small portion of their appointment power for a few members of the opposition party, perhaps as a protection against possible lean years for the party in the future.

Candidates for judicial appointments must be careful in soliciting support, but it can be said that ambitious lawyers will make it known to strategic friends that they are available and interested in a particular vacancy. The campaigning is done by others on their behalf, but it is still as intense as the indirect channels of activity permit. The stakes are high in salary, power, and prestige. The behind-the-scenes struggles are discreet but genuine.

In general, senatorial power to influence federal judicial appointments declines as one ascends the ladder of the federal judiciary. Circuit court judges and Supreme Court Justices serve jurisdictions which cross state lines. The subsequent dilution of the individual senator's power strengthens the hand of the President. Since a circuit covers at least three states, the combination of forces necessary to support a single candidate or group of candidates is extremely difficult to form. The President will have a wider range of choices, but the basic list of candidates will include many individuals enjoying senatorial support. On appointments to special federal courts and District of Columbia courts, the senatorial leverage is still less, due to an absence of a geographic constituency support, but a senator may resist the nomination of a man from his own state who is personally obnoxious to him.[10]

---

[10] Harold W. Chase, "Federal Judges—The Appointing Process," *Minnesota Law Review*, Vol. 51 (December, 1966), pp. 218–21.

Senator Hugh Scott has proposed that the selection of federal judges be left to a seven-man Judicial Service Commission composed of ABA members, former judges, and a balanced party grouping. He noted the general public dissatisfaction with the current method of political selection. But even Scott's plan leaves the final determination to the President. It is difficult to imagine that the President will not feel the pressures of party strong upon him.[11]

Appointment: United States Supreme Court

The issues confronting a state judge or a lower federal judge are often challenging and intellectually stimulating. Men of legal training and great competence are required for these positions. But the Supreme Court of the United States is, in many ways, an untypical body, and as one writer suggests, "in the selection of judges for a supreme tribunal in a federation, much more is to be looked for than conventional professional attainments."[12] Unlike his counterpart in the state supreme court, the federal member of the high court must weigh the impact of his court's decision on the whole nation, and upon the 50 state governments within it.

The power of the Senate over Supreme Court appointments is limited to rather negative activities. The Senate may combine against a Presidential nominee, but it cannot force a candidate upon him. However, the grounds for the Senate's negative actions are likely to be ideological or

---

. [11] Hugh Scott, "The Selection of Federal Judges: The Independent Commission Approach," *William and Mary Law Review*, Vol. 8 (Winter, 1967), pp. 173–84. The proposal was 1967 bill S. 3579. Scott refers to the tabulations of the American Bar Association which show that every President in this century has appointed more than 90 percent from within his own party, except Taft (82.2 percent), Hoover (85.7 percent) and Kennedy (88.9 percent). (*Ibid.*, pp. 177–78.) Wilson approached nearest perfection with 98.7 percent.

[12] Paul A. Freund, *The Supreme Court of the United States* (New York: Meridian Books, Inc., 1961), p. 109.

"philosophical," and a weak President may find his own party or the opposition party reacting against his candidate's ideology, even to the point of rejecting otherwise competent men.

Approximately one fifth of all Presidential nominees for the Supreme Court have been rejected by the Senate, but most of these were in the early years and have included notorious incompetents (Madison's appointee, Alexander Woollcott) and very able individuals (Roger Taney's 1835 nomination by President Jackson). Judge John J. Parker has been the only nominee rejected in this century.

In making his appointment, a President is likely to inquire deeply into the personal philosophy or attitudes of a Supreme Court candidate. Teddy Roosevelt was concerned enough to inquire into the beliefs of Oliver Wendell Holmes before he nominated Holmes to the Court. President Truman appointed men whose views he knew personally, like Tom Clark and Fred Vinson. Wilson admired the views of Louis Brandeis, while Lyndon Johnson seemed to find Abe Fortas' views congenial. But a nominee of outspoken ideological views, such as Brandeis, may find that senatorial opposition will be generated because of these views.

It is sometimes safer for a President to nominate a man of known conservative views. This will make him a more acceptable nominee to the Senate Judiciary Committee and the American Bar Association. The committee has often been led by southern conservative Democrats or, in the alternative, by conservative midwestern Republicans. The leadership of the Bar Association is of a similar persuasion.[13] Of course, the meaning of "conservatism," in this context, is quite unclear, but this term describes a common mode of perception among senators.

One of the less significant criteria for appointment is prior judicial experience. Over half of all Supreme Court Justices

---

[13] John R. Schmidhauser, *The Supreme Court* (New York: Holt, Rinehart & Winston, Inc., 1960), pp. 16–27.

have had some earlier experience on the bench, but only a few have had extensive legal careers. No doubt legal training is a definite advantage to a Supreme Court Justice, but as Justice Frankfurter said, "The Supreme Court is a very special kind of court," one in which "judicial service as such has no special relation to the kinds of litigation that come before the Supreme Court."[14] A President who, like Dwight Eisenhower, states a preference for experienced judges, may reveal a hidden bias for the safe or the more conservative appointment. Certainly, some of our most creative Chief Justices, for example, John Marshall and Earl Warren, have been men of very limited judicial experience (or none at all). Other examples are Story, Taney, Miller, Bradley, Hughes, and Brandeis. As we shall see, the political and partisan preferences of candidates are more significant factors in Presidential appointments.

Retirement, discipline, and removal

The nature of judicial service is such that a judge, whether appointed or elected, is generally beyond the independent scrutiny of the public. In the federal courts a judge is, as a constitutional matter, beyond the reach of the persons appointing him, because of virtual life tenure. In the states most elected judges are reelected without challenge. Appointed judges are usually reappointed without question. Even if judges are, at times, not reappointed or reelected, the reasons for their loss of position are usually traceable to political, rather than juridical, matters.

Probably the most common problem affecting the competence of judges is physical or mental disability incident to growing old. Deafness, loss of sight, loss of use of limbs, or

---

14 Felix Frankfurter, "The Supreme Court in the Mirror of the Justices," *University of Pennsylvania Law Review*, Vol. 105 (April, 1957), p. 785. Prior experience on a state court or on a lower federal court does not, according to Frankfurter, help in dealing with the peculiar problems facing the Supreme Court (pp. 785–87).

senility may impair the abilities of an older judge. Several Supreme Court Justices are known to have been mentally deranged in their latter years. The later opinions of Justices Baldwin, Grier, McLean, and Field may all have been infected by mental disturbances.[15] In one instance in the federal courts, a dishonest colleague actually wrote an opinion on behalf of senile Circuit Court Judge Joseph Buffington.[16]

Open corruption has sometimes been discovered in the personal conduct of judges. Misuse of court money, favoritism, drunkenness, fraud, conflict of interest, changing of records, and acceptance of "gifts" have each been found on particular occasions.[17] However, most of these misdeeds are hard to uncover, and harder to prove. Although probably very rare, they are also very embarrassing to the rest of the judiciary.

To the problem of old age, one solution has been compulsory retirement for age, which is now the law in about 20 states. Voluntary retirement for disability is available in 46 states, with varying age minima dependent upon the level of the court or the length of service. Voluntary retirement at full salary after reaching the age of 70 with 10 year's service, or at the age of 65 with 15 year's service, is the federal program. Of course, there have been many capable older judges, such as John Marshall, Roger Taney, and Oliver Wendell Holmes.

Impeachment is usually available as a remedy in cases of serious misconduct. Forty-three states and the federal government have the power to institute impeachment proceedings. However, this method of discipline has proven wholly unsatisfactory. There have been only eight congressional efforts at impeachment of federal judges, four of

---

[15] Charles Fairman, "The Retirement of Federal Judges," *Harvard Law Review*, Vol. 51 (January, 1938), pp. 405–29.

[16] Jack E. Frankel, "Removal of Judges—Federal and State," *Journal of the American Judicature Society*, Vol. 48 (February, 1965), p. 179.

[17] See Joseph Borkin, *The Corrupt Judge* (New York: Clarkson N. Potter, Inc., 1962).

which proved successful in achieving removal. The states have had a similar lack of success in using this cumbersome technique. In addition, impeachment has been periodically criticized as partisan and overly expensive because of its characteristic feature of "legislative justice."

In a few states removal of a judge by a governor upon the request of the legislature is available as an alternative to impeachment. It is simpler, because no trial is required. Removal by joint resolution of the legislature is even more uncommon and much easier. The most uncommon procedure for judicial discipline is the recall election, found in a few states, although judges are usually exempted from recall in states generally permitting that scheme.

Despite all of these techniques, the inadequacy of existing removal and disciplinary procedures is becoming increasingly obvious. The American Bar Association and other specialized legal groups have long been interested in these problems.[18] Voluntary retirement plans, such as that found in the federal court system, have proven unsatisfactory and only in unusual cases, like those involving District Judges Underwood and Chandler, would the judge's colleagues take action against the incompetent or incapacitated judge.[19]

Two methods of meeting these problems have appeared within the states and enjoy considerable popularity in the legal profession. The first, a "special court," involves judicial action in a public proceeding after a formal complaint

---

[18] Frankel, *op. cit.*, p. 181. See editorial in the same issue of this journal at pp. 163–65.

[19] Judge Underwood was requested to resign by the unanimous resolution of the Sixth Circuit Court of Appeals, in 1965, but chose to ignore the resolution at first. He finally retired within a year. Judge Chandler was ordered in 1965 by the Judicial Council of the Tenth Circuit Court of Appeals to cease performance of all judicial duties (but with salary continuing). No hearing was held, but the action of the council was in the name of a 1938 statute empowering it to "make all necessary and expeditious orders for the effective and expeditious administration of the business of the courts within its circuit" (28 U.S.C. Sec. 332). See Note, "Chandler Incident and Problems of Judicial Removal," *Stanford Law Review*, Vol. 17 (January, 1967), p. 448.

is filed by specified persons, such as the chief justice, the governor, the attorney general, or groups of lawyers or citizens. A special court is designated to preside over the issue. Physical or emotional disability are adequate grounds for removal by this court. This technique is endorsed by the American Bar Association.[20]

The second new method of judicial removal or discipline is the "commission" plan. This provides for a confidential investigation of complaints against judges by a special panel composed of judges, lawyers, and laymen. If there is adequate proof of judicial misconduct, the commission may choose to communicate privately with the judge to warn him. If it is a more serious matter, he may be asked to voluntarily resign without public disclosure. If the judge persists in his refusal, the proceedings will become public and more formal, as a complete hearing before the commission or another panel can be ordered. This group may make formal disciplinary recommendations to the state supreme court.[21]

These two new procedures for judicial reform appear to be prohibited on the federal level by the Constitution. The dilemma of the disabled or incompetent federal judge cannot be solved with current procedures unless, as in the situations involving Judges Chandler and Underwood, the other federal judges are willing to take collective action against these individuals. In practice, most federal judges choose not to retire and, consequently, die in office.

Social backgrounds

Although it is, as yet, impossible to attribute judicial decisions in particular cases to particular attributes of the

---

[20] *Journal of the American Judicature Society*, Vol. 47 (June, 1963), p. 11. Alabama, Alaska, Iowa, Louisiana, New York, New Jersey, and Texas now permit this procedure. Other legislatures are considering it.

[21] California inaugurated this plan in 1960; Louis H. Burke, "Judicial Discipline and Removal," *Journal of the American Judicature Society*, Vol. 48 (February, 1965), pp. 167–72.

judge's background and experience, it is now generally accepted that a judge's behavior pattern is not unlike that of other political actors and is subject to the influence of his social and personal habits and leanings. One should not leap to the extreme view that judges behave in identically the same fashion as politicians. The evidence does not support that view. However, many of the forces which motivate politicians *and* other people also move judges.

There is nothing new in noting that judges possess peculiar attributes which set them apart from other men. Detailed analysis of backgrounds of Supreme Court members discloses a definite upper-middle-class bias in patterns of judicial recruitment.[22] It is likely that these biases may be reflected in actual decisions, but the manner of their impact is not fully understood. Furthermore, we do not yet know very much about state court judges.

If one abstracts a single variable from the complex equation of judicial decision making, much that was obscure becomes more distinct. Political party affiliation is a good example. One study shows that among certain Supreme Court Justices, Democratic Justices were more prone to: favor defendants in criminal cases, administrative agencies in business regulation matters, the libertarian view in free speech cases, the government in tax cases, the tenant in landlord-tenant cases, labor unions in labor-management cases, and injured parties in accident cases, among other things.[23] Surely, this is useful, if not completely predictive, information. This finding is generally supported by others, with regard to lower federal courts and state courts.[24] This indicates that party affiliation and identification operates as

---

[22] John Schmidhauser, "The Justices of the Supreme Court: A Collective Portrait," *Midwest Journal of Political Science*, Vol. 3 (1959), p. 1.

[23] Stuart Nagel, "Political Party Affiliation and Judges' Decisions," *American Political Science Review*, Vol. 55 (December, 1961), pp. 843–50.

[24] Kenneth Vines, "Federal District Judges and Race Relations Cases in the South," *Journal of Politics*, Vol. 26 (1964), pp. 350–51. Republicans tended to favor more moderate racial policies; S. Sidney Ulmer, "The Political Party Variable in the Michigan Supreme Court," *Journal of Public Law*, Vol. 11 (1962), p. 352.

a "feedback reinforcement" for values already held by the judge.[25]

Membership in religious groups may have an effect upon judicial behavior, but probably not so marked an impact as party identification. It appears, on tentative evidence, that Catholic judges may be more "liberal" than Protestant judges. Of course, this analysis is limited by the fact that many Catholic judges are Democrats.[26]

If one selects a single judge, the impact of his personal background becomes more obvious, but this does not admit of much generalization. One may identify values of great importance to the particular judge, but these may be idiosyncratic or historically limited. Biographical information may be of great importance in grasping the thought of one man, but it is not necessarily sound to project those insights onto an entire period.[27]

Some surprising conclusions have appeared from examining judicial backgrounds. For example, contrary to the general impression, one study showed that the typical dissenter in Supreme Court cases, rather than being a radical, hot-blooded individual, was more likely to be a "tenacious advocate of traditional doctrines which were being abandoned."[28]

The variables of judicial background cannot be taken alone to predict likely judicial behavior. Interwoven with them are the subtle influence of later learning and the interplay of judges, judges and lawyers, judges and clerks. A man may change somewhat after he becomes a judge. The feedback effect of social conditioning and political experi-

---

25 Nagel, *op. cit.*, p. 847.

26 Stuart Nagel, "Ethnic Affiliations and Judicial Propensities," *Journal of Politics*, Vol. 24 (February, 1962), pp. 92–110; but read with care.

27 See David Danielski, *A Supreme Court Justice Is Appointed* (New York: Random House, 1964), pp. 180–99.

28 John Schmidhauser, "*Stare Decisis*, Dissent and the Background of the Justices of the Supreme Court of the United States," *University of Toronto Law Journal*, Vol. 14 (1962), at p. 209.

ence will vary from judge to judge or even from decision to decision, so that, though useful, information of this sort is not yet highly reliable.

Internalized behavior

The interaction of judges within a courtroom is another significant aspect of judicial behavior. Given the institutionalized setting of an American appellate court, the interplay of conflicting personalities and values is surely a vital key to an understanding of how judges behave. At the appellate level the attitudes of judges, combined with the individual personalities of each, as they impress each other, may be quite as important as the previous rulings of the court, or the literal wording of a statute or constitution. In a sense, then, each appellate courtroom is a subsystem of the legal subsystem itself. Each forms, in miniature, a feedback network internal to its own processes, as well as to the outside legal system.

It is especially true of the United States Supreme Court to say that it is a political body as well as a legal group. The search for neutral principles of constitutional law may be both fruitless, and itself a product of a particular political bias.[29] In certain evolving social problems, the modern Supreme Court has been in the forefront of policy making. But this is due to its relationship to the rest of the political system, which allows that Court a usually interstitial, minor role in policy making, but sometimes, by default, permits it to assume a major policy-making role. On these occasions, the judge's attitudes and beliefs will play a major role in formulating outcomes. This is especially the situation in the areas of legislative reapportionment, civil rights, and rights

---

[29] This point is well made in Martin Shapiro, *Law and Politics in the Supreme Court* (Glencoe, Ill.: Free Press, 1964). This is to be contrasted with the famous essay by Herbert Wechsler, "Toward Neutral Principles in Constitutional Law," *Harvard Law Review*, Vol. 73 (November, 1959), pp. 1–35.

of accused persons, in which other political agencies were either unable or unwilling to act.

The nature of the disputes brought to the attention of the Supreme Court may require its judges to formulate a set of attitudes, a "philosophy," or an "ideology" regarding the large social issues of the day. These attitudes may be both discoverable and measurable. They may allow for a certain amount of predictability in the analysis of patterns of decisions. It is possible to construct a diagram of political and economic liberalism and to describe judicial attitudes in a spectrum of "conservative" and "liberal" attitudes. Two outstanding attitudes can be discerned in this manner—the attitude toward personal rights and the attitude toward property rights.[30]

However, the examination of judicial attitudes may not apply to all appellate tribunals. On lesser courts the issues may not take the ready form of a "liberal"-"conservative" bipolarization or spectrum. It is still possible to measure judicial attitudes toward particular problems, by "scaling" voting patterns among judges according to a single attitude dimension.[31] Analysis by groups ("blocs") is a less sophisticated version of the same approach. This is a favorite journalistic device, as well, in which a court is seen as composed of competing subgroups with fixed ideas on certain issues, sometimes including a "swing-man" or marginal member who shifts from one group to another.

A more profitable method of perceiving appellate courts is the technique of small-group analysis. This school of thought, borrowing from sociology and psychology, prefers to concentrate upon the structure of the group itself as it

---

[30] Glendon Schubert, *The Judicial Mind* (Evanston, Ill.: Northwestern University Press, 1965). This is an expansion and improvement upon the bloc analysis of C. Herman Pritchett, *The Roosevelt Court* (New York: Macmillan Co., 1948).

[31] See explanations of Glendon Schubert in "The Study of Judicial Decision-Making as an Aspect of Political Behavior," in *The American Political Science Review*, Vol. 52 (December, 1958), pp. 1007–25. These methods could apply to any appellate court.

internally manages conflicts of opinion about law. The influence of one judge upon another, and the formation of opinion leadership, is more clearly understood as a result of these studies. For example, the way in which blocs are formed and the difficulties of maintaining solidarity on a single decision, and the role of a chief justice in forming blocs is now beginning to be understood.[32]

Despite the many ways of examining the judge as a political actor, several matters remain obscure. First, how free is a judge on a particular court to impose his views on a case decision? Second, is there a difference in different courts in the way in which a judge's personal motivations may be given expression? Writing opinions is only one way. Bargaining and lobbying are other ways. Merely examining the outcomes as an index of judicial motivation is a superficial technique. A sound student of judicial behavior will have to know what events preceded the outcome and be aware of the causal connection between these events and the particular outcomes. The relationship between input and output is more important than the output itself, if we are to understand the judicial process.

Jury trial: nature and purpose

The Constitution of the United States requires (Art. III, sec. 2, cl. 3) a jury trial in all criminal cases. The Seventh Amendment requires a jury trial in civil suits when the amount in controversy exceeds $20. State constitutions have similar requirements, although the variations among the states are extremely numerous. Each state legislature re-

---

[32] Eloise Snyder, "The Supreme Court as a Small Group," *Social Forces*, Vol. 36 (March, 1958), pp. 232–38, sets the pace for this type of research. It has been utilized by David Danielski in "The Influence of the Chief Justice in the Decisional Process," found in Walter F. Murphy and C. Herman Pritchett's, *Courts, Judges and Politics* (New York: Random House, 1961), pp. 497–508. Walter F. Murphy's, *Elements of Judicial Strategy* (Chicago: The University of Chicago Press, 1964), chap. iii, pp. 37–90 is a further refinement.

tains the power, subject to the state constitution, to determine the qualifications and method of selection of jurors; the number of jurors needed to report a valid verdict; and the powers of the jury to find facts, determine law, or fix sentence. In effect, there are 51 different types of jury systems producing 51 different patterns of interaction with the judges, lawyers and parties.

At common law the trial, or petit, jury consisted of 12 men chosen from the community, who were to serve as impartial arbiters of the facts in a case, with the judge himself passing upon all questions of law. Fundamentally, this is still true in all criminal and many civil cases. Many modifications have been made in the common-law jury, however. Now women sit as jurors in 45 states, civil trials by juries of less than 12 (usually 6) are found in 22 states, and 8 states have relaxed the criminal law jury requirement (excepting capital cases). Even more remarkably, half the states now require less than a unanimous verdict in civil cases, and eight apply this view to criminal, noncapital cases. Federal trial juries are required in all criminal cases and must issue a unanimous verdict in such cases. The greatest departure from the common-law jury concept is found in Maryland and Illinois, where juries serve as arbiters of law and of fact.

The frequency with which juries are employed varies significantly from state to state. In criminal cases the relative frequency of jury trials is determined by the amount of crime, the number of criminal acts for which states require jury trial, and the regional customs regarding waiver of jury trial. On a comparable base, for the year of 1955, for example, Georgia had 48 times as many criminal trials as had the state of Connecticut.[33] Significant variations in the frequency

---

[33] From the charts in Harry Kalven, Jr. and Hans Zeisel, *The American Jury* (Boston: Little, Brown & Co., 1966), pp. 502–4. This book is based upon one of the few empirical, controlled experiments concerning jury behavior, the University of Chicago's Jury Study Project based on a large sample of 3,576 cases.

of use of civil juries also exist. Obviously, factors other than statutory availability affect the decision to use a jury.

To some extent, recent studies reveal, juries do not act in accordance with their assigned roles of ascertaining the facts or applying the law—as it is—to the facts. Juries do more than merely engage in pure fact-finding, but in possibly one fourth of the cases in which they are employed, juries may substitute their value preferences in place of the legal principles described to them by the judge. This is rarely done in overt fashion, yet the jury may unconsciously seek to do justice by evading the literal meaning of the law. When this occurs, juries may reach different results from those which a judge, sitting without a jury, might reach.

On the whole, though, judges and juries do not often disagree in their perceptions of a case. The judge and jury usually share similar community values drawn from American social life. The occasions of their disagreements are explained far more by the different reactions of professionals and amateurs to the same stimuli. Juries do not seem to be especially defendant-prone, but they are probably more influenced than judges might be by racial or sexual factors presented in evidence, as well as by the type of crime (in criminal cases).[34]

Internal inputs: lawyers and judges

Among the other stimuli to which the jury is subjected is the personality, demeanor, and presentation of the lawyers for the respective parties. The extent to which the behavior of lawyers has impact upon the jury is the subject of a good deal of folklore. Lawyers themselves believe their tactics and style to be a major determinant of the verdict-outcome in jury trials.

It appears clear that the behavior of a lawyer is a con-

---

[34] *Ibid.*, pp. 396–400; pp. 78–80. Judges and juries seem to differ a good deal in their view of sexual offences affecting children.

siderable, but probably not a significant, input factor in jury trials. Jurors do not necessarily react in the fashion anticipated or desired by the lawyers. In fact, jurors may "try" lawyers as well as the parties in the dispute.

It also is established that a lawyer's facial expressions, his courtesy to court officials, his emotionalism, the number of his objections, all have weight in the jury's view. The tenor of the lawyer's arguments, the tone and flavor of his delivery may, indeed, have unexpected effect upon the jury.

Surprisingly, however, jurors seem to have a high tolerance for objections. It seems expected that lawyers will object. In some instances, however, it may be that jurors will attach special significance to objected-to evidence. Unfavorable inferences may be drawn from repeatedly overruled objections.

One other common error pointed out by jury studies is the failure of defense attorneys to argue the question of the amount of damages in civil suits. Lawyers for the defense fear to indicate to juries any hint of weakness in their cases. However, an unanticipated result may be a high award based on the plaintiff's theory of injury. The jury can only consider the plaintiff's version.[35]

Two important technical powers of lawyers which may have significant effect upon jury composition are *voir dire* and change of venue. In the first, lawyers for both parties are empowered by court rules to examine a juror for bias and to remove him from a prospective jury if bias is shown, or to some extent, for reasons of the lawyer's own tactics. Besides this, in a notorious case, lawyers may request a change of the place of trial (venue) in order to avoid a hostile or prejudiced jury. Intensive pretrial newspaper publicity which might inflame prospective jurors is a typical example. Obviously, both these powers are exercised before the jury is formed.

The role of the judge is, of course, critical in nonjury

---

[35] Dale W. Broeder, "The Impact of the Lawyers: An Informal Appraisal," *Valparaiso Law Review*, Vol. 1 (Fall, 1966), pp. 40–76, at p. 73.

cases. The judge's roles become more complex, even at times confused, in nonjury cases. Most judges attempt a settlement before trial, playing the role of arbitrator. If this fails, they must be determiners of facts, which involves them more intimately in the trial than if a jury were present. Finally, the judge must decide the dispute in terms of the facts as he perceives them and the law as he perceives it. Lawyers tend to argue more law to nonjury judges.

When a jury is employed, the impact of the trial judge depends upon the extent of his active participation in the trial. Jurisdictions vary on the issue of the kind of instruction which the judge may give to the jury, for example. There is also considerable variation in the form of the verdict which the judge may permit the jury to render. If the judge issues detailed instructions on the law *and* the facts, he may influence the jury more than if he were restricted to a brief discussion of applicable law. Similarly, if the jury cannot render a general verdict, but only answer specific questions, the judge has helped shape the outcome.

In England, the trial judge plays an active, vigorous role during the trial, but this is uncommon in the United States. The more the judge participates, the more likely it is that the jury would be impressed, one would expect, but there is no firm proof of this as yet.

On the whole, it appears that juries respond primarily to the input of the evidence, and much less to the influence of the judge and the lawyers. If the evidence is not regarded as a primary input, the jury is more likely to be influenced by internal jury sentiment than by the behavior of the official representatives of the court. As discouraging as it may be to future Clarence Darrows and Melvin Bellis, the most careful study of jury behavior produced an estimate of 1 percent as the degree of defense lawyer impact in an average criminal case.[36]

---

[36] Kalven and Zeisel, *op. cit.*, p. 372. This is not to say that in a close case the presentation of the lawyer could not be a determining factor in the outcome. Also, an extremely incompetent lawyer may not even present all
Footnote continued on next page

Jury selection and recruitment

It is practically impossible to create a completely representative jury, in the sense of a perfect mirror of the community, or a scientific cross section. Nevertheless, it is the goal of most judges to obtain a relatively impartial jury, and recent legal developments point toward that eventual end.

In the federal courts, as in the states, the method for the selection of a pool of jurors is left largely to local determination. Department of Justice surveys reveal a considerable variation from one district to another in the number of Negro jurors on recent jury panels. In one division of a deep South district in which 50 percent of the population is Negro, only 5 percent of the jury panels were Negro. Systems of jury selection in the North sometimes produce disproportionately white-collar, upper-class juries. Laborers, service workers, and semiskilled workers were disproportionately underrepresented, according to one study.[37] These results fly in the face of court rulings forbidding discrimination in jury selection on account of religion, sex, national origin, or economic status.

Federal legislation has been suggested which would eliminate many of the discriminatory jury selection processes at their starting point. Under the recommended procedure, jury commissioners would draw the names for prospective jurors from voter registration lists by random selection. Jurors would need only to meet the requirements of read-

---

the evidence available to him, so that the jury could not properly weigh the facts. These situations are not considered in the Chicago Jury Study Project. Furthermore, in more primitive societies, judges and lawyers may serve as major instruments of social change. See Irving Kaplan, "Courts as Catalysts of Change: A Chagga Case," *Southwestern Journal of Anthropology*, Vol. 21 (Spring, 1965), pp. 79–96.

[37] *Hill* v. *Texas*, 316 U.S. 400 (1942); *Swain* v. *Alabama*, 380 U.S. 202 (1965); *Labatt* v. *Bennett*, 365 Fed. 698 (5th Cir., 1966). See Edwin S. Mills, "A Statistical Study of Occupations in a United States District Court," *Maryland Law Review*, Vol. 22 (Summer, 1962), pp. 205–14.

ing, writing, speaking, and understanding the English language. Although versions of this procedure are to be found in many states, in a majority of jurisdictions this proposed technique is not found, and in a few it is bitterly opposed. There appears to be a feedback into the judicial system which may permit the same eventual result by slow judicial erosion on a case-by-case basis.

Once the jury panel is selected, a screening process is supposedly made available at the trial. This is done by the lawyers for both sides of the case, who ask a series of questions of the jurors in order to determine the existence of bias or some special disqualifying attribute. This *voir dire* is usually held in open court, and the judge may participate. It does not appear that the *voir dire* is an effective screening mechanism. Jurors often, consciously or otherwise, lie on *voir dire*. It is more effectively used as a means of indoctrination than as a means of sifting out biased or unfavorable jurors.[38]

The selection of a grand jury panel is not technically a different matter, although there is no requirement that a grand jury be composed of a representative cross section of the community. In fact, it is sometimes expected that grand juries will be composed of members of the more propertied, "substantial" classes. The United States Constitution does not require all states to employ grand juries, and even in the federal courts, where it must be used, it need not necessarily include a particular proportion of Negroes, women, or workingmen. Consequently, grand juries, which have considerable power not only to indict for particular offenses but also to investigate possible infractions of law which may lead to widespread investigations, do not have to comply with the same kind of screening and selection process as do petit juries of much more limited power.

Grand juries only rarely play an active role, but when they do, their efforts may result in a considerable input into

---

[38] Dale W. Broeder, *"Voir Dire* Examinations: An Empirical Study," Southern California Law Review, Vol. 38 (Summer, 1965), pp. 503–28.

the criminal law process. Otherwise, they usually serve as a minor restraint upon the input capacity of the prosecutor. The grand jury, composed of laymen, and usually lacking the direct testimony of the suspect, is dependent for its information upon the prosecutor, who is nominally merely the legal advisor to the grand jury. This situation usually renders the grand jury virtually powerless, despite its formal powers to generally supervise the peace in the community.

The extent of the effect of social background, racial, ethnic, and economic factors upon the jury verdict is still not understood. Studies of American voting patterns reveal that social and economic status are significant input phenomena in voting behavior. Since a verdict is a kind of small-group vote, the same factors would seem to be relevant. However, when a unanimous verdict is required, a single strong personality may be more important than the respective backgrounds of the jurors. Clearly, this question is both fascinating and important, since the effects of socially distorted panels must be known before useful remedies can be produced.

Extralegal officials

The final group of legal decision makers to be treated are the federal probation officers, a group of individuals who may have greater weight in the issuing of sentence than the jury itself. The probation officers in the states are not as well staffed, organized, trained, or studied, but the federal approach seems to be a model for the more progressive states.

Probation officers are appointed by the United States District Court for each judicial district. There are almost 530 probation officers now serving in the federal court system. In addition, there is a Federal Probation Training Center in Chicago, staffed by professional experts in relevant social sciences from nearby universities.

Probation officers are appointed with tenure or security according to variable practices from district to district. Sometimes the probation officer is the personal appointee of the judge, who has personal knowledge of the appointee. No particular qualifications are required for the post, although a college degree and some social service work is usual. Some probation officers fall below this standard, lacking even a high school education.

The probation officer possesses the power and responsibility to issue a presentence investigation report, on the basis of which the judge may be aided in selecting offenders for probation. Further, the report may serve as a guide to the type of institution appropriate to the offender and his mental and emotional attitudes. Approximately 85 percent of all convicted persons receive presentence investigations.

Very little use of psychiatric or psychological services has been made by the probation officers. In this respect, some states have taken the lead in establishing clinics and diagnostic centers. Psychiatric examination for serious sex offenders is mandatory in New York State.

Not all probation officers make specific recommendations, nor are the standards of recommendation clearly defined. Value preferences of the community, or the individual officer, frequently creep into the report. Independent judgments of probation officers need not be accepted, but they do serve to influence the judge's determination of the character of the sentence in a criminal case.[39]

Statistically valid prediction tables for failure or success of probation or parole have still not evolved. More accurate and sensitive indicators are required. Furthermore, probation officers need to know what factors judges consider to be significant in giving sentences. Comprehensive statistical services are lacking, resulting in a general confusion of

---

[39] A. Kenneth Pye, George W. Shadoan, and Joseph M. Snee, *A Preliminary Report of the Federal Probation System* (Washington, D.C.: Georgetown University Law Center, 1963).

information. Sentencing institutes, held from time to time for federal judges may help by providing judges with direct contact with probation officers and correctional institutions. As of the moment, sentencing procedure, the most vital stage of the legal process for the convicted criminal, remains a chancy and largely intuitive practice.

On the state level, decentralization is widespread. There are over 3,000 counties in the nation, most with their own probation laws. Centralization of control in the states does exist, and it is growing, but the majority of states permit great county autonomy, and a few, much city autonomy. Uniform parole and probation policies do not exist, saving those exceptional states which have state-centralized combined parole and probation agencies.[40]

Bar associations in many parts of the country have called for the elimination of long prison terms and for the greater use of probation and parole techniques, except for the most serious crimes. Even so, our knowledge of probation and parole policies is very limited. If this is the path of future public policy, it is not lighted by recent information and informed evaluation. What happens to a released prisoner during the period of probation or parole is not clearly known.

---

[40] David Dressler, *Practice and Theory of Probation and Parole* (New York: Columbia University Press, 1959), p. 27.

VI

Trial and appeal:
the conversion process

THE SERIES of processes which precede the occurrence of a
trial are each important events which, in many ways, determine the course of the trial, and later determine the course
of the appellate stage, if any. A dispute may be settled during the months or years intervening between the decision to
institute legal action and the beginning of a trial. Criminal
or civil cases may be dropped during this time, and the parties, the witnesses, and the evidence may have disappeared,
become lost, or otherwise transformed by time. The communication of the actual events to a trial jury becomes a historical problem, with the imperfections of any historical
recreation. Of course, other inputs have also intervened during the time between the litigated events and the trial. This
is summarized in Diagram A.

The trial is a formal event prescribed by law, as an official, socially sanctioned manner of determining facts, applying law to the facts, and pronouncing an official conclusion, called a *verdict*. In the simplest, and most common
situation, the verdict as an output terminates the dispute
for all official purposes. It may not be relitigated in the

same way again because of the criminal prohibition created by the American double jeopardy doctrine and the civil limitation (which is not the same) of *res judicata*.[1] The same facts and offenses cannot be retried, in normal circumstances. On the other hand, an appeal may be granted by a higher court on the ground of substantive or procedural error and a new trial ordered, if the appeal is not dismissed. These processes, trial and appeal, represent the public face of the law and constitute the official means of resolving disputes by converting them from inputs to outputs.

The conversion from input to output is the most dramatic aspect of the legal system. Novelists, playwrights, and "nonfiction novelists" have often utilized the trial scene, or even the appeal, as a climactic moment in the story's development. However, it should be realized that most disputes are never litigated, many are not tried in courts, and inputs and outputs are far more complex than these creative writers allow. Finally, the feedback loop between society and the legal system, between the political and legal systems and the internal feedback processes, tends to be misunderstood.

The adversary system

The lawyer in all legal systems serves as a counselor to his clients. He supplies advice in the writing of legal documents, the meeting of legal obligations, and the negotiation of legal differences. Litigation is usually a last resort, because it is relatively unprofitable, time-consuming, unnecessary, and it causes tensions within the profession. However, if a party or his attorney decides to go to court, the actual trial is conducted, in Anglo-American jurisdictions, according to the adversary system of justice, which requires an

---

[1] Jay A. Sigler, "Federal Double Jeopardy Policy," *Vanderbilt Law Review*, Vol. 19 (Spring, 1966), pp. 375-405; Jay A. Sigler, "A History of Double Jeopardy," *American Journal of Legal History*, Vol. 7 (November, 1963), pp. 283–309.

antagonistic bifold structure of disputation. This system is not inevitable, but it is a hallowed product of legal history.

The adversary system of justice regards the lawyer as both an officer of the court and a representative of a client, and also as the most active organizer of the most favorable version of his client's case. The lawyer, who is more naturally a peacemaker, must become an active partisan warrior for his client. The skills of negotiation and compromise become less significant, while the skills of examination, cross-examination, and verbal disputation become critical. The trial is the legal equivalent of limited war.

The limitations upon the trial advocate are professional and procedural. He cannot do anything he wants on behalf of his client. He may not inflame the jury, bribe the witnesses, or threaten the judge. He may not insult the other attorneys or concoct false evidence. He is bound by professional standards to present the truth, though not necessarily all of it. He is restrained by rules of evidence from presenting hearsay, or raising irrelevancies, or forcing wives to testify against husbands. On the other hand, he may cast aspersions against witnesses, challenge jurors or charm them, utilizing histrionic arts or audio-visual techniques.

The zeal with which the lawyer plays the role of a partisan advocate may affect future relationships with the lawyers and judges he confronts at his trials. Since his client may not soon relitigate, a lawyer may be more concerned to retain professional acceptance than to press his client's cause. Thus, incompetence or poor preparation may account for the generally colorless character of most trials.

The most important aspect of the adversary system is the claim of truth-finding upon which it rests. Defenders of the adversary system must maintain that by presenting two opposing versions of the facts and law to a neutral judge and jury, the truth will emerge from the contrasting versions of the case. By preventing the deciding tribunal from entering into the case prior to trial, the tribunal's impartiality is preserved, its flexibility is maintained, and the trial becomes an open, fresh conflict in which the facts can be sorted out by the tribunal. Some defenders have concluded that "partisan advocacy plays a vital and essential role in one of the most fundamental procedures of a democratic society."[2]

However, the adversary system does not necessarily upturn all relevant facts. The judge and jury are largely passive recipients of the facts presented by the advocates. Lazy, incompetent, uninterested, or corrupt lawyers may not unearth all the needed evidence. Highly competent lawyers may conceal some valuable facts. Elements of surprise, "coached witnesses," or simply the expenditure of money may affect the quality and completeness of factual evidence. By virtue of a combat theory of evidence, the facts may become hopelessly entangled, rather than clarified. Besides, it may be government policy *not* to zealously pursue a public claim.[3]

Under the adversary system, "proof of fact" means persuading a judge or jury to accept one version of the actual events. Even "proof of law" may be affected, as the trial judge accepts an advocate's version of the law, although the judge is supposed to act independently in that area.

Mitigating features of the adversary system do exist. The judge may independently participate in questioning witnesses. The judge may request an attorney to find more facts. Beyond that, the jury may independently appraise the credibility of witnesses or infer the probable occurrence of events.

There is no doubt that legal systems which do not employ the adversary system also have flaws. If the judge in conti-

---

[2] Report of the Joint Conference on Professional Responsibility, of the Association of American Law Schools and the American Bar Association, *American Bar Association Journal*, Vol. 44 (1958), p. 1161.

[3] Jerome Frank, *Courts on Trial* (New York: Atheneum Publishers, 1963), pp. 80–102. On a lack of zeal in antitrust prosecution, see Carl B. Swisher, "Federal Organization of Legal Functions," *American Political Science Review*, Vol. 33 (1939), pp. 973–1000.

nental Europe is the leading participant in the trial, if he
questions the witnesses, determines the direction of the trial,
calls for experts, and generally commands the trial, the true

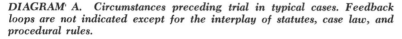

DIAGRAM A. *Circumstances preceding trial in typical cases. Feedback
loops are not indicated except for the interplay of statutes, case law, and
procedural rules.*

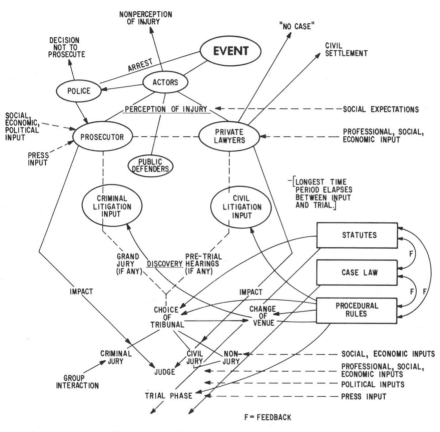

facts may still prove elusive. However, rules of evidence,
surprise, and money spent to retain lawyers become much
less relevant factors affecting the outcome of trials. The relative position of all the actors in the trial shifts significantly
when the lawyer's role is reduced, but it has not yet been
proven that either system will more effectively elicit facts.

Institution of criminal trial

The decision to begin a criminal trial, or not to begin it, is a choice which is usually considered to be within the wide range of discretion available to the prosecution in all states and in the national government. In one case, a Mississippi grand jury and a district court judge failed to force the United States attorney to bring suit against two Negro civil rights workers for alleged perjury. In another, some civil rights workers tried to force the Justice Department to prosecute white citizens for supposed deprivation of Negroes' civil rights. In both cases, the courts upheld the prosecutor's discretion.[4] The decision not to prosecute was seen as an executive choice which courts may not coerce. In effect, the input of a criminal trial must emanate from the prosecutor's office and from no other place.

Preceding the decision of the prosecutor, the police must have made an arrest and must also have decided to present the case to the prosecutor. For many reasons, the police may decide to free the arrested person without further action. The low visibility of their administrative decision to free the arrested individual renders the police prone to pressures and influences of an extralegal sort.[5] In addition, the police may be subject to different political direction than the prosecutor, who is often elected separately. If the police decide to present the case to the prosecutor, their responsibility and effective power cease at that point.

Once the file of a prospective case is in the hands of the prosecutor, he must make his choice in the light of factors

---

[4] *United States* v. *Cox*, 342 F.2d 167 (5th Cir., 1965); *Moses* v. *Kennedy*, 219 F. Supp. 762 (D.D.C., 1963).

[5] Joseph Goldstein, "Police Discretion Not to Invoke the Criminal Process: Low Visibility Decisions in the Administration of Justice," *Yale Law Journal*, Vol. 69 (March, 1960), pp. 543–94.

which he is aware will result in a socially or personally desirable outcome. For the most part, a prosecutor wants to win the government's case. His decision not to prosecute may involve a calculation of the likelihood of failure given the facts presented him.

The chances of success must seem more than just fair. Money spent on unsuccessful prosecution is money wasted. Besides, the prosecutor might like to gain a reputation as a successful advocate for the public. Access to higher political office might be available as a result of great "success," although this is not true at the national level. His status within the office is also at stake.

The decision to prosecute, then, involves a nice calculation of the probable behavior of the judges and juries in the jurisdiction who might be given the case to try. Caution is the byword. Although relatively unsupervised by superiors, the prosecutor in a particular matter is unlikely to gamble upon a close or dubious case unless other external factors are brought into play. These might be party, press, or personal factors which could counterbalance the professional caution of the prosecutor.

For more serious crimes, it appears more likely that trial will be sought than for minor crimes, although this needs further corroboration. Previous conviction of felonies might also provide a reason to prosecute a particular individual, even in the face of a merely fair set of information. On the other hand, it might be better for the prosecutor to await a better case against the accused, rather than embolden him by a flimsy prosecution.[6]

A prosecutor must be especially sensitive to the existence or the absence of jury appeal in his case. He must predict, with some accuracy, the probable behavior of a jury confronted with his facts.

---

[6] See John Kaplan, "The Prosecutorial Discretion—A Comment," *Northwestern University Law Review*, Vol. 60 (May, 1965), pp. 181–82.

The prosecutor must also make a judgment concerning the availability of facts he wishes to allege. Will the witnesses be available? Will the witnesses cooperate? Will they be believable? If the answers are unfavorable, the chances of success are sharply diminished.

Higher standards of proof may be required for particular offenses, such as mail fraud or murder, which require proof of the accused's state of mind. Certain defendants, because of their apparent middle-class respectability, may be especially hard to convict because of jury sympathy, as in embezzlement cases.

Also, the decision to prosecute may be conditioned on the competence of the defendant's attorney. An unskilled lawyer or an uninterested assigned counsel might, by his very presence at the defendant's side, invite prosecution. Some defense attorneys are prone to issuing guilty pleas on behalf of their clients. This, too, might be a habit of great significance to the prosecution.

Finally, the decision not to prosecute may flow from the prosecutor's judgment that the available sanctions are too harsh. Sometimes, the prosecutor becomes, by his behavior, a virtual legislator. Even if the defendant's guilt is easy to establish, the prosecutor may not institute proceedings if the magnitude of the penalty appears disproportionate to the offense. The input of the law itself may be less significant than the social factors which condition the personal value scheme of the prosecutor. If we could grasp this element of personality structure, we would know a great deal more about criminal law enforcement than we do at present.

There are some limitations upon the prosecutor's discretion besides the professional internal feedback mechanisms within the office. In some places it is possible for individual citizens to force the prosecutor to bring a suit, although this does not assure zealous effort. Then, too, it is not usually possible for a prosecutor to continuously harass an individual with repeated threats of prosecution. The constitutional requirement of a speedy trial is an ultimate barrier to this kind of misconduct.[7]

Institution of civil suit

The civil suit, unlike the criminal action, is instituted at the behest of one of the actors in an incident who becomes, as he solicits legal advice, a client. Many clients are not interested in suits but only wish advice in the conduct of their affairs. However, there are clients who, having perceived an injury, wish to receive the satisfaction, not only of some material recompense, but also of the symbolic rewards of a trial victory. There is also an increasing number of unwilling clients, such as insured persons whose companies wish to engage in a suit to protect the companies' interests. However it happens, the machinery of a civil suit must be set in motion by a private party, usually one who perceives an injury.

Since a private party selects his lawyer for the purpose of redressing an injury, it should be clear that success in recovery for injury is largely dependent upon the quality of legal service which is purchased. The more affluent should be more able to pursue their claims because they can buy better legal service. As with medical service, the less affluent are likely to endure more discomfort and pain than the more affluent, and unless protected by insurance systems, the victims of severe injury may have to surrender their legal claims because of their inability to afford legal service. This is mitigated somewhat by the contingency fee system, in which a lawyer may agree to receive as his fee a propor-

---

[7] Despite the constitutional requirement of the Sixth Amendment, delay of trials for several years is the common situation. This is especially true in civil cases. See Hans Zeisel, Harry Kalven, Jr., and Bernard Buchholz, *Delay in the Court* (Boston: Little, Brown & Co., 1959).

tion (usually one quarter) of an anticipated damage recovery, or by publicly supported legal services for the poor.

The nature of the party to be sued is one factor which a client and lawyer must consider. If the defendant is a well-staffed utility company, it may be able to prolong a case and make it expensive. The quality of legal service is likely to be higher among large corporations than in the average private law firm. This may discourage full-fledged suits.

One major problem to be overcome before a decision is made regarding suit is the obtaining of an accurate statement of the facts. The client must be induced to reveal all the facts surrounding the objectionable incident. Otherwise, evidence concealed at the interview will appear at the trial, to the detriment of the client. With a clear view of the facts, lawyers may appraise the value and validity of a claim.

Unlike the situation in criminal law, the practitioner has a wide range of tactical choices, including a choice of courts, a possible demand for a jury, and the negotiation of arrangements with other attorneys. He may even decide to refer his client to another lawyer, or join forces with other lawyers.

All of these calculations will be made in the light of the chances of success, and with a view to the amount of the fee involved. Generally, the lower the fee, the less anxious the attorney will be to institute suit. Days spent in court or preparing for trial are extremely costly to the lawyer, especially if he is working on a contingency fee. Hence, there is a strong incentive not to go to trial.

A client must also consider professional differences among law firms before deciding to press his claim. Very large law firms usually will not handle divorce cases, or defend professional criminals, or accept negligence cases from new clients. The very large firms serve the business community rather than individual persons. On the other hand, the very large law firm (often a New York City firm) is likely to have more prestige and influence in high government and business circles, since these law businesses tend to recruit the elite of the profession.[8] For the average client, though, it is best to seek out a small local firm, well reputed in the community, which is usually best equipped, by reason of experience, to deal with local courts and juries.

Settlement: the noncase

The input of a client in the civil matter or by the police, consequent to arrest in the criminal case, need not result in a thorough processing, by the conversion process, in the form of a trial with a verdict output. The process may be cut short by settlement, which is an informal bargaining process between the two sides of the dispute to reach a resolution without using the formal apparatus of trial or hearing. As should be evident, settlement can take place in a civil dispute at any time before the final verdict, but in criminal cases, once the trial has begun the prosecution must carry it through to conclusion, because of the effect of the double jeopardy rule of most states and of the federal Constitution.[9]

In a civil case, each party's attorney will probably seek settlement more actively than he will pursue trial preparation. Both efforts will be going on at the same time, unless the clients restrain the lawyers. Some lawyers settle virtually every claim which is brought to them, believing the certainties of settlement preferable to the expensive uncertainties of a trial outcome. Many lawyers believe that it is their job to keep their "client out of court just as the doctor's job is to keep his patient in good health."[10]

When a private lawyer in a civil case is ready to settle,

---

[8] Beryl H. Levy, *Corporation Lawyer: Saint or Sinner?* (Philadelphia: Chilton Co., 1961); Erwin O. Smigel, *The Wall Street Lawyer* (New York: Free Press of Glencoe, 1964); Charles A. Horsky, *The Washington Lawyer* (Boston: Little, Brown, & Co., 1952).

[9] *Kepner* v. *United States*, 195 U.S. 100, 128 (1904); *Green* v. *United States*, 355 U.S. 184 (1957).

[10] Walter P. Armstrong, "How and When to Settle," *Arkansas Law Review*, Vol. 19 (Spring, 1965), p. 20.

he will probably meet with the attorney for the other party face-to-face in order to work toward a dollar value of the claim, if it has some merit. In a sense, this bargaining is done under pressure, since if negotiations break down, a trial will ensue. Under the impending threat of trial, both sides are likely to engage in realistic bargaining.

As the day of trial approaches, both sides in a civil case will have a fairly complete idea of the strength of their respective positions. Pretrial pleadings will reveal the factual bases of the claims. Consequently, settlement is more likely in the days or weeks before the day of the trial than at any other time before or after.

Throughout the bargaining process the lawyers are the primary actors. The clients play a passive role. A good attorney will keep his client well aware of the current stage of the process, so that the client can soundly choose between trial or settlement.

Settlement of cases involving the national government or a large corporation may be a greatly different matter. Large corporations can better afford the expense of trial, and may wish, for business reasons, to avoid admissions of defects in their products or services unless proven at a trial. Settlement with the federal government is made more difficult because of the number of lawyers involved. It is common government practice to put a new lawyer on the case as it enters a new phase. Each lawyer represents a fresh start, and it is likely that each has never seen the case file before. It is usually necessary to deal with the head of the government department in order to reach a settlement.

Settlements with the federal government are most often obtained in the areas of antitrust violations, unfair competition matters, and, most especially, in income tax disputes. The Internal Revenue Service consciously prefers to reach administrative settlements whenever possible. In 1965, 87½ percent of the tax cases were settled, dismissed, or defaulted. Great pressure is also brought upon defendants by the Tax Court before a case is calendared. However, if the Internal Revenue Service is concerned with establishment of a legal principle, or a new statutory interpretation, the chances of settlement are minimal.[11]

In criminal cases, settlement takes the form of bargaining for a guilty plea. The accused person agrees to plead guilty to the charge rather than face a trial. This may be considered a settlement (although it has not been called that) because it is a way of avoiding trial incident upon a bargain reached before trial. A high proportion, perhaps 85 percent, of all convictions in criminal cases are obtained this way. The defendant is forced to choose between a "bargain" plea for a lesser offense or else run the risk of conviction in a trial for a greater offense flowing out of the same facts. If the defendant refuses to agree to plead guilty, the prosecutor may discharge him (because he knows the case to be weak) or he may go to trial. The defendant is in a very vulnerable bargaining position because only the prosecutor knows the strength of his case. Since the prosecutor's public reputation is often gauged by the number of criminal convictions, prosecutors usually prefer to "settle" by bargaining for a guilty plea.[12]

The reasons which favor settlement in non-criminal cases are simple ones. From the plaintiff's point of view, he gets his money promptly, rather than waiting years before final judgment. From the defendant's point of view, he may pare down the size of the plaintiff's claim and also achieve a financially certain conclusion of the dispute. Both parties may wish to avoid the psychological strains of trial, the costs of trial, and the loss of time and delay caused by trial.

From a social point of view, the informal operation of the

---

[11] Lester R. Uretz, "Settlement of Tax Controversies," *Taxes*, Vol. 44 (December, 1966), pp. 794–802. The author is Chief Counsel to the Internal Revenue Service.

[12] "Guilty Plea Bargaining," Note, *University of Pennsylvania Law Review*, Vol. 112 (April, 1964), pp. 865–80.

settlement process is highly desirable. It removes cases from congested court dockets, which pleases the judges. It makes jury trials less necessary, which pleases citizens subject to jury duty, and it pleases lawyers who have many cases to handle in their offices. Nonetheless, the flow of events reveals a typically legal process. The form of the output should not mislead us into underrating the settlement. The settlement is often a legally binding agreement having the force of a formal judgment. Although achieved informally, the output is given a formal sanction, should subsequent disputes arise. Settlement serves to abort a case; it resolves a dispute in anticipation of trial process which is otherwise available. Settlement is the most healthy manner of legal resolution.

Fact determination

No single element entering into a legal decision is as important as the factual input. The "facts" are the reconstruction of the initiating incident which ultimately led to the trial. "Facts" are, in a sense, a historical recreation of a past condition which, when combined with the rules and the law, produce a socially binding result through the conversion medium of trial, or the aborting settlement. The initial facts serve to limit the possible number of outcomes by limiting the applicable rules of law. If the facts are established with certainty, the dispute can be much more easily resolved.

Now, it must be emphasized that there are many meanings in the word "fact," and also noted that a legal "fact" is not the same as an empirical "fact." No lawyer or judge is concerned with a complete reconstruction of every element of a past occasion, since this would involve innumerable irrelevancies and enormous expenditure of time, energy, and money. The layman must consider that only in the most remarkable circumstances is it possible to reassemble the constituent parts of a past event to create a "true fact." The Kennedy assassination controversy illustrates the difficulty in a dramatic way, especially in view of all the available information. And the remarkable press coverage of the Oswald murder indicates the rare exception of a completely recorded event. In the Kennedy assassination, the facts remain obscure, but the whole television audience served as witness to the Oswald murder.

The development of legal facts takes place during, and as a part of, the conversion process. The "facts" perceived by an arresting officer may be seen differently by the prosecuting attorney. The insolence of the suspect and his suspicious behavior may seem critical to the policeman but are less meaningful to the prosecutor. He knows that a judge and jury will be more influenced by other aspects of the situation, or he may know that the fact situation does not sufficiently indicate a violation of a criminal statute.

Similarly, on the civil side, the lawyer realizes the differences existing between the quality of pieces of "fact" evidence. His client's statements, photographs, expert statements, statements by eyewitnesses, documents, tape recordings, and moving pictures are all parts of the jigsaw puzzle, but the true facts cannot be completely reassembled. It is increasingly possible to obtain a more balanced view of the offense through the use of pretrial discovery techniques, permitted by court rules. Thus, it is possible to get some idea of the opponent's view of the facts, and to avoid surprise, by the use of questionnaires and examinations before trial in civil and criminal cases.

The atmosphere of adversary proceedings, and the desire for victory, may lead to an incomplete presentation of facts at the trial. Each lawyer will try to present that view of the facts most favorable to his client. Cross-examination may reveal some of the gaps, but it is usually a partial version of the facts reconstructed by lawyers which the jury must consider. Furthermore, some of the evidence may have become

lost or be inadmissible for technical reasons, witnesses may
have disappeared, and the lawyers may not be fully capable
of presenting the evidence.

Evidence is essentially the raw material from which the
jury derives, by inference, the legally operative "facts." In
the final analysis, the "facts" are what the jury concludes by
way of a verdict. Sometimes the verdict does not require a
specific finding of fact, but it does indicate a preferred view
of the facts, in any event.

The law does not require a perfect reconstruction of the
facts. Guilt must be proven "beyond a reasonable doubt,"
but not with absolute certainty. In a civil case, the trier of
fact must be convinced on the basis of "a preponderance of
the evidence," which means something more than 50 percent probability.

The fact determination in one case is not controlling in
other cases involving other parties. If several people are
injured in a single accident, it is quite possible that some
will convince the triers of fact in their separate trials and
others will not. The fact outcome in one case is not considered to be evidence in another case flowing from the same
events.[13]

Seen from the point of view of our analysis, the outcome
of any case involves a conclusion both as to the law and
facts in a case dispute. "Facts," in a legal sense, are the
output of a trial. "Facts" are not the "true" events themselves from which the dispute originated. Evidence is the
input and facts the output in the trial process.

---

[13] "Estoppel by judgment" and *"res judicata"* have a limited effect of
barring suits on identical facts and causes of action. "Estoppel by verdict"
precludes the *same parties* from relitigating a fact which has been determined
in a suit between them. These are very narrow doctrines, however, and are
subject to many exceptions. In order that a judgment may operate to bar a
subsequent suit on the same legal theory, it must be based upon a complete
investigation of the merits of a case, *In Re Hoover Co.,* 134 F.2d 624 (U.S.
Ct. of Customs and Patent Appeals, 1943); *Estelle* v. *Board of Ed. of Red
Bank,* 97 A.2d 1, 26 N.J. Super. 9 (1953).

The rule input

Further restrictions upon the accurate reconstruction of the originating events are found in various rules of evidence which restrict a full presentation of all available information. The evidence rules are much more lax in situations where juries are absent. This is even more true when administrative hearings are being held. It can be said that the more formal the proceeding, the more restricted the flow of information to the trier of fact will be.

In the conduct of a trial, each party has the right to make an objection to the reception of any item of evidence. He may do so on the ground of irrelevance, or on several other bases. If his objection is sustained, the evidence is ruled inadmissible. This means that the jury (if any) will be told to disregard evidence it may have already heard or seen. Obviously, it is preferable to make an objection before the jury has been exposed to the evidence, because the jurors need not be asked to forget what they have perceived.

Evidence may be objectionable because the witness is incompetent or because a mere opinion has been offered rather than a perceived event. The hearsay rule is intended to restrict the use of secondhand evidence, but it is inconsistently applied. Other evidence may be excluded because it is "prejudicial," which means it could be emotionally upsetting to the jury. For example, evidence of prior convictions, evidence of insurance in an accident case, gory photographs, or lie detector tests may each be considered by the judge to be potentially misleading.

Beyond this, certain kinds of evidence are excluded because of some greater social interest apart from the trial. In this category fall various so-called privileges. The government need not reveal its secrets, clergymen need not tell what was revealed to them in the confessional, attorneys need not tell what their clients disclosed to them, wives need not testify against their husbands, and doctors need not reveal what their patients have told them. These "privileges" are intended to protect certain prized social relationships. The interest in protecting these may be stronger than the interest in finding facts in a trial.

Of particular interest in criminal law are the rules restricting the use of illegally obtained evidence. These rules are now on a constitutional plane. They are intended to protect accused persons against the powerful police and prosecutor by requiring a strict adherence to technical rules for finding evidence. Warrants must usually be obtained pursuant to a search for evidence. Confessions must be voluntary and must be made after being informed of a right not to confess. Wiretapping and other forms of eavesdropping, though effective means of finding evidence, may not be permissible, in the sense that the evidence obtained by these illegal means will be inadmissible as evidence to establish the fact of guilt in a criminal case.[14]

The feedback effect of exclusionary rules for criminal cases is considerable. Police must be trained to know the pitfalls of the rules of evidence. They must take care to know the rights of suspects. If guidance is not provided the police, invalid arrests, improper seizure of evidence, and undue violence may result in a guilty man's going free.[15]

Fact and law

The relationship between fact and law is central to the trial process. The two factors are tightly intertwined in the

---

[14] *Mapp.* v. *Ohio*, 367 U.S. 643 (1961).

[15] *Rochin* v. *California*, 342 U.S. 165 (1952), involved illegal entry and forcible extraction of swallowed material. Coerced confessions are clearly inadmissible, but a driver might be compelled to submit to a blood test in a medical environment (*Schmerber* v. *California*, 384 U.S. 757 [1966]). A right to counsel is guaranteed even before trial, and during interrogation (*Miranda* v. *Arizona*, 384 U.S. 136 [1966]).

average case. The issues of law arise initially out of the facts, but the law grows from distinctions made among fact situations. The law informs the lawyer which facts he must emphasize and which he may safely disregard. If the law is unsettled, the lawyer may introduce a novel kind of fact, but if it is very clear, he may be restricted in his use of facts.

Sometimes the recognition of unusual data as evidence of a fact may signal a major change in the law. This was certainly the situation in *Brown* v. *The Board of Education of Topeka*,[16] the 1954 landmark desegregation decision. When the Supreme Court agreed to admit the evidence of sociologists regarding the baneful social and psychological effects of segregation upon school children, the "separate but equal" segregation standard was on its way into the discard pile of legal rules.

In certain cases, the law is undisputed and the facts are in contention. When this happens, the output is determined by the trier of fact. The rule of law functions unambiguously and guides the ultimate sanction or penalty invoked. In a murder case, the nature of the legal offense is usually understood, but the issue revolves around the factual problems.

In other cases, the facts are agreed upon but the law is unsettled. When this occurs, the role of the judge is en-

---

[16] *Brown* v. *Board of Education of Topeka*, 347 U.S. 483 (1954). In later school desegregation decisions, the lead of the *Brown* case has sometimes been pursued to further horizons. Judge J. Skelley Wright, in *Hobson* v. *Hansen*, 269 F. Supp. 401 (D.C. Cir., 1967) issued decrees against *de facto* segregation in a District of Columbia neighborhood school plan. Empirical studies of the psychological effects of segregation upon the attitudes of Negro school children are cited profusely throughout the lengthy opinion. But Judge Wright has admitted elsewhere that "There can . . . be no mathematical formula to determine at what point . . . racial imbalance and *de facto* school segregation rises to constitutional dimensions": "Public School Desegregation: Legal Remedies for De Facto Segregation," *New York University Law Review*, Vol. 40 (1965), p. 303.

Heavy reliance upon historical material, including Negro history, is extensively found in *Poindexter* v. *Louisiana Financial Assistance Commission*, 275 F. Supp. 833 (5th Cir., La., 1967) against the Louisiana tuition grants system.

hanced and that of the jury sharply diminished. It may be possible to dispense with the jury entirely and dispose of the matter by a decision of the trier of the law.

In many cases, the law may be deliberately vague. This is often so with modern statutes which attempt to create legal flexibility by defining legal standards in very general terms. For example, contracts in restraint of trade violate the Sherman Antitrust Act, but the concept of "restraint" has been worked out on a case-by-case basis by federal courts. This method of delegating law definition to the courts is very popular with legislatures, which also frequently delegate this power to administrative agencies. The effect, however, is to make the law-fact distinction extremely obscure.

In most cases, both the law and the facts are in dispute. Both sides pursue different legal theories, that is, they construct their case preparations with different conceptions of the law to be applied and, as a result, differ in their views of the operative facts. This creates the complex texture of the average case, complicating the jobs of the triers of fact and the triers of law.

After all the evidence has been presented, the judge must decide whether there is factual dispute sufficient to merit sending the case to the jury (if any). If there is not, he will "direct" a verdict for the party which has made out an incontestable claim. This means that the jury will be instructed that it must, on the basis of the evidence and the law, find for the party who obtains the directed verdict. If there remains some ambiguity of *fact*, the judge will allow the jury to resolve it, giving them his instructions, which attempt to separate the fact input from the law input.[17] The jury is primarily the trier of facts. Jurors are not supposed to innovate legal principles. Of course, it is possible that jurors will violate their instructions, often unconsciously, by interweaving law and fact.

---

[17] How a judge decides to send a case to a jury is described in Joseph N. Ulman, *A Judge Takes the Stand* (New York: Alfred A. Knopf, Inc., 1933), pp. 52–66.

The stage of instructing the jury is possibly the most meaningless phase of a trial. Judges and lawyers know that juries pay scant attention to the usual set of heavily legal instructions. It is probably a feeble gesture, except as the instructions serve to impress upon the jury the solemnity and the significance of their task.[18] Instructions are usually written and are read to the jury verbatim, from a mixture of legal sources. The judge may comment upon the facts, but he will usually avoid saying very much about his own impressions, or else risk a mistrial.

The administrative process

A glaring exception to the usual practice of the judicial trial as a means of conflict resolution is the utilization of administrative hearings. The conversion process depicted in the paragraphs above must be regarded as a typical pattern, but the growing tendency to create administrative bodies with rule-making and quasi-judicial powers has shattered many standard concepts. A comprehensive examination of the legal process cannot neglect these newer patterns.

In the administrative process the legislative, executive, and judicial functions are mixed together, and many functions, such as investigating, advocating, negotiating, testifying, rule making, and adjudicating, are performed. The reasons for the breakdown of the separation-of-powers formula are not hard to find. It was felt by Congress and the state legislatures that certain regulatory tasks could not be performed efficiently, rapidly, expertly, and with due concern for the public interest by the traditional branches of government. Accordingly, regulatory agencies were delegated powers to consider disputes from the earliest stage of

---

[18] R. J. Farley, "Instructions to Juries—Their Role in the Judicial Process," *Yale Law Journal*, Vol. 42 (December, 1932), pp. 194–225. This subtle article also examines the ways in which instructions may be manipulated by lawyers and judges to suit ends other than the official one of guiding the jury.

investigation to the final stages of adjudication entirely within the agency itself, subject only to limited review in the regular courts.

Perhaps the most surprising feature of this new situation is the potentiality of the merger of the functions of prosecuting and judging. The agencies make the rules, institute investigations into violations, make complaints on violations, hear testimony, and then determine the proper application of the rules to a particular case.

One expert asserts, the problem is to ensure "that their judicial functions will be exercised in a truly judicial manner uninfluenced by the possession of inconsistent functions of investigating and prosecution."[19] But this assertion assumes that the adversary system of justice is the only or the best means of discovering facts and of adjudicating the legal effects of those facts. Instead, it appears that the administrative process is a very different phenomenon, based upon the view that a single-focused, controlled flow of information, managed largely by one agency, will provide a sounder legal result. The conversion process is largely managed by the administrative agency, even if affected parties are permitted to have lawyers to represent them. It cannot be said that this different conversion process is inherently unjust, merely that it is inherently different.

Since administrative agencies are usually staffed by experts in the regulated field, and since juries are not employed, the technical rules of evidence which restrict the production of facts are largely, though not completely, eliminated. Constitutional protections, such as the right to plead possible self-incrimination, are still accorded the parties. Many agencies have specialized rules of procedure which require skilled lawyers for affected parties, but on the whole the legal process is much more streamlined before these agencies.

---

[19] Bernard Schwartz, "Administrative Justice and Its Place in the Legal Order," *New York University Law Review*, Vol. 30 (November, 1955), p. 1410.

Hearings are usually instituted by the agency itself, though private parties frequently use their resources to settle disputes. The National Labor Relations Board, for example, acts on the complaints of either labor unions or management, receiving their inputs from these external group sources. Other agencies, such as the Internal Revenue Service, operate largely through the regular court system. The determination of the proper forum and of the means of instituting complaints is made by the legislative body which has created the agency.

Obviously, the expertise, staff, and procedures of the administrative agencies are bureaucratic in character. The government's view of the case is likely to be given some preference. The hearing is not an adversary struggle between legal equals. However, since the purpose of these agencies is not merely the resolution of individual disputes, but also the setting of general policy, it is likely that the administrative procedure leaves less room for chance, caprice, and error in the establishment of social policy.[20]

Curiously, the relative merits of the adversary system and the administrative process have never been subjected to careful empirical testing. The establishment of new agencies with new administrative authority has been largely unplanned and only dimly conceived. There may be cases to which one procedure is more appropriate than the other.

Appeals

Appellate courts have at least two major functions: they provide a place to which a party may go to correct a "mistake" in the trial, and they also must see to it that the law is kept uniform throughout the jurisdiction by settling differences of opinion over the law found to exist in the lower courts. Appeal is not merely a continuation of the trial

---

[20] See Kenneth Culp Davis, *Administrative Law and Government* (St. Paul, Minn.: West Publishing Co., 1960), pp. 1–11.

process. In addition, it provides a means of homeostasis within the judicial system by providing feedback to the lower courts.

To start the process of appeal, one party must complain about the result of the trial below. Usually, the party denoted the "appellant" is the party against whom an unfavorable judgment was rendered in the trial court.

The information input is called the "record on appeal." Usually, appellate courts will not consider matters which do not appear in the printed record of the case. This means that all the pleading papers, court orders, and transcripts of testimony (if it were taken at the trial) must be made available. All the motions, objections, instructions, and rulings of the trial court will also be made available.

Appellate tribunals employ the adversary system. Opposing parties prepare written briefs of legal points to supplement the record. The lawyers also present a brief oral argument to explain and expand upon the brief. The skill and cogency of the appellate lawyers may be a factor in decision making. The research of the judge himself or his law clerk may be other factors in the process. It is rumored that in appellate courts, which are comprised of a panel of judges, the judge most familiar with the area of law involved in the litigation will have some persuasive power over his colleagues. No matter how the judges approach the problem of resolving the appellate dispute, it is clear that they do not have adequate time or facilities to carefully research every case which comes before them. Some hasty decisions are inevitable.[21]

No witnesses are heard. No jury is present. No reconstruction of the facts is generally possible. This is the place where most of the common law is generated and where the statutory law is interpreted. The appellate tribunal provides the parties with outputs and the legal system with inputs.

---

[21] See especially, Mario M. Cuomo, "New York Court of Appeals: A Practical Perspective," *St. John's Law Review*, Vol. 34 (1960), pp. 197–218.

Depending on the needs of the case, an appellate court will affirm, reverse, or modify the judgment of the lower court. In order to lay the groundwork for the appeal, though, the appellant must await the final judgment of the trial court and must prove that the error of the trial court was prejudicial, and not merely harmless. If this is done, a new trial may be the result, and the process will be begun anew. Otherwise, the judgment of the trial court will be affirmed or modified, and the dispute will be finally resolved, assuming that all possible appeals have been exhausted.[22]

Distortion in information flow

That the legal process is fallible does not signify that justice is blind. On the contrary, it is difficult to imagine a mechanism for fact gathering, fact appraising, law gathering and law appraising which would not be fallible in many respects. The Anglo-American procedure is probably better than most, but it suffers especially from distortions in the information which it incompletely receives. The conversion process must treat as "evidence" a vast amount of information of uneven quality. It is this which, more than anything else, renders the prediction of trial outcomes so difficult. Prediction of appellate court outcomes is much easier because the "fact" element is not in controversy and the "law" element has been reduced to a fairly simple set of alternatives.

The most obvious distorting factor in a trial is the possibility of witnesses' lies. When witnesses falsify the events, a direct confrontation of opposite versions of the originating events is inevitable. Unless a lie is openly opposed, the jury must accept one version and reject another, based upon its collective appraisal of the most probable course of events.

---

[22] Criminal appeals by the federal government are looked on with strong disfavor by the Supreme Court: *Carroll* v. *United States*, 354 U.S. 394 (1957); *Peters* v. *Hobby*, 349 U.S. 331, 344–45 (1955).

It is interesting to note that before juries were in regular use, appeal to the supernatural was employed to determine who was telling the truth.[23]

Other factors affecting the reliability of information are possible misperception by the witness, loss of memory due to the passage of time, unconscious or conscious bias against a party (or in his favor), fear of the repercussions of testimony subsequent to the trial, incoherence of testimony at the trial, mental disturbance, coaching by attorneys prior to testimony, psychological intimidation caused by the courtroom situation, and merely careless observation. All of these variables are potentially present in all cases. In the adversary system it is the task of the lawyers to discover these possible flaws and to communicate them to the jury. In large part, this is the function of the cross-examination, when the lawyers attempt to challenge the testimony advanced on behalf of the other parties. Successful cross-examination may expose the weaknesses in the testimony of a witness, or if not done with sufficient skill, it may distort the information flow still more.

Obviously, the law's methods for gathering information from respondents is quite different from those used in the social sciences generally. The social researcher must be scrupulous about the selection of his respondent; he must be careful in the construction of his questions to avoid giving hints of a desired response. The social researcher must be neutral in appearance, demeanor, and aspect. He must try to work in an environment which is natural to the respondent and avoid interviewer bias as completely as possible. Survey interviews must avoid preconditioned conceptions and also avoid conditioning the responses. These aims

---

[23] Witnesses took oaths and were assisted by other oath-helpers. No cross-examination was used, but the oath-takers had to complete the ceremonies without signs of divine displeasure becoming manifest. Trial by ordeal was used in some serious cases. A battle could be ordered between the claimants or an accused could be placed in the water, to float if innocent in the sight of God. (Frederic W. Maitland, *The Forms of Action at Common Law* [Cambridge: Cambridge University Press, 1936], pp. 15–16.)

are largely absent in the legal conversion process, except as the judge may exemplify them. However, it should be stressed that the lawyers must take the witnesses as they find them and cannot sift out a desired sample. Moreover, opinion surveys do not seek out "facts" but merely views about facts. Such testimony is usually unacceptable in a trial.

Recognizing the deficiencies of the usual types of evidence, progressive jurists have encouraged the use of scientific data to supplement the facts available for use in the conversion process. Psychological evidence to show the influence upon children of the distribution of free Bibles in classrooms was admitted in a New Jersey case.[24] Anthropological findings were admitted as evidence in a California case involving miscegenation statutes and an interracial marriage.[25] Survey research data has been admitted as evidence in some cases, including patent, trademark, and misbranding litigation.[26]

The temptation to resort to "scientific" evidence in preference to the older types of evidence is very strong in the legal system. Clearly, if more convincing evidence of facts could be produced than that offered by partisan witnesses, the quality of the information flow would be greatly improved, and trials would be more predictable, less disturbing occasions. However, the accuracy of assertions in the social sciences is not yet very great. Experts disagree with high frequency. Even in the natural sciences some once fashionable ideas have become outmoded,[27] and controversy

---

[24] *Tudor* v. *Board of Education*, 14 N.J. 31, 100 A. 2d 857 (1963).

[25] *Perez* v. *Lippold*, 32 Dal., 2d 711, 198 P. 2d 17 (1948).

[26] Robert C. Sorenson and Theodore C. Sorenson, "The Admissability and Use of Opinion Research Evidence," *New York University Law Review*, Vol. 28 (November, 1953), pp. 1213–61.

[27] *Buck* v. *Bell*, 274 U.S. 200 (1927), provides an excellent example of the reliance upon weak scientific information. The Supreme Court upheld a criminal sterilization statute partly on the basis of some dubious assumptions about the genes of criminals, derived from some faulty information concerning eugenics.

still rages about the proper use of scientific evidence.[28] Finally, it is possible that the conflict of expert scientific evidence may also produce confusion in the minds of the jurors. We shall have to learn to live with imperfect trials.

Discovery and disclosure

Attempts to improve the flow of communication have been made periodically in the legal system. Today the mechanism of pretrial discovery has been constructed to inform attorneys in advance of part of the calculation of the value and strength of competing claims.

In a sense, the modern method of pleading before trial is a communication intended to improve the fact-gathering, fact-measuring process. Once the two parties are engaged in a suit, there will be an exchange of pleadings. The plaintiff issues his *complaint* setting forth the facts and law upon which the claim is based. The defendant replies with his *answer*, denying liability. Settlement may take place at this stage if the defendant's lawyer feels that his client's case is too weak. However, both the *complaint* and the *answer* are merely outlines of the dispute, since neither party wishes to reveal too much to the opposition in advance of trial.

Under the modern pleading a special series of questions, known as *interrogatories*, may be directed at each party. The answers are often evasive, but they do provide a more complete view of the event than the earlier pleading papers. *Depositions* or special requests to take written statements from witnesses are also common. Motions may be made to a judge in advance of trial to permit a party to interrogate the other or his witnesses.

The pretrial conference is usually the last formal com-

---

[28] Compare Edmond Cahn, "A Dangerous Myth in the School Segregation Cases," *New York University Law Review*, Vol. 30 (January, 1955), pp. 150–68, with Kenneth B. Clark, "The Segregation Cases: Criticism of the Social Scientist's Role," *Villanova Law Review*, Vol. 5 (1959–60), pp. 224–39.

munication between the parties prior to trial. The judge may try to induce each party to "disgorge completely and absolutely everything about its case."[29] He may try to get the parties to settle in advance of trial, but aside from the force of his personality, he cannot coerce a full, frank, and complete disclosure of information in advance of trial.

In criminal trials, discovery and disclosure in advance of trials is a relatively new development in America. As late as 1927, Judge Cardozo could say that a criminal defendant was not entitled to examination of the state's evidence in advance of trial.[30] Yet it should be obvious that pretrial discovery is more critical in criminal than in civil matters.

Today the main authority for discovery in federal criminal trials lies in the Federal Rules of Criminal Procedure. Under these Rules the Supreme Court held, in 1957, that a defendant had the right to examine certain FBI reports which formed the basis of an undercover agent's trial testimony.[31] Fearful of excessive generosity, Congress passed the Jencks Act, which imposed sharp limitations upon the examination of government documents in advance of trial.[32] It is not even clear that a defendant has the right, under the current view of the Rules, to examine his own confession made to government authorities.[33] The same kind of confusion exists on the state level.

On the other hand, there is an increasing tendency for prosecutors to disclose the weaknesses in their case. The existence of perjured testimony or falsified evidence may be admitted by the prosecutor more readily today than in the recent past. Prosecutors are officers of the court and have a duty to serve the interest of society, not merely to gain a

---

[29] Judge Skelly Wright in 28 F.R.D. 144–45 (1962).

[30] *People ex. rel. Lemon* v. *Supreme Court of New York*, 245 N.Y. 24, 156 N.E. 84 (1927).

[31] *Jencks* v. *United States*, 353 U.S. 657 (1959).

[32] 18 U.S.C. Sec. 3500 (1957).

[33] *Shores* v. *United States*, 174 F. 2d 838 (8th Cir., 1949); *United States* v. *Rothman*, 179 F. Supp. 935 (W.D. Pa., 1959).

conviction. Prosecutors may be held to this duty, regardless of the requirements of their adversary role.[34]

Despite these improvements in the modes of internal communication in the legal system, the atmosphere of the adversary system remains as a limitation upon fact-finding. The leading expert on evidence law puts it bluntly. He believes it axiomatic that a man will avoid revealing his strengths and weaknesses to an opponent before the contest. That exposure to an unscrupulous opponent would result in fraud or chicanery.[35] There is no premium for honesty in the adversary system.

---

[34] Note, "The Duty of the Prosecutor to Disclose Exculpatory Evidence," *Columbia Law Review*, Vol. 60 (1960), p. 858, and Note, "The Prosecutor's Constitutional Duty to Reveal Evidence to the Defendant," *Yale Law Journal*, Vol. 74 (1964), p. 136.

[35] John Wigmore, *A Treatise on the Anglo-American System of Evidence* (3d ed.; Boston: Little, Brown, & Co., 1940), Vol. VI, Sec. 1845.

VII

Primary outputs

THE END PRODUCT of most litigation is at least a verdict. Disputes cannot end in a stalemate. More specific forms of disputes include: acquittal or sentencing, fine, and imprisonment (criminal); an award of damages (civil); a decree of specific performance, injunction, quo warranto, mandamus, and the like (equity); a divorce decree or separation; declaratory judgment; probate; and several variations among these forms. The effect of each type of output upon the parties to the action is often dramatic, although it is not always immediate. Long years may intervene between a favorable verdict for damages and collection of the sum owed under the judgment.

Beyond the formal output, more subtle side effects may be produced which will have greater influence for others than for the particular parties to the action. These other effects are as much a part of the output as is the verdict itself. One such output is judge-declared law. Statutes or previous precedents are either reinforced, reinterpreted, or legitimitized by resting a decision upon a version of law announced in a case. Not every statute, rule, or executive order has force as law, but many do, and those which do are altered by the process to some extent. In a few cases, new political values may also be produced as an output, sometimes unconsciously, by the judicial process.[1]

Appellate tribunals produce a peculiar type of output. Rather than a verdict, which is the function of the trial court, the verdict below must be sustained or set aside. If it is set aside, a new trial may be ordered on the basis of the corrected law or procedure. It is also possible for some appellate courts to merely enter a favorable judgment for either party without recycling the dispute back to a trial court.[2] Further, an appellate court might be able to reverse part of a verdict or to reverse a judgment alone when the verdict is in a separable form. Nonjury trials may be reversed (the judgment overturned) both as to law and facts in most states. But the most significant output of appellate tribunals is substantive judge-declared law, because the lower courts are bound to accept the higher court versions of law, producing an internal homeostatic reaction in the judicial system.

The legal system, which is a subsystem of the political system, is typically used as an output channel for the political system. The laws, rules, executive orders, contempt orders, and other devices of achieving social order are often transacted through legal machinery. However, there is an increasing tendency not to include the ordinary judicial system in the procedure, but this proclivity to prefer the administrative process should not misguide us.[3] When the administrative procedure includes a conversion process or

---

[1] That the Fourteenth Amendment is violated when apportionment according to the basis "one man one vote" is not met is a new social value. It was announced in 1963 by Mr. Justice Douglas, and is not found in the Constitution or classical democratic theory. This view was announced in *Gray* v. *Sanders*, 372 U.S. 368 (1965).

[2] It is also possible in some jurisdictions to obtain review of intermediate orders made prior to a verdict. Thus, an error committed at the trial may be repaired prior to the conclusion of the case.

[3] See Julius Stone, "The Twentieth Century Administrative Explosion and After," *California Law Review*, Vol. 52 (August, 1964), pp. 513–42, for an explanation for this phenomenon and a discussion of possible future developments.

a rule output, there is a legal system operating. The legal system includes more than the judicial apparatus, and the clue is the nature of the output. Any output of a generalized character, intended to bind one or more persons in some socially sanctioned manner, is part of a legal process. Whatever output is law-like in intention and effect is law and part of the legal system. In this sense, a statute is law even if it has never been applied or judicially tested, and the statute stands as a part of the legal system.

Verdict

The delivery of a verdict may precede the conclusion of the entire trial by granting a motion for a directed verdict. This motion may be made by either party at the conclusion of its presentation of its case. It is usually made prior to the court's decision to send the case to the jury for its verdict. The question of when and under what circumstances a verdict may be directed is not yet settled, but it is assumed that a directed verdict granted to a party signifies that the opposite party has failed to make out a case warranting jury consideration. The effect of a directed verdict is to deny a trial to a party, on the ground that no jury could reasonably decide in its favor.[4]

In a civil case, at the conclusion of the submission of evidence, either side may request that the jury be directed to answer specific questions of fact. This form of output, rarely requested, allows the judge to apply the facts, as determined by the jury, to the applicable law, enhancing the judge's role in the trial process. The decision to permit a special verdict is largely within the judge's discretion.

The general verdict is far more commonly employed, although it arose at a later period of time than the original (now special) verdict. The general verdict allows the jury

---

4 John E. Bagalay, "Directed Verdicts and the Right to Trial by Jury in Federal Courts," *Texas Law Review,* Vol. 42 (October, 1964), pp. 1053–71.

itself to determine the outcome by applying the law given it in the judge's instructions to the facts determined by it. Under a general verdict, no one ever knows which facts were most determinative in the jury's decision, or whether the jury did, indeed, rest its verdict on the facts. Thus, it is impossible to discover whether the jury correctly understood or applied the facts, or applied them fairly.[5]

A recent compromise device has evolved under the Federal Rules of Civil Procedure, and in some states which adopted it. This method of combining a general verdict with special written interrogatories requires the jurors to state the factual bases for their verdict.[6] It is a useful way of checking the reasoning process of the jury against its general verdict, but it is regarded with suspicion still by many lawyers and judges, who fear possible bad side effects upon jury deliberation.

The vote required to reach a civil verdict is generally less than the unanimous verdict mandatory in criminal law. In many states the concurrence of 9 or 10 jurors will be sufficient to reach a verdict; it seems likely, until research demonstrates otherwise, that jury verdict outcomes are greatly affected by the number required to reach a verdict. The threat of a hung jury diminishes as the requirement of numbers diminishes. It would seem that the bargaining power of one nonconforming juror would be reduced in proportion to the number required to reach a verdict. Of course,

---

[5] It is well-settled law that jurors are not allowed to impeach their own verdicts, even if they use an improper means of agreeing upon a verdict, a view going back to early English law. See R. J. Nordstrom, "New Trial Use of Testimony of Jurors to Set Aside Verdict," *Michigan Law Review*, Vol. 41 (November, 1948), pp. 261–67. As to the supposed tendency of jurors to misunderstand, ignore, or distort facts, see Harry Kalven and Hans Zeisel, *The American Jury* (Boston: Little, Brown & Co., 1966), pp. 148–62, which asserts that research shows that jurors do understand the case and follow the evidence, while pp. 301–28 indicate exceptions to this general condition.

[6] The practice grew out of a common-law custom which required the jury to account to the judge for its reasons in reaching an unexpected verdict (William H. Wicker, "Special Interrogatories to Juries in Civil Cases," *Yale Law Journal*, Vol. 35 [January, 1926], pp. 296–307).

coalitions of nonconforming jurors could arise to offset this expectation.

Because of the greater risks to the individual inherent in the criminal trial, the verdict output is more carefully restricted than at a civil trial. The special verdict, which was used in criminal trials centuries ago, is now virtually discarded. The jury returns a verdict of guilty or not guilty. However, the meaning of a not guilty verdict is less clear than of a civil verdict, because it signifies only that the state failed to prove its case "beyond a reasonable doubt," not that the defense has established innocence.

The requirement of a unanimous jury verdict in criminal cases is retained in all but six states.[7] Failure to produce a unanimous verdict may result in a hung jury, which permits the prosecutor to bring the case anew at a later date. It is probable that the unanimous vote rule results in some acquittals, since hung juries are uncommon.[8]

The finality of criminal verdict outcomes is variable, depending upon who is attacking the verdict. A convicted criminal may request a new trial on the ground of newly discovered evidence, but a prosecutor is prevented from obtaining a reversal of any acquittal, except for minor offenses not involving imprisonment.[9]

A comparison of civil and criminal output channels reveals the relative social significance of each process. In the civil case, the legal system provides a largely neutral forum for weighing a dispute, with each side having nearly equal formal output access. Output access in criminal cases is unequal, with numerous advantages for the defendant. The fact that the state has exceptional advantages under the adversary process is apparent at all stages:

---

[7] In a few states, misdemeanors are excepted, and less than a unanimous verdict is required.

[8] It is also possible, in the federal courts and in a few states, for the judge to direct a verdict of acquittal if the jury is unable to agree upon a verdict.

[9] See *State* v. *Wickett*, 300 N.W. 268, 230 Iowa, 1182 (1941).

It is not possible to exaggerate the cumulative physical and psychological impact, in the contest between state and accused, resulting from arrest and interrogation by the police. For all but a few knowledgeable and self-assertive subjects of inquiry, no one of the constitutional safeguards, and not all of them together, can equalize or neutralize the initial advantage which follows from taking the accused into custody and subjecting him at a station-house to close questioning by skillful and experienced interrogaters, vested with formidable authority and energized by sense of duty or ambition . . . [and] the modern American prosecutor brings to the side of the law, enforcement processes powers and capacities no less impressive than those of the police.[10]

The Supreme Court has been attempting to balance the advantages by changing the conditions of police interrogation procedure and increasing the significance of the right of counsel. Yet, the narrow output channel remains the best protection for the accused person, requiring the state to produce an overwhelmingly convincing case to the jury. Nonetheless, if one regards conviction as a successful outcome after the commission of crime, careful study shows a very great attrition rate in the legal process beginning with the commission of a crime and ending in conviction.[11]

Civil judgments

Many different types of civil outputs are available in the American legal system. These range from money damages awarded the victorious party to the granting of a divorce. The social interest in the output is also variable, depending upon the intensity of the social policy being subjected to

---

[10] Bernard Botein and Murray A. Gordon, *The Trial of the Future* (New York: Simon & Schuster, Inc., 1963), p. 60.

[11] Phillip Ennis, "Crime, Victims and the Police," *Transaction*, Vol. 4, pp. 36–44. In the Ennis study of 2,077 crimes (as seen by the victim), only 50 resulted in conviction, with the greatest attrition at the first stage of notification of the police. Only 18 percent of the victims questioned said they were satisfied by the outcome.

test in the legal dispute. Divorce policy is normally of more moment to the society than most civil matters, so that the output is granted slowly, grudgingly, and under severe limitations. Obviously, no output is ever so insignificant that individuals other than the parties may not be influenced by the results, but for the sake of this analysis, the civil judgment will be treated at this point primarily as it adjusts the relationship which existed between the parties prior to the case.

The nature of the outcome depends upon the character of the court in most states. A multiplicity of civil courts is to be found, each with its own jurisdiction, differing largely in the outcome type (often called the "legal remedy") permitted by statute or state constitution. Some courts may grant only money judgments, some only probate wills, some only grant "equitable" decrees. These differences are an important factor in choosing a court in which to start suit.

The simplest types of output, in terms of the conversion process, are the judgment by default and the consent judgment. When the defendant in a civil suit fails to appear to defend against the action, the court has little choice but to enter a judgment for the plaintiff. If the output sought is money damages, the amount of damages, if unclear, will be fixed by the court at a hearing at which the plaintiff must appear. However, the most socially disapproved output in civil suits is the uncontested divorce action. In some states a special officer may investigate and participate in the trial of the divorce. Even if this isn't done, the quality of the output is questionable. Uncontested divorce actions are not entitled to legal recognition in other states, despite the "full faith and credit clause of the federal Constitution."[12] Still, collusive divorces do occur, and the courts are frequently used to evade the divorce policy of a state, where the divorce statutes are strict.

---

[12] *Vanderbilt* v. *Vanderbilt*, 354 U.S. 416 (1957), applies the reasoning to alimony actions flowing out of an uncontested divorce.

Full faith and credit is regularly accorded civil judgments as long as the judgment is awarded by a court having jurisdiction over the parties or over the object of the suit.[13] This does not mean that property in one state will be distributed in accordance with a judgment from another state,[14] but it does mean that a final judgment rendered by a state court of competent jurisdiction must be recognized by a sister state, which may not go behind the judgment and inquire into the merits of the controversy. On the other hand, this requirement does not extend to penal statutes. The determination of the character of the suit as criminal or civil is critical, and hinges upon the nature of the output. If the law is designed to punish an offense against broad public policy, rather than to provide a civil remedy for an injury, it is criminal and not entitled to recognition in other states.[15] States jealously guard the power to determine their own basic criminal law policy, and have been aided by Supreme Court decisions in this matter.

Most civil suits involve private claims for money damages. The method of ascertainment of damages is the same in federal and state courts,[16] although it varies from state to state. A common law of damages has evolved which, in the absence of contrary statutes, deals with court measurement of compensation for losses and injuries. Since each state court system has developed its own common law of damages, the state law to be applied will directly affect the outcome. Generally, in tort cases the law of the state where the injury occurred is applied, and in contract actions, the law of the state where the breach of contract occurred.

The amount of damages is a fact which the jury may determine as part of its fact-finding function. The judge issues

---

[13] *D'Arcy* v. *Ketchum*, 11 How. 165 (1850).

[14] *Clark* v. *Willard*, 294 U.S. 211 (1935).

[15] *Huntington* v. *Atrill*, 146 U.S. 657 (1892). A tax judgment is not considered penal and must be given credit in other states—*Milwaukee County* v. *M. G. White Co.*, 296 U.S. 268 (1935).

[16] An important result of *Erie R.R.* v. *Tompkins*, 304 U.S. 64 (1938).

the jury instructions on the issue of damages, based on the law of damages in the jurisdiction. If the amount of the damages is deemed excessive or inadequate, the judge may set aside the award and order a new trial. Thus, the jury is not truly in command of the civil trial output because the trial judge, or an appellate tribunal, can veto the jury damage verdict. This problem does not arise in criminal cases, since sentencing is almost entirely in the hands of the trial judge. Both practices remove the jury from part of the output determination.

Sometimes the damages awarded will only be a nominal one cent or one dollar, because the plaintiff cannot prove any particular damage. The real interest of the plaintiff in such cases may be vindication, as in libel and slander cases, rather than an actual sum of money, or an attempt to declare legal rights in an official way. Yet, the tendency is for increasing numbers of money damage awards, which spiral upward in amount throughout the country, creating indirectly a higher social cost in the form of increased insurance premiums, which pass on the cost of expensive verdicts to the general public.[17]

Today only four states—Arkansas, Delaware, Mississippi, and Tennessee—maintain separate courts for the granting of equitable decrees. In the rest, a party can request some general civil court for either money damages or something desired instead of money. A plaintiff may wish to get a court order forbidding a defendant from doing something, and would seek an "injunction." If he wishes to have a contract enforced according to its original terms, he would seek an order to "specific performance." Other equitable writs exist in many states, such as an action in "ejectment," to evict a nonpaying tenant and, in a modern addition to old equity powers, to issue a divorce decree. A judgment of a court in

---

[17] New records are set every few years, but the one-man current high recovery record in a personal injury case is $1,125,000 awarded a 17-year-old boy in a New Jersey court in 1964, for an accident in his school gymnasium. He sued his school.

equity is directed at the defendant himself. Noncompliance with the order could result in fine or imprisonment, an exceptional outcome, enforcing a civil judgment with quasi-criminal methods.

Many other civil outcomes are possible, mostly for highly special situations. Court orders for the custody of a child, the surrender of property, the determination of the value of condemned property, the adoption of children, and the distribution of property under a will are leading examples. Most of these are available only from a specialized court.

Last among the civil outcomes, and least common, are the "extraordinary writs." Among these are: "mandamus," which is a proceeding to compel a public officer to perform a legally required act; "quo warranto" which is a proceeding to challenge an election or an improper appointment, and "habeas corpus," which is a proceeding to release a person unlawfully held in private or public custody. All extraordinary writs are available only in higher courts, including the Supreme Court of the United States.

The range of civil outcome types is very wide, though not unlimited. It is possible to be injured in such a way that there would be no appropriate legal remedy. If so, the legal doctrine of *damnum absque injuria* comes into play. This signifies a loss, hurt, or harm without a legal injury, a loss which does not give rise to an action for damages because there is no appropriate legal category which includes it.

Criminal judgments and sentencing

The outcomes for criminal cases are much less varied. Fine, imprisonment, or both is imposed in the overwhelming number of cases. A suspended sentence may be issued for minor offenses, or an indeterminate sentence may be imposed in special categories of cases. Efforts to apply modern theories of correction in criminals have resulted in an increasing use of probation techniques, parole procedures, and periodic reconsideration of past sentences. Death is the ultimate sentence power.[18]

It must be admitted that the underlying purposes of criminal policy are much less agreed upon than the public recognizes. As a result, there is much less uniformity in criminal outcomes than the public expects, although it is the legislature which has the primary responsibility in these matters. The jury or trial judge may choose only those punishments which the legislature prescribes. There is no common law of criminal punishment. If criminal outcomes are not always satisfactory, the fault is widespread. The criminal statute input is the major determinant of criminal judgment outputs.

The legislature is forbidden to create certain forms of punishment under the "cruel and unusual punishment" clause of the federal Constitution and in some state constitutions. The clause covers obvious devices, such as torture and maiming, but also includes the deprivation of American citizenship. It does not include a situation in which a condemned man must risk execution several times.[19]

To a limited extent, the imposition of a criminal verdict is automatic. This occurs when the statute is self-executing, leaving no task for the judge or jury to perform once guilt is found. Premeditated murder is the best example, since conviction usually carries with it a mandatory death sentence.

Usually, though, the statutes allow great flexibility in the sentencing procedure. In the great majority of the states the precise penalty is determined by the judge, while in about 12 states the jury has most of the responsibility. In the federal courts the judge has almost complete control of the process.

Wide variation in sentencing patterns means that indi-

---

[18] It is the penalty for murder, treason, and giving defense secrets to foreign governments.

[19] *Louisiana ex. rel. Francis* v. *Resweber*, 329 U.S. 459 (1947).

viduals who commit the same crime could be subjected to different sentences. This discretion is not reviewable except in extreme cases of abuse or prejudice.[20] In order to assist the judge, affidavits are received from the prosecution and from the defense which may throw more light upon the commission of the offense or the character of the defendant. Since most convictions flow from guilty pleas negotiated between the prosecutor and the defendant, this may be the major factor in setting the sentence, although no judge is bound by such arrangement. Further, judges may cooperate with local political figures, and if the defendant has strategically placed political friends, it could be extremely helpful.

In November, 1960, the judges of the United States Court for the Eastern District of Michigan began to use new sentencing procedures. Under this new approach, the sentencing judge discusses proposed sentences with other members of his court prior to sentencing. In this way the disparities between sentences are mollified. There is a greater uniformity in sentencing from one judge to another, and by the same judge from one case to another.[21] It has been suggested that the function of sentencing be removed from the trial court and placed in the hands of a trained board of criminologists, but that day is far away.[22]

More enlightened output practices have been created by statutes in recent years. In 1925, Congress enacted the Pro-

---

[20] *Harris* v. *State*, 142 Miss. 342, 107 S. 372 (1926). Connecticut permits appeals from most trial court sentences.

[21] F. J. Gaudet, G. S. Harris, and C. W. St. John, "Individual Differences in the Sentencing Tendencies of Judges," *Journal of Criminal Law*, Vol. 23 (January, 1923), pp. 811–18; H. E. Lane, "Illogical Variations in Sentences of Felons Committed to Massachusetts State Prison," *Journal of Criminal Law*, Vol. 32 (July, August, 1941), pp. 171–90.

[22] Theodore Levin, "Sentencing the Criminal Offender," *Federal Probation*, Vol. 13 (March, 1949), p. 13. California has begun to do this by establishing its Adult Authority to which all commitments are made. The Authority determines the length and place of incarceration.

bation Act, which provides power for a judge to suspend
sentence and to place offenders on probation. In 1938, the
Juvenile Delinquency Act was passed, applying to all offenders under the age of 18, with a few exceptions. The act
provides for a noncriminal proceeding which results in a
court order of probation or commitment for a period of no
more than three years. In 1950, the Youth Correction Act
was passed, which enables judges to commit gang offenders
to special youth correction facilities, with the further power
granted the United States Board of Parole to release offenders under 26 at any time. The latest major change came
in 1958 with the passage of an indeterminate sentence law,
which permits a judge to sentence a defendant for the maximum term with eligibility for parole at any time or to impose a minimum sentence of one-third the maximum, after
which the defendant becomes eligible for parole. This important act also empowers judges to commit a defendant
for observation and study, enabling the Bureau of Prisons
to perform psychological, psychiatric, and other examinations which can aid the judge in his final disposition of the
case.

Despite these flexible tools for sentencing available to
federal judges, there remains a wide area of discretion, and
there are very few guidelines to the exercise of judicial
choice. Judges gain local reputations as "tough" or "easy,"
even if they have faithfully attended various sentencing institutes, held since 1958 for federal judges. The choice of
whether or not to place the defendant on probation is in
the hands of the trial judge, which he may make on the
basis of a background study of the defendant made preliminary to sentencing. These presentence reports which are
prepared by probation officers are being used increasingly
as a guide by judges, although their utilization is also
discretionary.

Attempts to standardize sentencing procedure have been

less than successful. Some outside limits upon discretion have been placed upon trial judges, but since the judges work in isolation, disparity remains. In the last analysis, it is "the judge's own character, as influenced by legal controls and advice of others, particularly specialists [which] will probably, in the course of time, produce some type of personal sentencing technique or the appearance of one, deceptive or otherwise."[23] Only by more careful recruitment of judges or boards can more precise techniques be applied in sentencing. Since someone or some group must issue sentences, the problem is the competence of the individual or group.

Administrative outputs

Administrative techniques of social control are still evolving. To some extent there is an overlap of administrative outputs with criminal outputs, such as in the use of fines and in the resort to the regular courts for more serious punishment, including imprisonment. Nonetheless, the already formidable armory of administrative output methods is being regularly increased. This proliferation of output techniques is not due to a ceaseless search for novelty but to the distinguishable purposes of administrative policies. Civil courts try to regulate private disputes. Criminal courts seek to control antisocial and deviant behavior. The administrative purposes are more subtle, since they are addressed primarily to modulating social and economic behavior rather than punishing or rewarding behavior.

The licensing power was historically the first administrative output method used in America. Using its maritime powers, the First Congress sought to license vessels, crew, and pilots. In the 20th century, licensing grew apace. The marketing and processing of agricultural products, radio

---

[23] B. J. George, Jr., "Sentencing Methods and Techniques in the United States," *Federal Probation*, Vol. 26 (June, 1962), p. 38.

transmission, television transmission, and air transportation have proven most important. State and local licensing is more widespread, with liquor licenses, professional licenses (law, medicine, barbering), business licenses, and automobile licenses the most common varieties. In all these circumstances, administrative officials, rather than judges, now hold primary or even sole responsibility.

The licensing power carries with it the negative output of license revocation. This major means of state law enforcement is almost entirely administrative. Formal hearings are usually required before the negative output of revocation can be invoked. This power, while not criminal in nature, may be used to deprive individuals of substantial economic privileges.

Penalties are the administrative equivalent of fines. The imposition of a penalty does not require greater formality than other administrative hearings. The power to issue an administrative penalty is considered to be an aspect of general regulatory powers and only incidentally punitive. From the point of view of the defendant, he loses the same amount of money, whether it be called a criminal fine or an administrative penalty. At least, no criminal record is produced by an administrative penalty. Fines and penalties are both issued by administrative bodies today.

Some administrative techniques are unique to the particular agency. Only the Post Office is concerned with the power of "nonmailability," which forbids certain goods being sent through the stream of the mails. Whiskey, certain firearms, and explosives are nonmailable. In addition, the Post Office and Customs Bureau have limited power to survey and hold foreign communist political propaganda.[24] Forbidden use of the mails, such as for mail fraud, could result in criminal prosecution in the Federal Courts. Deportation is another example of unique administrative

---

[24] This power is limited somewhat by constitutional problems raised in *Lamont* v. *Postmaster General*, 381 U.S. 301 (1965).

powers shared by the Immigration and Naturalization Service and the courts. The Service also administers the admission and exclusion of aliens.

The strengthening of the Interstate Commerce Commission in 1906 created the power to issue administrative orders. Disobedience of the orders is punishable by penalty. The Federal Trade Commission provides a typical example of this very broad power. Cases are instituted by the Commission with the issuance of a complaint charging a person or group with the violation of some of the statutes under its responsibility. If the charges are uncontested, or are proven true, an order is issued requiring discontinuance of the unlawful practices. Complaints may begin with consumers, competitors, state or federal authorities, or the agency itself. The agency may also strive to reach "voluntary" action before issuing an order, or it may issue trade regulation rules.

The "cease and desist" order is today the most powerful federal administrative output. It is sometimes accompanied by fines or penalties in order to secure compliance. Further, many respondents against whom orders have been issued are required to file periodic reports which demonstrate compliance with the order. The power to issue cease and desist orders to prohibit unfair competitive practices is possessed by the Interstate Commerce Commission, the Federal Reserve Board, the Federal Power Commission, the Federal Communications Commission, and the Civil Aeronautics Board, each within its own economic fields.

The tensions of the cold war have given rise to new approaches. One of the most controversial is that of the Subversive Activities Control Board. The Board, which is relatively inactive, was created in 1950. The five-man Board has virtually no other function than to determine which organizations in the nation are "Communist action" or "Communist-front" or "Communist-infiltrated." Upon reaching this determination, the group must register with the Attorney General. Board decisions are subject to judicial review. The curious aspect of this administrative output device is that it is very indirect. The group is not fined or ordered to change its practices; instead it is exposed.[25]

The administrative injunction is employed by several agencies. The Securities and Exchange Commission, for example, may enjoin the sale of a security. Obviously, the injunction is not unlike a cease and desist order.

The seizure of property is another available administrative output. The Food and Drug Agency may choose, through the federal courts, to seize goods failing to meet statutory standards of purity, quality, or safety. The same agency possesses extensive powers to control the access of new drugs to the market. It tests the safety and effectiveness of new drugs and evaluates them before permitting them to be generally sold or dispensed.

The withdrawal of administrative benefits is another output method. Eligibility for unemployment insurance, welfare payments, and payment under government contracts are subject to administrative controls. Violators may find that they will not receive the full amount of the expected benefits until the improper conduct terminates.

Finally, although it is not often thought of as an output, administrative declarations are the frequent conclusion of administrative studies, investigations, and hearings. No sanctions are attached to the statements, but it is hoped that improper conduct will be voluntarily curtailed. A good example is provided by the Office of the Surgeon General of the Public Health Service, which has been carrying out a long campaign to warn of the dangers of cigarette smoking. When it proved that warnings were insufficient, the Fed-

---

[25] Registration of party members is unconstitutional—*Albertson* v. *Subversive Activities Control Board*, 382 U.S. 70 (1965). Registration of the Communist party as a foreign-dominated action organization is not unconstitutional—*Communist Party of the United States* v. *Subversive Activities Control Board*, 367 U.S. 1 (1961).

eral Trade Commission required a warning to be placed on the labels of cigarette packages.

Many administrative outputs are nonlegal. Some agencies are devoted to research, some to personnel recruitment, some to purchasing, some to national defense, and the like. However, increasing political support for expanded social and economic controls has resulted in ingenious output techniques directed at individuals and groups within society. Little information is available which demonstrates the comparative effectiveness of various techniques. A survey of administrative output methods would be difficult to fashion, but would be very useful to policy makers.

Advisory opinions and declaratory judgments

Two rather uncommon forms of output have recently become important. The advisory opinion and the declaratory judgment are powers of preventive jurisprudence, or outputs which occur in advance of an actual injury as a way of mitigating or preventing the injury. In addition, the advisory opinion frequently deals with matters beyond the single individual, in permitting the justices of the highest courts to advise the legislature and the executive upon the constitutionality of proposed action. In this advisory capacity, the courts are most clearly announcing policy norms, an activity which is usually disguised in the normal output process.

At the current moment, 11 states permit their highest courts to render some form of advisory opinion.[26] Generally, the request may come from either the executive or the legislature (only from the governor in Delaware, Florida, Oklahoma, and South Dakota). The function is usually restricted

---

[26] Alabama, Colorado, Delaware, Florida, Maine, Massachusetts, New Hampshire, North Carolina, Oklahoma, Rhode Island, and South Dakota. Several other states have experimented with it. The International Court of Justice also issues advisory opinions, as do the high courts of many foreign nations.

to pending legislation, and it is not exercised upon abstract or theoretical questions of law.

The judges may decide whether the question is within their power to answer. They may refuse to issue an answer for virtually any reason. On the other hand, if they do issue an opinion, it is not considered binding for future occasions. The doctrine of *stare decisis* is not supposed to apply to them, but they are frequently cited in later cases as valid judicial authority. Consequently, the advisory opinion output is at least of the same significance as any other judicial output.[27]

The executive and legislative branches generally accept the judicial output. The newly declared norm provides a guide to policy making at the moment that the policy is being constructed. This partnership means that the ultimate statutory output itself enjoys automatic legitimacy.

The advisory opinion has been used most in questions of structure of government, intergovernmental relations, taxation, and finance, rather than in questions related to property rights or personal liberties. It has minimized the uncertainty and delay to which most statutes are subject. Instead of the usual lapse of time between enactment and decision, which is seven and one-half years, the average lapse of time in advisory opinions between request and opinion is less than 30 days.

There has been a steady growth in the use of the advisory opinion from 1790 until the present. The number of these opinions is still less than 90 a year throughout the country, but some of the most important issues in the states are treated in this way.

Since 1793, the federal Supreme Court has considered the advisory opinion unconstitutional at the level of the national courts. The first President asked his Chief Justice for an opinion regarding a pending neutrality proclamation.

---

[27] Oliver P. Field, "The Advisory Opinion—An Analysis," *Indiana Law Journal*, Vol. 24 (Fall, 1948), pp. 203–30.

Chief Justice John Jay, feeling that an advisory opinion was inconsistent with the judicial function and violative of the principle of separation of powers, refused President Washington's request. This refusal has become the foundation of the Court's opposition to an advisory function.[28] In addition, the absence of an adversary proceeding, as may be required by the language of Article II of the Constitution, is a barrier to the use of advisory opinions in the federal courts.

In 1934, however, the Congress passed the Federal Declaratory Judgments Act, which was declared constitutional three years later.[29] A declaratory judgment simply declares the rights of the parties to the suit. It involves particular individuals, and expresses the opinion of the court regarding the rights existing between them. A person who is unsure about the effect of a future course of activity may be able to get an adjudication of his legal position in this way. Thus, by providing individuals with advance information regarding their rights and duties, a socially beneficial result is produced. The output has the force of law.

The declaratory judgment differs from the advisory opinion in that it presents a dispute between two parties at least nominally adverse to each other. Again, jurisdiction is discretionary, and the court (federal or state) may refuse to issue a judgment. If the judgment is issued, no damages or other further awards are issued. The injury not having occurred, the judgment is anticipatory of actual harm.

Both the advisory opinion and the declaratory judgment provide graphic illustrations of policy making in advance of actual injury. The creative role of the judiciary in adjusting legal relationships prior to a concrete dispute is nowhere more evident. The role is unfamiliar, but the form of the output has met the same acceptance as more tradi-

---

[28] *United Public Workers* v. *Mitchell*, 330 U.S. 75, 89 (1947); *Coleman* v. *Miller*, 307 U.S. 433, 462 (1939); *Muskrat* v. *United States*, 219 U.S. 346, 354 (1911).

[29] *Aetna Life Insurance Co.* v. *Haworth*, 300 U.S. 227 (1937).

tional outputs in those states where these procedures are available.

Judicial review and norm output

The critics of the United States Supreme Court are fond of quoting the phrase of Charles Evans Hughes, "We are under a Constitution, but the Constitution is what the judges say it is." However, the complete context demonstrates the normative role which high courts feel that they must play in the United States. Hughes indicated his normative guides by concluding, "and the judiciary is the safeguard of our liberty and of our property under the Constitution."[30] The Constitution itself provides a body of political norms, and in this nation, it has become the prerogative of the courts to serve as a decisive agency of constitutional norms. This was not an inevitable development, but it is now a fundamental characteristic of the legal system. Together with outputs which directly settle the claims of the parties to a legal dispute, a court may, on occasion, apply a constitutional norm newly interpreted to meet the needs of the case and to act as a guide to future cases. This norm output may even signify a conflict between the policy of another political agency and the courts, leading to the exercise of the power of judicial review.

The highest courts of the states also possess the power of judicial review. The practice is universal in American high courts and is even enjoyed on an exploratory basis by lower courts. In all states the practice is permitted.

It is customary for American courts to assert that an enactment, administrative order, or executive action is presumed to be constitutional, and that repugnance to the constitutional text must be clearly apparent. If this were true, then there would be little reason for a split of opinion among

---

[30] In Merlo J. Pusey, *Charles Evans Hughes* (New York: Macmillan Co., 1951), Vol. 1, p. 204.

members of the same court; unanimous decisions would be commonplace. But a cursory analysis of state and federal exercises of judicial review displays sharply divided courts. Conflicts of policy norms are reflected by these divisions.

There are three possible variations upon the exercise of judicial review. A state court may find an enactment contrary to state or federal constitutional provisions, and a federal court may find an enactment contrary to the national Constitution. The exercise of state judicial review of enactments as contrary to state constitutions became so excessive as to produce a reaction in the early part of this century.[31] The state courts are under a duty to enforce the provisions of the federal Constitution as they apply within the states. This includes a duty to comply with Supreme Court views of the clause in question.[32]

The exercise of judicial review by federal courts may be directed at either federal or state enactments, though the purposes are clearly divergent. Judicial review against state enactments numbers over 800, although no accurate count has been made recently. Most of these exercises of judicial review have occurred since 1890, and many have been based upon the "due process" or the "equal protection of the laws" clauses of the Fourteenth Amendment. More recently the "interstate commerce" clause of the First Article has been of renewed importance.

The voiding of state policy upon grounds of repugnance to the Federal Constitution is based upon different norms from those involved in voiding federal policy through judicial review. The primary value has been called "umpiring the federal system." By this is meant the settling of disputes between the states, the assurance of conformity of para-

---

[31] Three state constitutions now require unanimous concurrence of judges to employ judicial review power. These are: Nebraska, North Dakota, and Ohio. For the reasons, see Francis Aumann, "The Course of Judicial Review in the State of Ohio," *American Political Science Review*, Vol. 25 (1931), p. 367.

[32] *Martin* v. *Hunter's Lessee*, 1 Wheaton 304 (1816).

mount national policy, and protection of individuals against encroachment upon fundamental rights. The first two are especially important to the maintenance of a federal system. As Justice Holmes crisply put it:

I do not think the United States would come to an end if we lost our power to declare an Act of Congress void. I do not think that the Union would be imperiled if we could not make that declaration as to the laws of the several states.[33]

Today the power of judicial review of state policies includes the supervision of such matters as state welfare practices, to insure the enforcement of federal policy in jointly sponsored programs.[34]

Judicial review of federal policy involves a direct confrontation between coordinate branches of the national government. The judicial branch, by asserting that power, must issue a policy norm which differs from that already advanced by the executive or the legislative branch. Consequently, the exercise of the power against federal action is much less common. Fewer than 100 federal laws have been declared unconstitutional, and only two or three times, guardedly, has the President been criticized on constitutional grounds. When the Supreme Court acts in this manner, final outputs are set, and the borderline between political and legal outputs becomes blurred.

The claim of the power of judicial review probably rests upon the idea of a "higher law," a superior set of norms to ordinary rules, laws, and customs. The belief in a "higher law" is deeply ingrained in American traditions, and it can even be traced as far back as the ancient Romans. This higher law has been used to protect many kinds of social

---

[33] "Law and the Court," in Mark De Wolfe Howe (ed.), *The Occasional Speeches of Justice Oliver Wendell Holmes* (Cambridge, Mass.: Belknap Press of Harvard University Press, 1962), p. 172.

[34] Note, "Federal Judicial Review of State Welfare Practices," *Columbia Law Review*, Vol. 67 (January, 1967), pp. 85–129.

interests against governmental encroachments. At times it is used in defense of property rights, at others, of individual rights. It provides a legal limitation upon political action. But the content of higher law is vague, the idea is becoming increasingly unfashionable, and judges cannot overtly appeal to a higher source of norms without risking criticism or ridicule. The history, development, and impact of some of these norms is treated in the final chapter, since it is best illustrated by examining the operation of the Supreme Court, which issues the highest norms in the American legal system, aside from the Constitution itself.

Judicial review is a dual output. In part, its effects are feedback in character, since it corrects an activity of another organ of the political system, of which the courts are a part. The legal output becomes a political input in its feedback capacity. In another light, the announced norm value becomes available to the whole society, not just to the litigants or to the government. The Constitution takes on a different normative meaning as a result of this generalized output. If the output is sufficiently sweeping, the social results may be dramatic, as with the still unfolding results of the desegregation decisions.

Legitimitization

The power of judicial review is rarely employed. It is a weapon of enormous potential and must be sparingly used if the courts are not themselves to be corrected by feedback. The normal flow of legal policy is through the courts, with minor additions to the legislative meanings supplied by judicial interpretation. The courts are essentially supportive of policies announced by other branches of government. The effect of judicial support is to reinforce the legitimacy of the original policy. The courts provide the procedural and psychological atmosphere which makes public policy more acceptable to members of the society. Rather than ruling by executive edict, Anglo-American legal systems utilize the courts as a regular matter, not merely because custom and the Constitution require it, but because the public expects and desires it. The output of legitimitization generalizes the law. The plaintiff and the defendant have received their verdicts, while the nonlitigant public is assured that their verdict is in accordance with public policy embodied in the law. The courts support the democratic expectations of the mass public.

If the courts were perceived as mere agents of the other branches of the government, rather than neutral tribunals open to the public and the government, they could not play this psychological role. The public may be cynical or dubious about government at large, and a fair trial and a fair application of the law are not entirely anticipated. Yet the law will not be imposed by fiat. It will be channeled through the courts in such a way as to prevent completely arbitrary and capricious action. For most people the law in action is the law decided by a court.[35]

Even for members of the political system the function of legitimitization is important. Legislation is often couched in deliberately vague language in the expectation that the courts will supply the missing meaning. For many administrators the law or rule is not complete until it has been tested in a court, or at least in an administrative tribunal. So, aside from the particular outcome of a dispute between two parties, the legal decision supplies substance to a public policy.

The best way to obtain a glimpse of the nature of legiti-

---

[35] Edmond Cahn has stated that democratic jurisprudence requires a new perspective on the law, a "consumer's perspective," gained by examining a legal problem from the standpoint of the individual affected by the outcome. See "The Consumers of Injustice," *New York University Law Review*, Vol. 34 (November, 1959), pp. 1166–81.

mitization is to consider the problem of retroactivity. When a statute is passed which implies rights and duties arising out of past events, it is retroactive in nature. If my trip over the Golden Arm Bridge has been free for several years and now it is subject to a fee, combined with a fee for trips taken earlier this year, the law is retroactive in effect. Retroactive laws refer to prior conduct, changing the legal meaning of acts already completed.

The Supreme Court has tested retroactive civil legislation against three standards contained within the Constitution: due process, equal protection of the law, and impairing the obligation of contract. Of course, retroactive criminal legislation is forbidden by the ex post facto clause.[36]

Actually, a constitutional clause such as "due process" is of little meaning in this area. The courts are forced to balance conflicting social interests in determining whether the law is to be upheld. A bar to retroactive legislation will be placed only as a protection against an undue loss of property, especially if a great deal of investment is involved, or as protection from the demand of officials of the government who might be encouraged to act irresponsibly. The retroactive operation of statutes is normally supported by the courts, thus lending legitimacy to a rather questionable tactic. The courts are especially likely to uphold retroactive tax legislation because it is half anticipated by the public and does not upset normal expectations. But if a retroactive statute, or even a retroactive judicial decision, drastically upsets social expectations, the courts are much less likely to permit that result, to give it the cachet of judicial legitimacy.[37]

---

[36] *Calder* v. *Bull*, 3 Dall. 386 (1798).

[37] Bryant Smith, "Retroactive Laws and Vested Rights," *Texas Law Review*, Vol. 6 (June, 1928), pp. 409–31. *Johnson* v. *New Jersey*, 85 Sup. Ct. 1772 (1966), prevented the retroactive effect of the *Miranda* and *Escobedo* cases which would have freed thousands of incarcerated individuals. These were men who had not been informed of their right to counsel or their privilege against self-incrimination at the time of interrogation. Evidently this drastic change in police procedure is prospective in effect.

Case law output

In a day when statutory law is most prevalent, courts are largely involved with interpreting it, enforcing it, and legitimitizing it. Even now, however, there are occasions when judges can improvise. Then a creative judge may do more than merely comment upon or ring changes upon a statute. There are a few areas left for judicial innovation, and most of these are on the frontiers of the law. But when they appear, an imaginative judge can do more than participate in a routine verdict output. He can help make law. In the common-law countries, this process is continual, and it has been the life of the common law.

Although it is easily forgotten and ignored, most of the categories of contemporary law are of recent vintage, a mere two or three hundred years old. Most of these categories, in terms of which our legal rights are best understood, were originally created by some judge, adopted by others, eventually hardened into precedent, and today form substantive law. The history of the common law is replete with examples of this creative output process.

The evolution of the rules for libel and slander provides a good example of case law output because very few statutes intervene to complicate the story. Slander was considered a criminal matter in church courts of 12th-century England. The word "defamation," which is now essential to a slander suit, is a church term for a man's evil reputation. Gradually, local courts began to give remedies to plaintiffs not merely insulted to their faces, as in church law, but behind their backs. In a novel 1333 case, an action was allowed in which the plaintiff claimed that the defendant called him a false and faithless fellow, which horrid language prevented him from securing a loan. The slander of government officials was made a statutory offense in 1275, triable in the King's courts, but this was a criminal matter.

The distinction between libel and slander had not yet been made by the beginning of the 17th century, although by then slander had become a civil matter, because many common-law courts had made it so by expanding upon early precedents. The common-law courts captured slander actions from the declining church courts and subjected the suits to their procedures, as available cases show, by the middle of the 16th century.[38] Libel had a separate history, connected with the regulation of printing and the attempt to suppress sedition by statute. The law of libel was part of the criminal law administered by the Court of Star Chamber until 1641, when Star Chamber was abolished. Again, the common-law courts moved into the breach, transforming an action which had been statutory and criminal in origins into one that was neither one nor the other. This took place by the end of the 17th century, so that the Court of King's Bench, a civil court which succeeded the Court of Star Chamber, was able to administer both the law of slander, as it had developed, and the new law of libel. Both types of law began to influence each other in the decisions of this court, and a systematic law of defamation, including both libel and slander, began to emerge in the 18th century.

Unfortunately, the court records of the early years of the creation of the common law are scanty. We cannot say with assurance which cases and which judges made the new departures. It is obvious that many judges, acting over a long period of time, collaborated in the law making process, and many experiments failed; many opinions did not persuade other judges. The fundamental distinction between libel and slander—between written and oral expression—had been made by 1670, but Judge Hale failed in his effort to use the law of libel to shore up a weak case of slander. Today, they are on equal footing as legal doctrines.

---

[38] *Somers* v. *House* (1693) Holt, K.B. 39. For a good brief history of libel and slander, see Theodore F. T. Plucknett, *A Concise History of the Common Law* (Boston: Little, Brown & Co., 1956), pp. 483–502.

In our own day we can watch the slow growth of new doctrines from case to case on the margins of the older parts of the common law, or in the sudden dramatic rejection of an old common-law rule. The newer law of privacy shows this kind of creativity.

Compliance

The full impact of a legal output is not always produced by a verdict or a sentence. For the convicted criminal, there may ensue a long period of imprisonment or probation, during which time he is subject to the restraint of a public officer, who sees to it that the terms of the sentence are faithfully met. For the successful civil plaintiff, it may be necessary to pursue his judgment beyond the trial court, especially if the defendant is elusive or short on cash. In a rare but dramatic situation, it may even be necessary for federal Marshals or federal troops to be used to secure compliance with court orders, but since this situation usually involves the Supreme Court, it will be treated at a later point. However, in all these situations some type of force is needed to support an output, if only the force of an additional court order together with a veiled threat of a contempt of court citation.

Failure to comply with a judgment can result in punishment for contempt of court. The forms of punishment may resemble criminal penalties, and include fine and imprisonment. Sometimes the punishment may exceed that of the similar criminal statutes. The party injured by noncompliance carries the burden of showing that the losing party has defaulted or failed to perform his legal obligations under the earlier judgment. The proceedings for criminal contempt matters generally follow those of other cases, with a required notice, hearing, and verdict. In most states the judge is relatively free to impose whatever punishment he thinks appropriate, although in the federal courts the usual limitation is $1,000 fine and imprisonment of six months at the maximum.[39] Trials in contempt matters do not usually utilize juries, because they are not regarded as "criminal" in the sense of a violation of a criminal statute, which means that the constitutional requirement of jury trial is inapplicable.[40] Judgments are subject to appeal.

Civil contempt differs from criminal contempt in that it is not intended primarily as punishment. If the threat of punishment is inadequate, the injured party may request that the noncomplying party be detained in custody until the court order is honored. A not-so-clever defendant can find himself in a civil jail, which looks and smells like any other jail, until he does what is required of him. As some say, he has the key to the jailhouse door in his own pocket. He can get out any time he decides to honor the original judgment.

The judicial power of contempt has been used by Congress to help enforce civil rights in America. For example, a 1957 statute compels election officers, at the risk of contempt hearings, to register individuals without discrimination due to race or color. Jury trial is available in these cases if the fine exceeds $300 or the imprisonment sought is for more than 45 days.[41] In effect, the Constitution is being enforced through the contempt power, under this sort of statute. Federal courts may be empowered to do more of this policy enforcement in the future, thus directly enforcing constitutional norms under congressional mandate.

In bankruptcy matters the court takes a direct hand in supervising the enforcement of the order which declared a man bankrupt. The federal act allows the court to take cus-

---

[39] In 1947, John L. Lewis and the United Mine Workers were cited for criminal contempt in the amount of $750,000 together with a contingent fine of $2,800,000. See *United States* v. *United Mine Workers*, 330 U.S. 258 (1947). This violation of an injunction did not fall under the federal statute, 18 U.S. Code, Sec. 402.

[40] *In re Debs*, 158 U.S. 564 (1895). Jury trial is required, though, if the act constituting contempt is also a criminal offense under federal or state statutes.

[41] 42 U.S. Code, Sec. 1995.

tody of the property, liquidate it, and distribute it among his creditors. In fact, so flexible is the enforcement procedure that the debtor's property may be operated directly as a means of paying off the debts. The Golden Slipper Hotel may really be under the management of a court-appointed officer as part of a bankruptcy proceeding.

One common compliance problem is that presented by the traveling debtor. This unscrupulous gentleman makes contracts, defaults, and skips to another state when the collection agencies pursue him. He may be poor or may even live rather royally on the largess of a credit economy. The debtor may calculate that the cost of pursuit and collection in another state is not worthwhile for his creditor, and he is often correct in this estimate. If the creditor is tenacious, he may sue on his judgment obtained in the original trial in the courts of the debtor's new state of residence. Usually, the out-of-state judgment is given full faith and credit in the other state, unless its policies are contrary to the first state in some fundamental way. Nonetheless, the creditor has the problem of assembling the evidence anew, sending lawyers and records to the second state, and perhaps even recalling witnesses from the first trial. The expense of collection mounts annually and is passed on to the regular bill payer in the form of higher prices and high interest rates on credit accounts and small loans.

In the criminal law the problem of compliance with the sentence output is rarely met. The convicted person is held in prison or placed upon probation and, unless he leaves the jurisdiction, that is the end of the matter. If the convict does leave the jurisdiction, usually by escape from prison or flight before being jailed, the obligation of the state receiving him to hand him over to the authorities of the first state is incomplete. The governor of the second state may decide not to honor the conviction and sentence of the first state for a variety of reasons, but whatever the justification, there is no way to force compliance by the second state. The reason is essentially due to the political operation of the federal principle, which leaves each state free to disregard the criminal policy of other states because of conflict with their own.[42]

Variable outputs

The level and type of output may sometimes vary in accordance with the nature and identity of the parties, rather than according to the merit of the claim. This kind of variable output may be related more to community bias or prejudice than to any other factor, but the existence of this kind of variable output is very hard to prove. It is sometimes said that jurors dislike insurance companies and minority groups or arrogant individuals, but the impact of these feelings cannot easily be discerned in most verdict outputs.

Recently, Maryland judges have been accused of dealing more harshly with Negro men convicted of rape than with whites convicted of that crime. A Negro bar association claimed that the death sentence for rape had been used exclusively against Negroes "and those few whites who perpetrated the most extreme and aggravated sexual assaults."[43] This accusation of a double standard, though clearly asserted, is qualified by the explanatory phrase regarding the death penalty issued against some whites. Thus, the variable output is not entirely proven, even if it may be highly probable. The report does go on, though, to cite more impressive statistics tending to show that the average sentence for Negroes in rape cases was influenced by the race of the rape victim.

Much controversy surrounds the question of the factor of

---

[42] *Kentucky* v. *Dennison*, 24 How. 66 (1861), held that the constitutional phrase "it shall be the duty" is not mandatory and compulsory, but is declaratory of a moral duty.

[43] *New York Times*, September 18, 1967, p. 33, col. 1.

race as it affects sentence outputs. Experts are not in agreement on this issue.[44] But this is the kind of analysis which could produce socially useful information. It should be possible to find out more about the sentencing process, at least, by careful statistical analysis of sentence outcomes over a span of many years.

Unfortunately, analysis of outcomes alone will not explain the process which preceded it. A variable outcome is merely an example of the uneven treatment given cases at all stages of the legal process. At no point, whether in input, conversion, or output does the system work with mere mechanical equality. Many other political, social, and economic factors impinge on the process. However, it is to be hoped that these departures from strict equality can be at least observed carefully so that those outcomes which affront our social values can be largely eliminated. Outputs need not be equal to be just, but they should be fair, according to the current standards of fairness.

---

[44] See Hugh A. Bedau, "Death Sentences in New Jersey," *Rutgers Law Review*, Vol. 19 (Fall, 1964), p. 1, for a careful appraisal of various factors, including race, which may help explain the reasons behind the sentence of death in one state.

VIII

Final outputs: the Supreme Court

THE UNITED STATES SUPREME COURT is the most powerful court in the nation and perhaps the world. On some issues it stands at the apex of the entire American legal system. But this power is both a blessing and a curse, because it requires the Court to make decisions which often border upon, or directly involve, politics, and on many of these issues the Court's word is virtually final. How the Court came to obtain final output authority, the extent to which it is able to control outputs of other parts of the legal system, and the ability of the Court to set basic social policy are important to an understanding of the legal system. Once these are grasped, the picture of the legal system becomes complete.

When the work of the Supreme Court is examined, the limitations of the legal system become more apparent. In America, many political questions are resolved through legal channels, because "every question about official action which is not a judicial question is a political question in the sense that it is a question to be decided by one or the other of the political departments of government, or by the electorate."[1] Potentially, most political questions can be con-

---

[1] Henry Hart and Herbert Wechsler, "The Federal Courts in the Federal System" (Brooklyn: Foundation Press, 1953), p. 192.

verted to legal questions, but many are not, and in determining why this is so, we can find out why the legal system is often inappropriate to the treatment of social problems. For example, the Supreme Court has had a very limited role to play in American foreign affairs. As will be shown, the Supreme Court is incapable of appraising and managing foreign affairs issues, so it must confess its weakness and accept policy leadership from another branch. In many other less obvious ways, the Supreme Court has proven to be inept, incompetent, or inappropriate. Critics may blame the judges for these shortcomings, but the fault is not purely personal. The intrinsic limitations of the legal system prevent the Court from being omnicompetent.

In many other areas the Supreme Court has proven extremely successful in setting legal and social policy. At times, the Court has captured the initiative from the other branches of national government. Since we are living through such a period today, it is especially necessary that we recognize the achievements of the Court and explain how they came about.

A careful analysis of the work of the Supreme Court will show that it acts differently within each of the areas of law that comes to its attention. In some it is "active," overturning the views of other state and federal agencies. In other areas of law, it is more or less passive, accepting the outputs of other agencies almost as an automatic gesture. These variations demonstrate that the Court is subject to many of the same political considerations as are other parts of the national government. The Supreme Court is forced into a dual position of legal and political responsibility which may cause it frequent embarrassment from one or the other quarter. No simple generalizations or mathematical formulas will entirely explain the subtlety of its behavior.

The English legal system has permitted its courts to avoid the dilemma of the Supreme Court. The principle of parliamentary supremacy makes the legislature's judgment the last word on the legitimacy of outputs. In the United States, the actions of the President, the Congress, and the states are not the last word. All are subject to at least the threat of the judicial review power of the Supreme Court. The outputs of all these officials and groups could fall under the scrutiny of the Supreme Court. Is it any wonder that the Court may at times be perplexed about its proper function in the American legal and political systems? Justice Jackson once expressed his sense of frustration caused by this excessive responsibility:

Of course, it would be nice if there were some authority to make everybody do the things we ought to have done and leave the things we ought not to have done. But are the courts the appropriate catch-all into which every such problem should be tossed?[2]

It is the purpose of this chapter to separate the various output rules of the Supreme Court. In this way, it is possible to see what the Court has done, what it can do, and what it cannot do both as part of the legal and as part of the political system.[3] The relationship of the Court to the society itself has often been exaggerated and misunderstood. It cannot perform miracles, nor command ethical standards for all Americans. Its marble palace is not on Mount Sinai, but in the political capital of the nation.

The birth of judicial power

In 1790, President George Washington appointed six men to serve on the new Supreme Court of the United

---

[2] Robert H. Jackson, *The Court in the American System of Government* (Cambridge, Mass.: Harvard University Press, 1955), p. 53.

[3] As Robert McCloskey points out, it is erroneous to treat the Supreme Court as either a purely legal or purely political organization. It is both "and the Court's power is accounted for by the fact that the mixture is maintained in nice balance; but the fact that it must be maintained in such a balance accounts for the limitations of that power." Robert McCloskey, *The American Supreme Court* (Chicago: University of Chicago Press, 1960), p. 20. Many legal realists have tended, wrongly, to treat the Court as merely another kind of legislature.

States. Only four of the six men designated actually arrived for the first session of the Court. Robert H. Harrison declined the appointment, preferring to keep a judicial post as chancellor of Maryland. John Rutledge never attended a single session in three terms of membership, resigning from the Court in 1793 in order to become chief justice of South Carolina. These two men did not expect much from the United States Supreme Court, believing their state judicial positions to be more significant. They were in error, but it did not appear so in 1790.

For the very perceptive judge the possibility of the future power of the Supreme Court could be detected in the Judiciary Act of 1789, the most important piece of federal legislation affecting the federal courts. The Framers of the Constitution did not clearly indicate their intentions regarding judicial power in the language of Article III. They may have intended, as their debates indicate, to provide a broad grant of judicial authority, but they did not explicitly say so. Section 25 of the Judiciary Act of 1789 settled some of these ambiguities. It gave the Supreme Court power to reverse or affirm state court decisions which denied claims based on the federal Constitution, treaties, or laws. But the act did not say what would happen if the state court resisted or if the state court and the Supreme Court both found a national act contrary to the Constitution. The act said nothing about either situation.

The claim of the power of judicial review had been advanced by Alexander Hamilton in Number 78 of the *Federalist Papers*. Some Supreme Court judges had hinted at the existence of such a power in an early 1793 case. Various state supreme courts had claimed the power to declare state legislation void at still earlier periods. The 1780 New Jersey case of *Holmes* v. *Watson* declared invalid an act of 1778 which created special six-man juries for confiscation matters, contrary to a state constitutional provision which, the earlier court claimed, guaranteed a jury of 12. Yet John

Jay refused to accept President Adams' 1801 reappointment to the Chief Justiceship of the Supreme Court of the United States on the grounds that he doubted that the Court would have enough "energy, weight, and dignity" to play a significant role in the nation's affairs.

But not until 1803 was the Supreme Court to become a major factor in American government, a role which by the 1820's had become confirmed and solidified. The rise of the Court came in reaction to a threat to its independence. In its hour of greatest danger, the Supreme Court found a masterful tactician in the person of its fourth Chief Justice, John Marshall.

Marshall was appointed Chief Justice in 1801 only after John Jay declined reappointment. Marshall, although a member of the Federalist group, had criticized the more extreme measures of his party, even voting with Jefferson's Republicans to repeal the Alien and Sedition Acts when a member of Congress. However, the Federalist defeat in the elections of 1800 meant that the party was in deep trouble. In desperation, the outgoing Federalists passed the Judiciary Act of 1801, which created many new federal judgeships, to be filled by worthy Federalists.

Marshall's appointment to the Chief Justiceship was part of the Federalist scheme to capture the national judiciary. The new Republican Congress struck at the heart of the plan by repealing the 1801 Judiciary Act. Then Jefferson's party sought to deny the Federalist judges their posts whenever possible.

When William Marbury sued Secretary of State Madison to secure his judicial commission, which had been denied him by an oversight, Marshall was faced with a painful political dilemma. The Court could grant Marbury his request, but risk exposing its weakness when the court order was ignored by Madison. On the other hand, the Court could accede to the pressure of the dominant Jeffersonians, denying brother Marbury his position.

Marshall found a middle way, and, not incidentally, discovered a power of judicial review over federal legislation. Since Marbury required a writ of mandamus from the Supreme Court to get his appointment, he relied upon the Judiciary Act of 1789 which seemed to grant the Court the power to issue that writ. Marshall attacked the act, not the Jeffersonians, saying that the portion of the act which created writ-granting power was in violation of the Constitution, because the jurisdiction of the Court defined in Article III did not include the possibility of additional original jurisdiction power. The federal act was unconstitutional.[4] The court was powerless to intervene on the behalf of Mr. Marbury. The Federalists had conceded the loss of Judge Marbury but had obtained the greater victory of establishing the power of judicial review. It should be noted that the 1789 Act was not Jeffersonian in origin, so the political motivation of the decision was not blatant.

However strained and arbitrary Marshall's reasoning process may have been, the decision was not a total novelty. Earlier courts had begun the process of building the power. In 1804, Marshall admitted privately that Congress might be able to reverse unsound legal opinions, indicating his uncertainty about the extent of the Court's power. The Jeffersonians did not react very sharply to the decision. *Marbury* v. *Madison* was not a bombshell, it was a delayed action bomb.

The other major aspect of federal review power is that over state legislation. Again, the brilliant Marshall was cautious in asserting the new power. The 1810 decision in which the principle was announced rests upon several explanations, only one of which is the judicial review power.[5] Then too, it is difficult to perceive which portion of the national Constitution was violated by the state law. Marshall left for the future the articulation of specific limitations upon the states.

---

[4] *Marbury* v. *Madison*, 1 Cranch 137 (1803).

[5] *Fletcher* v. *Peck*, 6 Cranch 87 (1810).

The point had been made. A state law was stricken down by the Supreme Court, and the central place of the Court in the federal system was established.

In order to secure the Court's primacy in the federal system, one fact had to be firmly established: the superiority of the Supreme Court over the state courts. In 1816, Justice Story, a close colleague of Marshall, completed the nationalist foundation of Supreme Court power by the language of his opinion in *Martin* v. *Hunter's Lessee*,[6] which argued that the people, and not the states, had created the Constitution, making the states subservient to a proper expression of national power, even if the interpretation of national power arises in a state court. The final arbiter of national power over the states on behalf of the people is the Supreme Court. In later years this view was expanded to support enhanced national powers at the expense of state sovereignty.

The feedback response during the early years of Supreme Court discovery of power was considerable, but ineffective. In 1803, the year of the *Marbury* decision, Congress impeached an incompetent Federalist district court judge. Having succeeded with the unfortunate John Pickering, the Congress proposed to impeach Samuel Chase of the Supreme Court, the most noxious of Federalist judges. Mismanagement by Congress led to Chase's acquittal, but Marshall had fearfully offered to permit Congress appellate jurisdiction over the Supreme Court. Demands came for Marshall's impeachment following his interpretation of the treason clause of the Constitution which made the conviction of Aaron Burr impossible. Finally, the states' righters in Congress continually sought to reverse the Supreme Court opinions regarding state power by statute and constitutional amendment. These efforts to curb the Court failed for many reasons, but primarily because the political significance of the Court's opinions largely escaped the politicians of the day. By the time they awakened to the situation, the

---

[6] 1 Wheat. 304 (1816).

Court had firmly established its legitimacy. It was too late to curb the Court by radical measures. The Court had claimed the Constitution as its own province.

By the 1820's, the Supreme Court had become the most powerful judicial body in modern history. The ambit and significance of the power were not clear, and as some saw it, the power could amount to government by judicial veto. The power could make the court a virtual supervisor of the American system of government. But this untenable, undemocratic use of power was not used in so ambitious a fashion.

Avoiding inputs

The power of judicial review is awesome. In the hands of John Marshall, the constitutional duty of the judge seemed clear:

The judiciary cannot, as the legislature may, avoid a measure because it approaches the confines of the constitution. We cannot pass it by because it is doubtful, with whatever doubts, with whatever difficulties, a case may be attended, we must decide it if it be brought before us. We have no more right to decline the exercise of jurisdiction which is given than to usurp that which is not given. The one or the other would be treason to the constitution.[7]

But the Court has learned to ignore Marshall's advice in the interest of self-preservation. It has learned to control itself by regulating the inputs. Today virtually no constitutional issue can be forced upon the Supreme Court against the will of its members. The Court is capable of avoiding sensitive, uncertain, and embarrassing matters by the use of an arsenal of doctrines which it has developed since Marshall's day. It is difficult to predict when the Court will accept a case, but merely agreeing to hear a dispute is a vital stage in the development of legal policy. The Supreme

---

[7] *Cohens* v. *Virginia*, 6 Wheat. 264, 403 (1821).

Court cannot process all social disputes, and it may refuse to handle even those which it could adjudicate.

The Constitution itself provides the justification for certain judicial rules to avoid inputs. The so-called "case or controversy rule" interprets the literal language of Article III to mean that there must be two real parties and a genuine controversy between them in order for the Court to consider the dispute. An actual adversary condition must exist, so that friendly, fictitious cases and advisory opinions are barred. At times, the Supreme Court has winked at this rule and permitted cases to be heard in which the dispute was merely nominal.[8]

Another rule requires that the complaining party be really injured, not merely hypothetically involved in the dispute. In an extreme situation, this may mean that to test the constitutionality of a law an individual must first violate it and then suffer a punishment.[9] This rule, too, can be ignored by the Court if it is anxious to consider a particular case. In one unusually sensitive application of this rule of "standing to sue," 18 electric power companies were denied the right to sue even though they could prove a direct injury from the competition of a federal agency (TVA).[10]

The doctrine of political questions is even more obviously a method of controlling input in sensitive areas of public policy. The principle stems from the 1842 case of *Luther* v. *Borden*[11] in which Chief Justice Taney confessed that it is the duty of the Supreme Court "not to pass beyond its appropriate sphere of action, and to take care not to involve itself in discussions which properly belong to other Forums." As advice to the Court to mind its own business, the maxim

---

[8] *Bailey* v. *Drexel Furniture Company*, 259 U.S. 20 (1922); *Barrows* v. *Jackson*, 346 U.S. 249 (1953).

[9] See *United Public Workers* v. *Mitchell*, 330 U.S. 75 (1947), which was an attempt to test a statute which prohibited political activity by federal civil servants.

[10] *Tennessee Electric Power Co.* v. *Tennessee Valley Authority*, 306 U.S. 118 (1939). In *Pierce* v. *Society of Sisters*, 268 U.S. 510 (1925) the Court did choose to ignore its stringent views on standing.

[11] 7 Howard 1 (1849).

seems sound, but what is the Court's own business? Perhaps the rule means that separation of powers requires the Court to honor the views of a coordinate branch of government. Perhaps it means that the Court may not intervene in a naked struggle for domestic political power, or in foreign relations. Whatever it means, it has been manipulated by the Court first to avoid decisions in legislative apportionment matters, and later ignored in the same kind of case.[12] Probably, the doctrine is available for the judicially modest or the timid, when all else fails, as a way of avoiding a touchy question which borders on the arena of active politics.

Vaguest of all the standards of judicial input restriction is the idea of "ripeness." An unused criminal statute might not be examined for this reason. A statute that is new and vague may not yet be "ripe" for judicial scrutiny. In essence, "a case may be ripe for one judge but not for another, depending not on their understanding of the fixed concept of ripeness but on the contours of the ultimate constitutional principle each would evolve and apply."[13] Ripeness is a kind of constitutional hindsight applied in advance.

A statutory device for avoidance is provided by the writ of certiorari. Since the writ is used in 90 percent of cases reaching the Supreme Court, it is the most important procedural method of obtaining a Supreme Court hearing. The denial of the writ terminates the history of the case and avoids hearing the issue. No reason is usually given for the denial, and the decision of the lower court is left standing. In this way, the Court may postpone a controversy until a later date, when hot passions surrounding the issues may have cooled or when its own views may have become clari-

---

12 Compare *Colegrove* v. *Green*, 328 U.S. 549 (1946), with *Baker* v. *Carr* 369 U.S. 186 (1962). Of course, the end result of the latter decision is that the Court is now intimately involved in the politics as well as the principles of apportionment, which it might have avoided simply by abiding by the earlier case.

13 Alexander M. Bickel, *The Least Dangerous Branch* (Indianapolis: Bobbs-Merrill Co., Inc., 1962), pp. 169–70.

fied. The entire Court membership votes secretly to grant
or deny the petition for certiorari, with a vote of four sufficient to grant the writ. The denial of the writ cannot fairly
be read to signify approval of the decision of the lower
court, since the Supreme Court is motivated by many factors, aside from the merits of the particular case.

Since only about 13 or 14 percent of certiorari petitions
are granted, the Supreme Court must have special reasons
for accepting a case on its crowded calendar. An accepted
case will usually involve a fundamental and unresolved issue, often of a constitutional nature. If there has been a
conflict of opinions in the lower courts on the matter, the
chances of acceptance are enhanced. If an individual right
is clearly involved, the case takes on additional importance;
and if it involves a fresh interpretation of a statute, the
chances are strengthened further. Another factor influenc-
ing the grant of the writ is the possibility of a lower court
deviation from a decision of the Supreme Court.

Despite the apparent intent of Congress, the Supreme
Court also regulates the use of appeals from lower courts.
The language of the appropriate statute appears to be mandatory, but the Supreme Court has treated it as discretionary. The Court often refuses to accept what may seem to
be legitimate appeals on the ground of a "lack of a substantial federal question." Nonetheless, this kind of input restriction is probably as necessary as any other kind. The Court
is limited by time and manpower. In order to avoid a deluge
of cases, it has attempted to consider only the most significant ones. Sometimes it may choose to avoid important
cases, too, but that may be for reasons other than the pressure of the business of the Court.

Avoiding issues

John Marshall, the powerful fourth Chief Justice of the
Supreme Court, led the Court into its current position of potential power by enunciating the doctrine of judicial review.

However, aware of the dangers inherent in the power, Marshall did not invoke the doctrine again against congressional acts during his remaining 34 years on the Supreme Court. Generally, the infrequent use of judicial review against federal legislation and its much more frequent use against state legislation is less typical than the unsensational cases in which judicial review is not invoked. Although the threat of judicial review hangs over most legislation, it is possible for the political system to operate on the assumption that the statutes are valid and the actions of governmental officials are constitutionally proper. Indeed, no political system could operate if it were in constant and imminent danger of repeated interference from the judges in the legal system. The homeostatic operation of the political system requires an infrequent intervention by the judicial branch of the legal system, and then only when the judges perceive a social imbalance or injustice.

In order to avoid constant interference in the political process, the Supreme Court has evolved a series of rules which permit it to resolve a case without calling into question the most fundamental portions of a statute or governmental action. As Marshall himself saw it, "the question whether a law be void for repugnancy to the Constitution is, at all times, a question of much delicacy which ought seldom, if ever, to be decided in the affirmative in a doubtful case."[14] As a rule of thumb, this approach is generally followed, but it happens that at times the issues may seem too important to avoid, and then the strictures of judicial self-restraint will be cast aside.

Among the most popular formulations by which the Supreme Court can avoid issues is the "rule of the clear mistake." This means that a statute can be considered unconstitutional only when the mistake made by the legislature is so clear that it is beyond rational question. The rule, derived from the writings of James Bradley Thayer, has been

---

[14] *Fletcher* v. *Peck*, 6 Cranch 87, 90 (1810).

adopted by certain Justices in particular. Holmes, Brandeis, and Frankfurter were especially fond of this rule and used it with great frequency. This rule implies that even if the judges personally disapprove of the policy or the statute under scrutiny, they should uphold it if the policy is reasonable. Of course, great latitude is possible concerning the meaning of "reasonable," so judges may disagree about the relative rationality of a statutory scheme. The product of an emotionally overexcited legislature or executive might be irrational, and then the Court might intervene by employing judicial review.

Another rule is that the Court "will not anticipate a question of constitutional law in advance of the necessity of deciding it." This would seem to mean that the Court could postpone consideration of questionable statutes for years, or even indefinitely. Certainly, in interpreting the Smith Act in 1950, the Supreme Court evaded a pressing obligation to examine the possible infringement of free speech, and the Smith Act is still largely unchallenged on constitutional grounds, even though it is a direct restriction of speech and assembly. The Court preferred to resort to interpretation of the statute rather than inquire into the basic constitutionality of the legislation.[15]

The Court "will not formulate a rule of constitutional law broader than is required by the precise facts to which it is to be applied."[16] An imaginative judge may choose to ignore the implicit advice of this maxim, and reasonable men may not agree upon the meaning or relevance of the facts. If the disagreement is profound, an inconclusive result may ensue, as in *Youngstown Sheet and Tube Company* v. *Sawyer*.[17] Still, the rule is generally employed with success to narrowly confine the ambit of the decision, if only to pro-

---

[15] *Dennis* v. *United States*, 341 U.S. 494 (1951); *Yates* v. *United States*, 354 U.S. 298 (1957); *Scales* v. *United States*, 367 U.S. 203 (1961).

[16] This and many other rules appear in Justice Frankfurter's concurring opinion in *Ashwander* v. *T.V.A.*, 297 U.S. 288 (1936).

[17] 343 U.S. 579 (1952).

tect the Court if it should choose to change its mind in the future.

The Court has held less firmly to its rule that it will not pass upon a constitutional question in any way if there is some alternate nonconstitutional ground upon which the case may be decided. In the days when the Supreme Court actively championed a conservative view of economics, it frequently attacked federal and state policies head on—even when confrontations were avoidable. In a 1908 case, the Court went so far as to inject the principle of laissez-faire into the due process clause of the Fifth Amendment, while also delivering a lecture to Congress on the meaning of the commerce clause.[18]

It is a pleasant pastime to determine who among the judges of the Supreme Court is an "activist." While some generalizations can be made, caution must be employed. In a particular case the desire to avoid an issue may be felt differently in different cases. The point at which the input is rejected may vary with the judge and the case. This is clearly indicated in *Polk Co.* v. *Glover*,[19] a case in which the majority of the Court agreed, without opinion, to hear a case involving a Florida law prohibiting out-of-state producers from marketing orange juice within the state using the word "Florida" unless the juice had been produced in Florida. The majority seemed to agree (without saying so) that the plaintiff should at least have a chance to prove that the law was unreasonable. Mr. Justice Black dissented from the *per curiam* decision on the ground that Florida should not be forced to prove the legitimacy of a state act when the legislature was convinced of its rationality.

---

[18] *Adair* v. *United States*, 208 U.S. 161 (1908).

[19] 305 U.S. 5 (1938). On the other hand, see Black's concurrence in the decision of *Morgan* v. *Virginia*, 328 U.S. 373 (1946), which also involved the commerce clause in use against state legislation. Unlike the Polk case, the issue at stake was racial segregation rather than economic rights. Black said he had feared the Supreme Court might become a "super-legislature" in commerce clause cases, but he acquiesed in the use of the commerce clause against racial segregation.

Adopting Black's view would mean that the plaintiff would never get a chance to raise the question of constitutionality. Black sought to avoid the input rather than only avoid the issue. However, having heard the case the Court might still choose to avoid the issue in constructing its decision. The case shows that the choice of methods to control the output is extremely wide and will depend on the attitude of the judges toward the problem as well as on their attitudes concerning self-restraint. Black is not known as an advocate of self-restraint, but he is generally opposed to using the due process clause to protect property interests. This explains his behavior in *Polk Co.* v. *Glover*, and helps illustrate the tactics of the Supreme Court when preparing to consider an issue. The rules provide an escape hatch from either receiving an input or deciding a constitutional issue. If the input is rejected by the Court, they are saved the necessity of considering the issue at all. But if the issue is considered, it can still be avoided, once heard.

Regulating federalism

The Supreme Court is probably most effective in its use of judicial review power when it serves as "umpire of the federal system." The Constitution, in Article VI, seems to place the Court in a strategic position in the federal system, since the Court was probably intended to supervise the superiority of federal law over the states. The reason for the Court's effectiveness in this role is that it has little competition. Neither the President nor Congress is forced to come to grips with conflicts of federal and state law as a normal matter. Of course, a severe conflict between national and state government cannot be resolved in the courts, as the Civil War demonstrates, but in the daily skirmish for federalism, the Supreme Court is in the front lines.

The Tenth Amendment of the national Constitution is the cornerstone of the legal doctrine of federalism. Despite the fulminations of ardent states' righters, the amendment does not provide a firm basis of state power independent of national government. Since 1937, the Supreme Court has held that the Tenth Amendment does not provide a grant of authority to the state, but merely indicates that the national government may use its power as fully as need be within its area of power. The Tenth Amendment is, in itself, no barrier to national law.[20]

In particular, the national government has used its powers derived from the commerce clause and the taxing clause to expand its authority and responsibility. From these grants of power to the national government the Supreme Court has implied a limitation upon the states. The Supreme Court goes to great lengths to support these exercises of national power at the expense of the states. Indeed, Justice Jackson suggested that the Court is virtually unable to restrain the national government in these areas.[21] In effect, the Court, while efficiently restraining the states from interfering in these areas, has become the captive ally of the other two branches of government. The Court simply does not strike down federal legislation under these headings unless individual rights are involved, although it might strike down conflicting state legislation.

The Supreme Court has assumed the power to strike down state legislation which burdens interstate commerce, even though the Constitution is silent on the issue. States still may act on purely local matters, but even if Congress does not act, no state could legislate on a matter which could require a uniform national rule.[22] The Court has evolved specific rules to guide state legislatures in these matters.

---

[20] *United States* v. *Darby*, 312 U.S. 100 (1941).

[21] Robert Jackson, *The Supreme Court and the American System of Government* (Cambridge, Mass.: Harvard University Press, 1955). As will be seen, the Court does interpret these statutes in a manner which helps shape economic policies.

[22] *Cooley* v. *Board of Wardens*, 12 How. 299 (1852).

The supremacy of federal power even against state governors has been demonstrated by the Supreme Court at key occasions in its history. In 1958, the Court, in insisting upon the requirements of its desegregation decisions, reprimanded the governor and legislature of Arkansas.[23] However brave the unanimous Court may have been in its reiteration of the principles of desegregation, it must be remembered the case grew out of the use of federal troops to assist in school integration. The Court needed the aid of the President to secure compliance with its view of the duties of the states in the area of education. Nonetheless, the theory of interposition—the supposed authority of a state to suspend within its borders the binding effect of federal law—was again rejected, as it has been in numerous cases.

One of the few areas of independent policy carved out by the Supreme Court has been the issue of the immunity from state taxation of the property and, at one time, the employees of the federal government. The supremacy clause (Article VI) has provided the tool to permit the Court to protect national property. The scope of this immunity has expanded and contracted several times and depends upon the current view of the status of government contractors. The same lines have not been drawn for state immunity from federal taxation, since it does not rest upon the supremacy clause. Only essential state functions receive the tax immunity and not, for example, state-run liquor stores.[24]

On the other hand, the most extreme example of judicial deference to the other branches of government concerning federalism involves the meaning of Article IV, section 4, the guarantee of a republican form of government and the guarantee against domestic violence. In both areas Congress has delegated authority to the President, while the Supreme Court has virtually refused to examine these kinds of cases. As a practical matter, these powers appear to be more ap-

---

[23] *Cooper* v. *Aaron*, 358 U.S. 1 (1958).
[24] *South Carolina* v. *United States*, 199 U.S. 437 (1905).

propriate to the executive because the Court would not be able to enforce a contrary interpretation against a determined President, especially if he were supported by Congress.

The directly opposite situation occurs within federalism when one state sues another in the Supreme Court. Since the interests of coordinate branches of national government are not involved, the Supreme Court has virtually a free hand in this class of cases. Then the Supreme Court can hope to have an impact upon the state through interpretations of the full-faith and credit clause, interstate compact clause, and the privileges and immunities clause. Discriminatory state legislation and conflicting state policies can be regulated by the Court to a considerable extent.

Correcting the Congress

The power of judicial review implicitly involves the possibility of correcting the errors of the federal Congress. However, examination reveals fewer than 100 exercises of judicial review directed against the Congress. From the first important decision of *McCulloch* v. *Maryland*[25] until today, the Court has generally supported congressional assertions of power against most challenges.

Despite the reapportionment decisions, the internal operations of congressional decision making remain largely beyond the reach of the Supreme Court. The reapportionment decisions are aimed at the state legislatures, and Congress retains the power to set requirements regarding the method of districting, if it chooses to use it.

The power of Congress to expel its members, or to otherwise discipline them, will not be interfered with by the Court. Of course, Congress may set its own rules, which are not ordinarily subject to judicial control. Furthermore, as long as a bill has been duly signed by the Speaker of the

---

[25] 4 Wheat. 316 (1819).

House and the President of the Senate, approved and signed by the President, and deposited in the Department of State, the regularity of the passage of the law is assumed. No man may say that Congress has not followed the proper procedure outlined by the Constitution unless there is a clear and obvious error apparent on the face of a statute.

At one point the Congressional subsystem may directly impinge upon the rights of citizens. It is in this area of congressional investigation that the weakness of the Supreme Court vis-à-vis the Congress is most clearly revealed. Although generous in its interpretation of civil liberties in the main, even the Warren Court has bowed before the authority of Congress to conduct investigations of the activities of private citizens. By elaborate pretense, the Court has largely evaded the issue of the rights of witnesses before such committees, although upholding a few basic rights, such as self-incrimination. The necessity of congressional power has to be recognized by the Court or else risk political retaliation and the charge of judicial intrusion into the prerogative of another branch.

The best that the Supreme Court could accomplish was to forbid the use of investigatory power as "exposure for exposure's sake," after a silence of nearly one hundred years on the subject.[26] This language has proven to be nearly useless as a protection to private persons appearing before such committees, since the Court persists upon presuming a valid legislative purpose to be present in investigations, refusing to go behind the ostensible purpose of an investigating committee to reveal the true motives of publicity and exposure sometimes present. The appearance in the cold war of a new kind of congressional inquiry previously unknown to the nation has not given rise to new protections as a judicial feedback. Consequently, congressional investigations some-

---

[26] *Watkins* v. *United States*, 354 U.S. 178 (1957). It must be admitted that the Court retreated from *Watkins* in *Barenblatt* v. *United States*, 360 U.S. 109 (1959), perhaps because communism was involved.

times display the runaway, uncontrolled pattern of positive feedback, feeding upon themselves to encourage further investigations until other external forces cause them to terminate.

It is interesting to note that a recent Supreme Court case has held that the state must justify any potenial invasion of First Amendment rights by demonstrating a "crucial relation to a proper governmental interest."[27] But First Amendment claims have been bluntly rejected by the Court when sought against congressional investigation. This double standard is partly explained by the fact that the state investigation involved favored legitimate groups, such as the NAACP, which were being exposed by the Florida legislature.

The judicial modesty with respect to congressional power is in part due to a misreading of the principle of separation of powers. When a legislature acts in a judicial manner, it could expect to be reprimanded for wandering into irrelevancies. No court should exercise the sweeping power of an investigating committee, but the need of informing itself about impending legislation could be satisfied behind closed doors and away from the glare of the news media. A fair and frank hearing could result without the freewheeling tactics of many committees. Further, to reprimand a committee is not to condemn the whole Congress, since some committees embarrass the Congress itself by their conduct. The Court has not provided salutory negative feedback.

Regulating the Presidency

Of all the branches of national or state government the Presidency is the office least subject to judicial review. The prevention of arbitrary executive action is not entirely beyond the power of the Supreme Court, but the Court has recognized its essential inability to check the most powerful and popular branch of the government, especially in war-

---

[27] *Gibson* v. *Florida*, 372 U.S. 539, 549 (1963).

time or other so-called "emergencies." For the sake of executive power, the Court has expanded the periphery of power beyond the text of the Constitution itself. On the very rare occasions when it has reacted against a claim of executive power, the Court has sought the support of Congress to sustain it. It appears, then, that Presidential power is not subject to negative feedback regulation, but must be self-regulated by the incumbent President, who may be restrained by the values of earlier Presidents and the political values of the American community.

The Supreme Court has held that, even in the absence of congressional authorization, the President has inherent power to maintain the "peace of the United States" and secure the enforcement of the laws.[28] In seeing to it that the laws are faithfully executed, he may use national force against any lawbreakers, even if the governor of a state does not desire it.

As Commander in Chief, the President appears to have extremely broad powers of action. Although Congress must "raise and support Armies" under the Constitution, the President may be able to secure ample funds for the military. Yet President Lincoln issued a proclamation in 1861 which called for volunteers for the Army and Navy, even though no statute authorized the latter action. The Congress ratified Lincoln's action, and the Supreme Court held that the President's action was authorized from the beginning.[29]

Repeatedly, the Supreme Court has accepted claims of executive power in wartime, especially if Congress has subsequently ratified the Presidential action. The doctrine of retroactive effect of congressional action has permitted the Court to avoid most direct confrontations with the Presidency. When, for example, the President issued an executive order in 1942 excluding persons of Japanese ancestry

---

[28] *In re Debs*, 158 U.S. 565 (1895); *In re Neagle*, 135 U.S. 1 (1890).
[29] *United States* v. *Hosmer*, 9 Wall. 432, 434 (1870).

from designated military areas, the Supreme Court upheld this action on the ground that Congress passed an act relating to such military areas later in the same year.[30]

Even the President and Congress acting together may, at rare times, receive a judicial reprimand. In *Ex parte Milligan*[31] the Court held that military trial could not be prescribed for civilians who are not in war zones. Martial law cannot be created by Presidential action where the Courts are open. However, this deviation may be partly explained by the essentially judicial nature of the challenged conduct, an area in which the Supreme Court can feel it is on safe ground even against the other two branches.

The discretion of the President to use force overseas is probably not subject to congressional control nor to that of the Court. This is a power of the greatest consequence and endangers congressional control of the power to declare war. The Presidential power to use force to protect American interests abroad appears to rest solely in his own discretion.[32] Presidents may dispatch warships to foreign ports and land soldiers on foreign soil even in the absence of congressional authorization. The President may seek a congressional resolution in support of his action, but it is doubtful that the Supreme Court would require this of him. It never has.

When faced with a naked claim of executive power in the absence of constitutional authorization, the Supreme Court has hesitated to act. When President Truman seized the steel mills, which were about to be shut down by a strike, the President claimed that his action was essentially based on wartime emergency conditions, rather than upon any specific statute. The Court did decide that the steel seizure order was invalid, but the grounds upon which the Court

---

[30] *Hirabayashi* v. *United States*, 320 U.S. 81 (1943).

[31] 4 Wall. 2 (1866).

[32] Only *Little* v. *Barreme*, 2 Cranch 170 (1804), lends support to the view that Congress could at least restrain the President's choice of conduct by prescribing a particular procedure.

acted are unclear.[33] No single unified result appeared. A close reading of the decision does not reveal that the President's claim of prerogative authority was expressly rejected. The Court did agree that there was a statute available; the President could not claim to act in a manner contrary to the statutory procedure. Nonetheless, President Truman has since stated that the President must have this broad prerogative power, "whatever the six Justices meant by their differing opinions about the Constitutional powers of a President."[34]

When caught between conflicting pressures of congressional policy and Presidential claims of power, the Court may waver. In one leading case, the Court reversed a position it had taken just nine years before by restricting the President's removal power to members of the executive branch. The Court leaned upon the intention of Congress in creating certain regulatory agencies, saying: "the authority of Congress in creating quasi-legislative or quasi-judicial agencies, to require them to act in discharge of their duties independently of executive control cannot well be doubted; and that authority includes, as an appropriate incident, power to fix the period during which they shall continue in office, and to forbid their removal except for cause in the meantime."[35] As a result, Presidential removal power may be limited by Congress if it can establish a new office outside the executive branch.

On the whole, the power of judicial review is more likely to be employed against congressional statutes than against executive orders of the President. There is a constitutional basis for this distinction in that the Constitution does appear to make a general grant of executive power to the President, while Article I restricts Congress to specific

---

[33] *Youngstown Sheet and Tube Co.* v. *Sawyer*, 343 U.S. 579 (1952).

[34] Harry S Truman, *Memoirs: Years of Trial and Hope* (Garden City, N.Y.: Doubleday & Co., Inc., 1956), p. 478.

[35] *Humphrey's Executor* v. *United States*, 295 U.S. 602, 629 (1935).

powers enumerated in Section 8. Since Congress has increasingly delegated its powers to the President, there has been a vast expansion in the President's law-making authority, beyond that inherent in his office. A major change in the balance of power among the branches of national government has taken place without substantial feedback from the Supreme Court. Thus, the modern political system has changed, achieving a new homeostasis in which the President, interest groups, public opinion, and the voters operate as a loosely integrated system to control national government, with occasional intervention by Congress, and in a few fields by the Supreme Court.

Regulating administrative agencies

The growth of administrative law has been noted in other chapters. Nothing in the Constitution says that judicial power belongs exclusively to the regular courts. Congress is free to bestow investigatory, rule-making, and adjudicating power to whatever agencies it wishes. Congress has been investing administrative officials with judicial power for over one hundred years and has been supported by the Supreme Court in this process, at least in recent years.

Until 1937, the Supreme Court resisted the development of administrative power by renewing the decisions of these agencies and substituting their own views of administrative policies in the name of the "rule of law." However, since the Supreme Court fight of 1937, when it successfully resisted FDR's court-packing plan but conceded the validity of New Deal programs, the Court retreated from the business of supervising government administrators.

In 1946, the Court received a congressional signal that suspicion of the administrative process was growing. The Administrative Procedure Act of 1946 required each adjudicating agency to judicialize itself. Judging and examining were to be separate functions of separate officials. However, the act does not require judicial review of administrative actions, although it does permit review except so far as precluded by statute and denies it where agency action is committed by statute to agency discretion. In effect, the question of judicial review is left up to Congress, which may provide for it as a means of checking agency power.

The right to judicial review of administrative action stems more from statutory than from constitutional law. If the statutes preclude judicial review, then the courts can take a case involving an agency only if they perceive that a constitutional right is involved, which is a rare happening. If the statute is silent on judicial review, the courts may decide the matter either way.

Even if judicial review is permitted, or is discovered in the silence of a statute, there is no assurance that the Supreme Court will review the entire case, including the facts upon which the agency's action is based. The Supreme Court has tended to create additional review powers over administrative agencies but to reduce the scope of review to a narrow range. In order to reach this ambivalent position, the courts have evolved the "substantial evidence" test by which they will uphold the findings of administrative agencies as long as these are supported by substantial evidence in the agency hearings, even if the judges may not have independently reached the same decisions of fact. Of course, the courts are free to examine all questions of law, if they can review the matter at all.

In fact, the members of the Supreme Court have evolved different attitudes toward different agencies and use these broad tests as a means of manipulating agency decisions if they are suspicious of the particular agency. This was tacitly admitted by Justice Frankfurter in a 1951 labor relations case. He found that the Supreme Court had greater responsibility to review NLRB decisions than those of some other agencies, even though the statutes involved were vague. As Frankfurter stated:

Some scope for judicial discretion in applying the formula can be avoided only by falsifying the actual process of judging or by using the formula as an instrument of futile casuistry. It cannot be too often repeated that judges are not automata. The ultimate reliance for the fair operation of any standard is a judiciary of high competence and character and the constant play of an informed professional critique upon its work. . . . Since the precise way in which courts interfere with agency findings cannot be imprisoned within any form of words, new formulas attempting to rephrase the old are not likely to be more helpful than the old.[36]

Frankfurter seems to be saying that the Supreme Court will review the scope of agency findings, not according to any hard and fast rules, but according to judicial attitudes. If the Court goes too far, it may be corrected by the feedback of "informed professional critique." Generally, it will honor congressional intention to preclude review, but in ambiguous situations review may be found. The way in which review power will be used will vary from agency to agency. Sensitive readers can almost predict how particular judges will react to cases involving certain agencies. It should be possible to develop a scale of judicial attitudes toward regulatory agencies and other administrative bodies, although this has not yet been done.

All in all, the Supreme Court does regulate the regulators to a limited extent. The limitations are created primarily by statute and somewhat less by the Court itself. The agencies usually lack strong political support, so the Supreme Court is in a strategic position to act to restrain them.

Property versus individual rights

Undoubtedly the most important turnabout in recent Supreme Court history has been the Court's virtual abandon-

---

[36] *Universal Camera Corp.* v. *N.L.R.B.*, 340 U.S. 474, 479 (1951). See Joseph Tanehaus, "Supreme Court Attitudes Toward Federal Administrative Agencies," *Journal of Politics*, Vol. 22 (1960), pp. 502–24.

ment of activism on behalf of property rights and its acceptance of leadership in the recognition of individual rights. At two points in its history the Court has championed different versions of rights guaranteed by the Constitution, and, to some extent, thwarted the policies of national, state, and local government. In this fashion, more than any other, the Court has served as a primary source of legal outputs. The whole society has felt the force of these decisions regarding the meaning of rights.

The Supreme Court does not have a monopoly on the conception of rights, but it is in the best position to assert and legitimatize a claim of a right. Does the Bill of Rights extend to the actions of the States? How far does it extend? Who is the guardian of the Bill of Rights? The answers to all these questions are provided by the Supreme Court. Until 1937, the public was not sure of the answer to the second question. In 1937, the answer was given. Those parts of the Bill of Rights which applied to the states are those "implicit in the concept of ordered liberty." Implicit to whom? To the Supreme Court.[37]

Somewhat by coincidence, in the same year of 1937, the Supreme Court abandoned its treatment of the commerce clause as a barrier to federal regulatory legislation. Although not exactly clear in the matter, the Court had previously held that Congress could regulate only harmful or deleterious property.[38] Other property was protected by the invisible effects of the commerce clause upon property rights. Even more useful than the commerce clause, because it was vaguer, was the due process clause of the Fifth and Fourteenth Amendments. From 1900 to 1937, the Supreme Court used a due process or equal protection ground to strike down over 180 state laws, and a few federal laws of a regulatory nature. The restraining effect of this negativism upon

---

[37] *Palko* v. *Connecticut*, 302 U.S. 319 (1937).

[38] Compare *N.L.R.B.* v. *Jones and Laughlin Corp.*, 301 U.S. (1937) with *Hammer* v. *Dagenhart*, 247 U.S. 251 (1918).

state legislators and congressmen cannot be calculated, but it is certain that the Court was one of the century's instruments of economic reaction prior to 1937. The defense of economic liberty aided many a businessman and caused more laboring men to suffer than might otherwise have been the case. But the Court was not alone. The political atmosphere was also pro-business and pro-property during most of these years. The Court merely rode the tide, until 1933.

In one of the most outrageous uses of judicial review on behalf of business, Justice Oliver Wendell Holmes filed a dissent which reached the heart of the matter and which has set the tone for current Supreme Court attitudes regarding property:

I think that the word liberty in the Fourteenth Amendment is perverted when it is held to prevent the natural outcome of a dominant opinion unless it can be said that the statute proposed would infringe fundamental principles as they have been understood by the traditions of our people and our law. It does not need research to show that no such sweeping condemnation can be passed upon the statute before us.[39]

The Court has withdrawn its protection of property against the will of the legislatures and the majority of the people. It has bowed to the verdict of the voters and accepted the regulatory–welfare state view of property.

This act of judicial realism or judicial humility in the area of property rights has not been matched by a general deference to the majority on questions of minority rights. On the contrary, the Supreme Court has become an active agency in the promotion of civil rights, sometimes in the face of a hostile majority. Fortunately, the majority has never become organized in its opposition to Supreme Court activism. It is much more difficult politically to oppose minority rights than it is to oppose business or property rights.

---

[39] Dissent in *Lochner* v. *United States*, 198 U.S. 45, 76 (1905).

Consequently, the Supreme Court has escaped with verbal criticisms and little political feedback as a result of its civil rights decisions. There is no counterpart to the Roosevelt court-packing scheme on today's horizon. The majority political party is not openly or clearly in opposition to the Court's definition of rights. The Court is in a very strong position. It may define civil rights rather strongly, as long as it is cautious on the most sensitive issue of all, the rights of the Communists. As long as the Court treats Communists differently from other minorities, as it does now, it is reasonably safe from political feedback.

The power of the Supreme Court to define a right is best illustrated in the recent case of *Griswold* v. *Connecticut*.[40] An 1879 Connecticut statute was the crux of the case. The statute made it a punishable offense to use or (under another statute) to aid or abet in the use of any drug or device "for the purpose of preventing conception." The Planned Parenthood League of Connecticut deliberately violated the statute by setting up a clinic in New Haven. The League claimed that the statute invaded the right of marital privacy, since family planning was a personal matter. The Court agreed with the League, but inconveniently, no right of privacy was listed in the Constitution. This problem was overcome by finding the right of privacy to be implicitly "a zone of privacy created by several constitutional guarantees." Justice Douglas did not say which sections he had in mind. Justice Harlan agreed, but on different constitutional grounds, believing that the due process clause of the Fourteenth Amendment was violated. Three other Justices concurred in another, more radical view, that the right of privacy was included within the completely undefined contours of the Ninth Amendment. In any event, the law was an invasion of privacy wherever that right could be discovered in the Constitution. If the Ninth Amendment argument is accepted—and no one knows its status—then the Supreme

---

[40] 381 U.S. 479 (1965).

Court may add new rights at will as it uncovers other rights "retained by the people."

In the years since 1937, the Supreme Court has made a conscious attempt to set a pattern for civil rights in America by pouring meaning into the Bill of Rights and the Fourteenth Amendment. It developed the doctrine of "clear and present danger" which is often (not always) used to protect First Amendment freedoms. It hinted at a preference for the First Amendment over all other sections of the Constitution by suggesting, inconclusively, that the amendment enjoyed preferred status and that laws invading the First Amendment must bear the unique burden of a special and more searching inquiry into their constitutionality.

Since 1938, the Supreme Court has pioneered in the field of racial discrimination, most notably since 1954 in its school desegregation decisions.[41] Here the Court has had its greatest social and political influence. The brave work of the Court preceded the later action of legislatures and Presidents. These decisions, supported by subsequent executive actions, shattered traditional patterns of segregation in public housing, public education, and transportation, and in privately owned public accommodations. Discrimination in voting rights had been attacked as early as 1941, but it continued throughout the fifties and sixties.

Negro voting right decisions helped, through the Fourteenth Amendment equal protection clause, to encourage the Court to enter the less certain area of legislative malapportionment. The "one man one vote" rule was discovered to

---

[41] *Missouri ex. rel. Gaines* v. *Canada*, 305 U.S. 337 (1938), began the chipping away at the "separate but equal" line. The Court gave warning of the change away from the doctrine that it had created in *Plessy* v. *Ferguson*, 163 U.S. 537 (1896). "Separate but equal" was unmolested for 41 years after its creation. It was undone gradually over another period of 16 years. Two *per curiam* decisions in 1948: *Sipuel* v. *Oklahoma*, 322 U.S. 631, and *Fisher* v. *Hurst*, 333 U.S. 147, were followed by two 1950 cases: *Sweatt* v. *Painter*, 339 U.S. 629, and *McLaurin* v. *Oklahoma State Regents*, 339 U.S. 637, which clearly challenged "separate but equal" and made *Brown* v. *Board of Education of Topeka* all but inevitable. By 1954, the desegregation battle was launched.

be a right which required relatively equal representation in state legislatures and in Congress. The political balance of power began to shift from the rural areas to the suburbs as a result. The end of the apportionment controversy is not in sight, and the impact cannot be as satisfying as have been the decisions supporting racial equality. Sadly, Negroes in northern cities may have lost as much as they gained, since the cities have become increasingly Negro, but have not gained substantially in representative power.

Judicial intervention on behalf of the Negro and the underrepresented voter has more recently been matched by decisions restricting the police on behalf of accused persons. This minority group enjoys little social support, and even less is given to the incidental beneficiaries, the individuals already in prison. Nonetheless, the Supreme Court has entered this field since the early 1960's. Before that time the Court was interested primarily in the general "fairness" of a criminal proceeding. Today the Court is setting higher standards of state and federal procedure. More and more the states are being required to meet federal rules of procedure and investigation, while both are being held to more stringent standards. Gradually, the entire Bill of Rights is being applied, on a piecemeal basis, to local police and to state courts. The right-of-counsel decisions almost require something like a public defender system for accused persons. Even during police lineups, a lawyer must be present. Lawyers must also be present during interrogation, and persons arrested must be informed of their rights to counsel and not to incriminate themselves. Confessions received in violation of these rules are inadmissible as evidence in a state or federal court, as is now true of all other illegally obtained evidence.

No doubt there will be further attempts by the Supreme Court to protect the rights of Negroes, unrepresented voters, and accused persons. Having gone this far to create policy, the Court shows no sign of retreat as yet. The Court has the advantage of defining the context of the policy by defining the nature of the right. It has acted successfully in these areas because no coalition could provide a focused feedback restraint.[42] Many writers have observed that the Supreme Court has acted in these three areas because the normal political agencies have neglected them. While this is probably true in general, it cannot be forgotten that there are many other neglected policy areas (transportation, air pollution, Indians, consumer protection) in which the Supreme Court is inactive. Conditions are most favorable for judicial policy making in these three zones of individual rights, and the Court moved into the policy gap because it is best equipped to establish rights and to fend off its opponents, who lack a national political base.

Primary policy outputs

In few areas other than civil rights is the Supreme Court able to play the role of prime policy maker. In most areas of adjudication, the Court must interact with primary political agencies, such as the Congress and the Presidency. Its output tends to be supportive of the political output of the other branches. Even in the decisions regarding the federal system, the Court, with some notable exceptions, has tended

---

[42] In school desegregation, defiance and subterfuge were the first reactions in hostile southern states. Finally, President Eisenhower called for a show of military force in support of court desegregation orders. In 1957, he called out federal troops and nationalized the National Guard. In 1962, President Kennedy deployed 25,000 federal troops in Mississippi to overcome the resistance of the governor to desegregation of the state university. But resistance to school desegregation was divided, while the federal courts were relatively united in support of the Supreme Court. (See Jack W. Peltason, *Fifty-Eight Lonely Men: Southern Judges and School Desegregation* [New York: Harcourt, Brace & World, 1961]).

The passage of the federal Civil Rights Acts is another story, related to the discontinuous history of desegregation legislation throughout the country. In this field the states preceded the national government efforts, and the Supreme Court added the force of its rulings.

Throughout the post-1954 period, efforts were made to punish or restrain the Supreme Court, but because of allies in the White House and in Congress, the Supreme Court was not forced to retreat. The feedback was significant, but sufficiently divided to prevent restraint of the Court.

to advance the work of other branches,[43] especially in recent years since the abandonment of the doctrine of dual federalism. In most of its decisions the Court accepts the political lead of other agencies, modifying them where possible and when the Justices hold strong views contrary to the policy of the other agencies.

Probably the Court is able to operate most freely when a political void exists into which it may move. The Constitution creates several such areas in which judicial policy making by the Supreme Court is of primary importance, so that the Court may take the lead in policy formulation. The clearest example is provided by issues arising under the general maritime law. The federal courts are now involved in the creation of a series of rules in maritime matters, with the Supreme Court playing a major role in the process. In one famous case the family of a stevedore who had been killed while loading a vessel in New York was denied workmen's compensation under a New York State law on the ground that the law invaded maritime matters under the control of the national government.[44] Ever since this 1917 decision, the Supreme Court has tried to erect a uniform law of admiralty. This is an area from which the states are, to a large extent, excluded and in which Congress has not chosen to act. The invitation to create policy has been accepted by the Supreme Court.

Another area in which the Supreme Court is relatively free to act is in the cases to which a state is a party. Article III, Section 2, of the Constitution gives the Supreme Court original jurisdiction over this class of cases. This means that, in the absence of applicable treaties or statutes

---

[43] One of the most glaring exceptions was the decision in *Pennsylvania* v. *Nelson,* 350 U.S. 497 (1956), in which the Court surprised the Congress by deciding that the federal Smith Act occupied the field of protecting the country against sedition, even though no such intention was expressed by the statute. Congress missed by one vote amending the statute to correct the Court. This preserved the right of the Court to balance local and national interests in this type of legislation.

[44] *Southern Pacific* v. *Jensen,* 244 U.S. 205 (1917).

(and they are usually absent), the Supreme Court must decide these disputes on the basis of self-created principles. To handle these cases the court has turned to principles of international law and to the common law generally. But these rules have been carefully selected, in accordance with the Court's current policy views. The rules of international law and common law provide an array of legal garments as varied as the choice of clothes in a department store. And if the choice does not please the Court, it may cut another garment, deciding a case as a matter of expediency and fairness because "the issue is not controlled by constitutional provisions."[45]

Undoubtedly, some other areas of judicial independence exist in which the Supreme Court may initiate public policy. These areas seem to be expanding.[46] However, as has been shown earlier, the Court prefers to avert constitutional issues and to avoid clashes with political branches.

Compliance

The term "compliance" may be applied to the problem of securing adherence to Supreme Court rulings. Although "accommodation" or "adjustment" may seem to be more neutral in tone, "compliance" is generally understood to cover those situations in which lower state and federal courts apply (or evade applying) the literal rule or the spirit of a decision of the Supreme Court.

Forcing recalcitrant states to comply with Supreme Court rulings has always been a major area of difficulty. The relationship between state courts and the Supreme Court has been an area of great sensitivity. Even in cases appealed to the Supreme Court from the highest state court, there is no assurance that after a reversal of the state court's rulings a

---

[45] *Texas* v. *New Jersey*, 379 U.S. 671, 683 (1965).

[46] Some are suggested by Alfred Hill in "The Law-Making Power of the Federal Courts: Constitutional Preemption," *Columbia Law Review*, Vol. 67 (June, 1967), pp. 1024–81.

new trial will produce a new result in conformity with Supreme Court outputs.

The mechanics of this problem are simple. After reviewing the decision of a state court, the Supreme Court may reverse and remand the case for further proceedings. The Supreme Court output is an interpretation of rights under the federal Constitution, statutes, or treaties which serves as a dominant input in the retrial of the original case. The retrial takes place in state courts, largely beyond the zone of federal activity.

From 1941 to 1951, approximately 175 Supreme Court cases were disposed of by reversal and remand. In 46 of these, there was further litigation. In 22, the party who was unsuccessful in the Supreme Court was unsuccessful in the state court, despite the reversal.[47] This is a quantitative hint of a small amount of noncompliance.

Not every case in which the remand–new trial output was contrary to the Supreme Court output is an instance of noncompliance. The Supreme Court has long ago upheld the refusal of a state court to alter a judgment reversed by the Court.[48] In order to justify a different output, the state court must be able to find an independent, nonfederal ground to support a judgment previously reversed by the Supreme Court. The high court generally doesn't review state decisions when there is a valid nonfederal ground supporting those decisions. Since the Supreme Court is not capable of examining local law extensively and is not willing to review cases resting on local law, it is possible for a retrial to produce results contrary to their ruling if, by clever research, a nonfederal ground can be discovered in the state court reexamniation of the original dispute.

The decision of the Supreme Court does not give complete assurance of the final output of a case appealed from

---

[47] Note, "Evasion of Supreme Court Mandates in Cases Remanded to State Courts Since 1941," *Harvard Law Review*, Vol. 47 (1954), pp. 1251–59.

[48] *Davis* v. *Packard*, 8 Pet. 312 (1834).

the state courts. Evasion is possible if state courts are determined and ingenious enough. The Supreme Court does
have the power to remand a case to a state court with direc-
tions to enter a particular judgment. This power, dangerous
in a federal system, is rarely exercised, but could be used in
a situation of anticipated noncompliance.[49] The power to
issue special writs, such as mandamus and certiorari, appears
to exist in federal statutes, but it is largely in abeyance. In
essence, the Supreme Court could order a final disposition,
imposing its will upon state courts by issuing a final output,
but the Court prefers to reserve this power for extreme
emergencies, trusting to the general high level of voluntary
compliance by state court judges.

Securing compliance from lower federal courts is easier,
but it is by no means automatic. The Supreme Court may
issue orders to lower federal courts and expect that they
will be carried out on the remand. The new trial can hardly
reverse the Supreme Court view. The Supreme Court output is generally honored by lower federal courts because
the judges, though often local residents with local ties, are
usually immune from the pressures of local politics. Even
though they may not agree with the Supreme Court, lower
federal judges more readily accept its lead than do state
judges. When the Supreme Court narrowed the interpretation of the Smith Act, as used against Communists, Judge
Chambers of the Court of Appeals bitterly attacked the Supreme Court's restriction of the act. Nonetheless, his court,
the Court of Appeals for the Ninth Circuit, reversed a previous conviction of a pair of Communist leaders on the basis
of the new Supreme Court ruling.

In addition to its policy leadership, the Supreme Court
has special powers over the federal judiciary. Under various
federal statutes the Supreme Court can promulgate rules of
procedure governing the lower courts. Under substantive

---

[49] 28 U.S.C. Sec. 2106 (Supp. 1952). See *Stanley* v. *Schwalby*, 162 U.S.
255 (1896).

headings, such as "criminal law," "bankruptcy law," and "maritime and admiralty law," the Supreme Court may set the boundaries of the decision-making process within the federal courts. These rules are usually drawn up by groups of lower federal judges, lawyers, and law professors but are subject to the final approval and final interpretation of the Supreme Court. In addition to this, in recent decades the Court has issued direct instructions to lower federal courts concerning the type of evidence to be received in criminal trials. These informal rules are intended to indirectly control the federal attorneys and the various quasi-police agencies of national government. These orders serve, more directly, to limit the discretion of federal trial judges in the admission of evidence.

One illustration of the complexity of the compliance and enforcement problem is presented by the Bible-reading decisions of the Supreme Court. The simple doctrine that Bible reading in public schools violates the First Amendment cannot be easily misunderstood. One study shows that 60 percent of the states initially continued to practice school Bible reading to some extent, and were acting contrary to the Supreme Court view.[50] A later survey revealed a reduction of 60 percent in Bible reading in the first three years after the Supreme Court decision.[51]

In some complying states, authorities at the state capital made efforts to bring school districts into line with the Supreme Court ruling. But as of this writing, New Jersey, one of the supposedly complying states, includes many school districts which still defy the Supreme Court ruling. "Bible story sessions" have replaced Bible reading in a few more

---

[50] Ellis Katz, "Patterns of Compliance with the Schempp Decision," *Journal of Public Law*, Vol. 14 (1965), p. 396. Noncompliance seems to be highest in southern states. The best study is Richard M. Johnson, *The Dynamics of Compliance* (Evanston: Northwestern University Press, 1968).

[51] Based on replies to mail questionnaires sent to 2,320 teachers, of whom 1,712 replied. The results appear in H. Frank Way, *Liberty in the Balance* (2d ed.; New York: McGraw-Hill, Inc., 1967), pp. 83–84.

sophisticated schools, but open Bible reading is also found. Enforcement by state officials is awkward, both in a legal and political sense. Local school boards, which are in effective control of the situation, can compel recalcitrant principals to comply with their illegal views. Unless there is countervailing pressure by local interest groups, especially civil liberties groups, noncompliance is likely to continue in many places for many years. Under consistent pressure from state officials, local school boards have begun to bow, but this pressure is unusual.

The reapportionment problem provides another vivid example of the compliance dilemma. The political restructuring of state governments implied by reapportionment has gone on grudgingly and imperfectly. In order to regulate the speed and direction of reapportionment (a difficulty encountered in earlier desegregation decisions), the Supreme Court has set timetables for the completion of reapportionment. In the interim, malapportioned legislatures may continue to enact legislation, but after the deadline has passed, all their deeds are subject to a potential assertion of illegality.

The state of Georgia was given until May 1, 1968, to reapportion its legislature. Even so, the Court permitted the malapportioned legislature to choose the state governor after the general election had produced a deadlock. This decision reversed a three-judge district court which had enjoined the state legislature from holding its election for the governorship.[52] Despite this reversal, the lower federal courts have been in the front lines of the reapportionment struggle and have usually been supported by the Supreme Court in a joint alliance to secure compliance with the "one man one vote" principle.

No issue has been the object of recent noncompliance as

---

[52] *Tombs* v. *Fortson*, 384 U.S. 210 (1966), set the timetable. *Fortson* v. *Morris*, 385 U.S. 231 (1966), upheld the legislative election of the governor, reversing *Fortson* v. *Morris*, 262 F. Supp. 23 (N.D. Ga., 1966).

consistently as the racial desegregation of public facilities. By 1963, nine years after the basic school desegregation decision, only 1.17 percent of the Negro children in the 11 former states of the Confederacy attended desegregated schools. Over 2,000 legally segregated school systems existed in the South.[53] The federal courts and state courts were flooded with litigation challenging various aspects of southern recalcitrance. In the state supreme courts and the federal district courts compliance was quite high,[54] but these cases were of limited value, since state legislatures and local boards continually invented new evasive schemes.

In 1964, Congress supplemented judicial enforcement with the passage of Title VI of the Civil Rights Act.[55] This title provided that federal assistance could be withheld from federally assisted school programs. Every department in the national government involved in the administration of federal assistance, but especially the Office of Education, was given the task of ensuring that recipients of funds under their jurisdiction were not practicing racial discrimination. Compliance under Title VI is by no means complete, but the pace of desegregaton has been greatly accelerated since this new approach was adopted.

In March, 1966, the United States Office of Education issued a set of Guidelines for school desegregation. These Guidelines indicated a positive duty by southern school officials to complete the desegregation of schools and faculties. Southern school officials contend that under the prevailing "free choice" plans, desegregation is left in the hands of white and Negro school children and their parents. All the state need do is to provide open schools, they claim. But it

---

[53] Southern Education Reporting Service, *Statistical Summary of School Segregation-Desegregation in the Southern and Border States* (1965).

[54] Kenneth Vines, "Southern State Supreme Courts and Race Relations," *Western Political Quarterly*, Vol. 18 (March, 1965), pp. 5–18, and Robert J. Steamer, "The Role of the Federal Courts in the Segregation Controversy," *Journal of Politics*, Vol. 22 (August, 1960), pp. 417–37.

[55] 42 U.S.C. Secs. 2000d to 2000d–4 (1964).

is likely that the Office of Education and other federal agencies will impose a standard which requires the correction of racial imbalance, even if it means that students be assigned to schools to achieve desegregation. Compliance with the 1954 Supreme Court ruling may eventually be coerced by the financial power of federal agencies in the executive branch of government.

Under current regulations, the Secretary of Health, Education, and Welfare is the most important official concerned with school desegregation. By a 1966 directive, it is required that every application for federal financial assistance must, as a condition for its approval or extension, be accompanied by an assurance that the program or the facility involved will comply with desegregation requirements. In lieu of this assurance, school districts can become eligible for assistance by submitting a plan for desegregation of the system which is determined by the Commissioner of Education to be "adequate to accomplish the purposes of the Act."

School districts will often find themselves under the watchful eye of both the local federal court and of Washington agencies. This joint effort at compliance shows the significance of political support for a total program of enforcement of judicial orders.[56] The proposed Civil Rights Act of 1966 would have permitted the United States Attorney-General to take independent action through the federal courts to compel desegregation of schools and other public facilities, but this most ambitious effort at compliance was defeated by a cautious Congress, against a backdrop of Negro riots, demonstrations, and outcries for "black power."

Meanwhile, the problem of achieving racial balance in the schools remains very confused by the absence of any generally understood formula. A school in the North or

---

[56] Interestingly, it is becoming fairly common for federal courts to utilize administrative guidelines and rulings as aids in judicial decision making in this area.

South which is predominantly white or Negro by reason of geographic, demographic, ethnic, or economic factors is clearly imbalanced. But what is to be done about it? Is school busing a requirement of the Constitution? Are neighborhood schools inappropriate means of education in the light of geographic maldistribution of Negroes and whites? Some lower federal courts have taken the lead in this troubling area, but a great difference of opinion on these matters separates the lower courts. Leadership from the Supreme Court is clearly needed if these more subtle forms of school discrimination are to be managed. On the whole, the Supreme Court has recently avoided its responsibility to clarify its earlier rulings.[57] Desegregation is being accomplished in the schools by the combined, if piecemeal, efforts of the district courts, the courts of appeal, and agencies of the executive branch of the national government. The scale of the compliance problem is probably unparalleled in Supreme Court history. The completion of the process remains far distant.

The Supreme Court and social change

Undoubtedly basic social changes are not caused by court decisions alone. The changing political and social life of the South is due as much to economic changes and to organized Negro action as to the impact of Supreme Court opinions.[58] Desegregation has been hastened by Supreme Court and lower court decisions. The 1954 decision of the Supreme

---

[57] See *Bell* v. *School City*, 213 F. Supp. 819 (N.D. Ind., 1963), aff'd, 324 F. 209 (7th Cir., 1963), *cert. denied*, 377 U.S. 924 (1964). The contrary result was produced in *Blocker* v. *Board of Education*, 266 F. Supp. 208, 229, *rehearing on remedy question*, 229 F. Supp. 709 (E.D.N.Y., 1964). The Supreme Court has hinted at its concern for faculty desegregation but has left the matter for the district courts to decide on the basis of available evidence: *Bradley* v. *School Board*, 382 U.S. 103 (1965) (*per curiam*) and *Rogers* v. *Paul*, 382 U.S. 198 (1965) (*per curiam*).

[58] Multiple causative factors are explored in Daniel C. Thompson's, "The New South," *Journal of Social Issues*, Vol. 22 (January, 1966), pp. 7–19.

Court accelerated other social trends in the region by removing the formal barrier of state-supported segregation in the schools. Outside the region other political and social forces were set in motion, triggering the explosion of the civil rights movements, a flood of civil rights legislation, and an inevitable reaction, in Negro and white groups, against the pace and direction of these changes.

At the most, an output of the Supreme Court can have a kind of chain reaction effect, as illustrated by the civil rights movements. But the Court can only initiate such a process when other social agencies are in stasis, unable to move from previously held positions. Then the Court may, by a single decision, help start a series of changes unanticipated by the original decision. The total effect of the decision may be contrary to that desired by the Court, but once launched, the process seems to move by a self-generating force. The vast population shifts from southern to northern cities and, of the whites, from cities to suburb, are very important demographic decisions, although this was neither expected nor intended by the Court. The consequences of the decisions may be considered as a very complex variety of feedback, initiating a series of new inputs and reshaping the social environment of the courts.

It is very difficult to show direct causation of social changes flowing from judicial decisions. Usually, other variables intervene to prevent a confident or complete explanation. One of the few clear examples of causation which does exist is the "released-time" decisions, and they bear a closer examination.

In 1948, the Supreme Court declared that state tax-supported public school buildings could not be used for the dissemination of religious doctrines and that releasing children from regular class work to participate in religious exercises violated the First Amendment.[59] The released-time movement, which began shortly after World War I, was dealt a dramatic blow.

---

[59] *McCullom* v. *Board of Education*, 333 U.S. 203 (1948).

Reaction to the Court decision varied from compliance, to verbal opposition, to open noncompliance. Experimentation with novel types of released-time programs began in an effort to discover some other legal means to reach the desired end of weekday religious instruction of schoolchildren during normal school hours. New York state created a system of "voluntary" released-time religious instruction off school grounds, and to the surprise of many legal experts, the Supreme Court upheld the validity of this new practice.[60] Four years separated the two decisions.

Widespread public enthusiasm greeted the latest decision. The glee of released-time supporters was matched by the disappointment of religious liberal groups, but the former were in the majority.

The empirical impact of these two Supreme Court opinions should have been readily apparent. In the four years separating the two decisions, you would expect to have found a decline in released-time programs, with a resurgence of a new type of program after the second decision. Statistical evidence appears to support this expectation. The raw data on attendance in released-time programs indicates a dip from 1948 to 1952 (although not a steady decline) and a rise since 1952. Yet the impact upon state legislatures has been much less than might have been expected. In most states no New York–type program has been created. It seems to be carried on increasingly at the local level, with a slight legal check on the legality of the specific program provided by the state attorney general. However, it is likely that many varieties of illegal released-time programs exist in school districts throughout the country, exemplifying both noncompliance and an incomplete social causation flowing from the Supreme Court opinions.[61]

Ignorance, lack of interest, and the activity of local pres-

---

[60] *Zorach* v. *Clausen*, 343 U.S. 306 (1952).

[61] Frank J. Sorauf, "*Zorach* v. *Clausen:* The Impact of a Supreme Court Decision," *American Political Science Review*, Vol. 53 (September, 1959), pp. 777–91.

sure groups all account for the limited impact of the two Supreme Court opinions. These intervening factors have not been measured yet, and they are difficult to weigh. Yet they are not beyond the understanding of scholars, and it is likely that a depth survey analysis approach, common in public opinion work, will yield valuable insights in this interesting area.

No doubt social change can also be retarded by Supreme Court opinions. From 1890 to 1937, a majority of the Supreme Court deliberately sought to thwart state and national legislatures which attempted to regulate the economy or to protect individuals against the injuries caused by industrialism. Armed with a laissez-faire view of the due process clause of the Fifth and Fourteenth Amendments, the Supreme Court was extremely successful in slowing the pace of social change by legislation. This negative view was, in time, abandoned as the Court personnel changed and as political pressures grew more intense. However, during those negative years the Courts were not alone in their conservatism. Large numbers of people and social leaders shared their views and supported the Court's opinions. The interaction of conservative opinion leaders and the conservative judiciary was sufficient to offset many (not all) reformist efforts over a 47-year span. Again, the judicial outputs were merely a part of a larger social process and, in time, the Supreme Court was forced to yield to the social feedback produced by post-Depression reformism in the New Deal.

The moral and symbolic output

The Supreme Court is an aristocratic agency within a democracy. Its nine members serve not only as judges who preside over the annual business of the Court but also as sources of moral and symbolic leadership in many secular zones. As Justice Cardozo once put it:

The restraining power of the judiciary does not manifest its chief worth in the few cases in which the legislature has gone beyond the lines that mark the limits of descretion. Rather shall we find its chief worth in making vocal and audible the ideals that might otherwise be silenced, in giving them continuity of life and expression, in guiding and directing choice within the limits where choice ranges.[62]

Above the ordinary legislation of Congress and the states, as above all else in the secular sphere, looms the American Constitution. The imprecise guarantees of the Constitution, "Delphic provisions" Justice Frankfurter called them,[63] invite judicial construction. In the hands of the Supreme Court, the vague phrases of the Constitution have become filled with moral notions.

"Due process" of law now incorporates the idea of a "fair trial," where formerly it protected "liberty of contract." Equal protection of the laws now implies the necessity of the moral principle: "one man one vote." The loss of American citizenship is now considered a "cruel and unusual punishment." The states are forbidden to act in a manner which "shocks the conscience" in the conduct of their criminal law policies.

These moral outputs are not unique to the American Supreme Court, but that Court is more deeply involved in moral language than most other courts in the world. As guardian of a supreme Constitution, the Court has had to elucidate the mysteries of its meaning. In doing so, the Court has sometimes served as the conscience of the nation, or as a prime source of symbolic leadership. Its moral standards may surpass those of the average citizen, but, as in the

---

[62] Benjamin N. Cardozo, *The Nature of the Judicial Process* (New Haven, Conn.: Yale University Press, 1921), p. 94.

[63] Felix Frankfurter, "John Marshall and the Judicial Function," in Arthur E. Sutherland (ed.), *Government under Law* (Cambridge, Mass.: Harvard University Press, 1956), p. 23.

area of the rights of accused persons, its symbolic leadership serves as a corrective upon harsh official practices.

Perhaps, in an increasingly secular society in which religious feeling (not observance) is on the decline, the Supreme Court serves as a generally accepted moral critic. The recent activity of the Court on behalf of individual rights may indicate an unconscious awareness on the part of the Justices that in a time of increased moral relativity there should be one section of the secular order which provides some firm guides to conduct. Although moral rules are a minor output of the Supreme Court, this activity does reveal much about contemporary American society and its search for moral guidance.

It is true that no court can save a society. Professor Dahl's suggestion that protection is not to be found in constitutional forms is sound.[64] The Courts can only help sustain the values of a social system. But one Supreme Court more than another may assist in the process of social and political integration. The *Dred Scott* case was disintegrative, and the school desegregation cases were integrative. By selecting among and manipulating competing moral values, the Supreme Court may assist in the democratization of American life.

---

[64] Robert A. Dahl, *A Preface to Democratic Theory* (Chicago: University of Chicago Press, 1956), p. 134. The homeostatic role of the Supreme Court in its internal operation is explored by S. Sidney Ulmer's "Homeostatic Tendencies in the United States Court" in *Introductory Readings in Political Behavior* (Skokie, Ill.: Rand, McNally & Co., 1961), pp. 167–88.

Afterword

THE EMPIRICAL examination of the nature of the legal system is a relatively new enterprise. Despite the existence of legal institutions over three thousand years of civilization, no scientific study of the place of law in social life was made until the 19th century. From then until today, great changes have taken place in this area of specialty. Fortunately, American writers have been in the vanguard of the new studies, and it is hoped that this book will lend them assistance by consolidating gains already attained, while suggesting future tasks. Political science and sociology are especially concerned with these developments, but they are sure to enrich our understanding of history, economics, and of the substantive law itself.

All peoples have formed some notions of the nature of law and justice. In Plato's *Republic* the first Western philosophy text, several conflicting views of justice were examined, and a mystical, nonrational definition was adopted. Aristotle, more of a realist, examined the existing constitutions of Greece before concluding that different social systems required different types of legal systems (and economic systems). Undoubtedly, ideas of justice and law existed prior to the writings of the Greek philosophers.

The Romans expanded the ideas of law by creating the concept of a natural law shared by all human beings by their very nature. The natural law concept is among the most influential ideas of Western history. It was developed by St. Thomas Aquinas into a comprehensive theology relating man to God. In the Renaissance it was secularized by Grotius, Spinoza, and Vattel. For Americans the natural law was communicated in the writings of John Locke and enshrined in the American Constitution, which is regarded by many as a source of "higher law."

But the legal thought of the writers prior to the 19th century were heavily laden with ethical precepts and moral values. These legal philosophers were less concerned with what the law *is* than with what it *ought* to be. At first, the Greeks sought to discover an ideal legal system for an ideal society. Even later, natural law writers, such as Locke, were concerned with absolute metaphysical "rights" which were superior to ordinary law. But these eminent thinkers were not especially concerned with the law in action—with examining the way the system actually worked at the time they were living in it. It must be said that early legal philosophy is essentially prescientific. In an age of science some of this legal philosophy seems inappropriate, although it is of prime interest to historians of thought.

The limitations of prescientific legal writing are illustrated by the work of Sir William Blackstone, one of the most famous writers in Anglo-American history. Blackstone's *Commentaries on the Laws of England* served as a textbook for lawyers for more than a century. America's leading jurists were once trained by virtually memorizing Blackstone. Like most enlightened men of the 18th century, Blackstone assumed that there was an eternal law of nature from which all human laws derived their authority. He even stated that human laws contrary to the law of nature were invalid. Yet Blackstone was a practical lawyer, and he knew that the English Parliament had virtually absolute power, and no force in England could ignore its laws. Blackstone never perceived that his legal philosophy contradicted his legal experience.

The philosophy of George Wilhelm Friedrich Hegel may be regarded as a turning point in the development of modern legal analysis. Hegel developed a massive theory at the end of the 18th century which embraced all elements of human life. Hegel declared that there was an objective force in history which shaped all events from epoch to epoch. This evolutionary force brought about social change and with it legal change. The system of law was, he thought, designed to realize the inevitable development of the state. The state was not merely a lawmaking institution, but it was also a molder of society, needed to regulate the ethical life of the citizens, their art, religion, and community values.

Hegel attempted to examine the historical relationship of the law to society. His conclusions may be authoritarian, but at least they are based upon some external observation. The role of law in initiating social change is exaggerated, but it is not static. While it can't be said that Hegel was a realist, he must be credited with a fairly modern, secular outlook.

In the early 19th century, a German writer, von Savigny, launched a historical school of legal analysis which was to dominate the thinking of scholars for over a hundred years. Building upon the Hegelian evolutionary view, the historical jurists believed in a unique national version of law related to the gradual development of legal institutions and practices in each country. Detailed investigations into primitive and early periods of legal history were undertaken, but the results were of limited value.

In the middle of the century, the writing of Sir Henry Maine provided the greatest attainments of this approach to legal analysis. Maine went beyond Savigny in undertaking broad comparative studies of the development of legal institutions in primitive and advanced societies. This "cross-cultural research," as it might be called today, led him to the conviction that there were recurrent patterns of evolution which appear in different societies under similar historical circumstances. This led Maine to the general conclusion that all progressive societies tended to enhance the role of the individual and to decrease the significance of family status.

The generalizations of Maine are no longer accepted by

experts today. They were in accord with the evolutionary scientific method developed in the natural sciences at the time, but they were not sound. The problem is not that Maine wasn't a careful researcher. He was. Instead, the difficulty is that the method of research was too limited, too value-laden, and too personal. Historical facts are not so certain as current perceivable facts. Historical method is not the same as modern, empirical scientific method, which depends upon observation, measurement, testing, hypothesis, and general theory. Maine had a theory but no means of verification of the theory.

Karl Marx was also influenced by Hegel. Marx, too, adopted an evolutionary view of law and society. However, Marx stressed the primacy of economic forces. Law was viewed as a mere superstructure imposed upon economic reality. With a change in the economic relationships, there would be a change in the legal system. Law was a reflection of economic class patterns. It was an instrument by which the dominant economic class controlled inferior classes.

The Marxian view of law is not unscientific, according to Marx. But he adopted a special definition of science which was essentially Hegelian and not based upon the natural science approach. The assertions of Marx regarding the social role of law are worthy of testing and verification, but as they appear in Marx's writings, they are supported by biased history and some limited statistical evidence. The ideological motivation of Marx was greater than his scientific integrity. That is why he was led to predict the withering away of the state and the disappearance of law. It was a prediction based on little evidence and intense faith.

In the 20th century, legal philosophers have sought to free themselves from the shackles of abstract reasoning, but a gap between jurisprudence and modern empirical research continues to exist. Hans Kelsen, for example, has tried to create a "pure theory of law" which would be devoid of irrational or ideological elements. Even the use of the word "justice" seems to him incompatible with the scientific method. Kelsen insists that only the positive law itself is the proper subject of study, but he excludes as extraneous the subject matter of psychology, sociology, and politics. He conceives of the legal order as a self-contained entity consisting of interrelated norms. Kelsen denies the existence of natural law or any ethical content in law. Law is merely the apparatus of social control, neutral in character and neither good nor bad in itself.

Kelsen's views are one of the most extreme versions of legal positivism in existence. They are objective and rational, but not necessarily scientific. In insisting on the isolation of law from other social phenomena, he has created a highly artificial analysis. It is, in part, to correct that analysis that this book was written. In many ways, the "pure theory of law" is a major contribution to legal thought, but it is unconnected with the reality of social experience. In an effort to remove the ethical and moral impurities which have clung to the idea of law, Kelsen has sterilized it.

Sociological and psychological theories of law appeared at the end of the 19th century and dominate current American legal philosophy. Sociological jurisprudence, as it is now called, has even influenced judicial opinions and interpretations of statutes and constitutions. This school holds that the positive law cannot be separated from the prevailing values of society. Law is seen as only an attempt to realize social goals. Each area of law is only a portion of real life hardened into a code. Law and social values must be examined as an interwoven fabric of experience and desire.

In America, Roscoe Pound captured the leadership among legal philosophers. Combining the native, practical tradition of pragmatism with sociological jurisprudence, Pound saw the law as an effort to maximize individual wants. As time goes on, the law recognizes more and more human wants and demands. The wants and demands are grouped into "interests," which must be balanced by judges in order to properly apply the law. Pound distinguished between "individual interests," "public interests," and "social interests." Some interests will have priority over others at particular times.

Unfortunately for Pound and for sociological jurisprudence, no method of evaluating competing claims was proposed. Pound left it to the judge to determine the relative value of each claim. Since most legal disputes will contain legitimate competing claims of "interests," it is difficult for this analysis to aid in either the prediction of outcomes or the making of decisions. The measurement of the "public interest" concept would be of enormous value to politicians, judges, and citizens, but it has not yet been done. In fact, the "public interest" may be a value term which merely states a preference, rather than a piece of objective reality.

The sociological jurisprudence movement is by no means a failure. In operation it has humanized the law and made it less rigid. Sociological jurisprudence has made relevant the testimony of psychiatrists, sociologists, economists, and other social scientists whose evidence was formerly considered extralegal or worthless. The law and the social sciences have entered into an uneasy partnership. But the purpose of the blending of law and the social sciences is not the gaining of new insights into the role of the law in the social system; it is merely for the social sciences to serve as a tool of the law. Sociological jurisprudence is not a method of analyzing the operation of the law; it is a system of applying the law. For the social scientist it provides little assistance or guidance. The gap between jurisprudence and social science continues to exist.

Several American judges have contributed insights into the way in which judges do their work. The realistic insights of Oliver Wendell Holmes, Benjamin Cardozo, and Jerome Frank provide a frail bridge between legal philosophy and the empirical analysis of the legal system. In examining the judicial process these men used their intuition and experience to reach their conclusions. All these realists attacked the traditional view of law as a stable and certain phenomenon and insisted on its variability and uncertainty. Frank went so far that he doubted that any legal rule ever exactly fit the facts of real social experience. He was more aware than most legal writers of the importance of the judge's social and economic background and of his psychological quirks.

Jurisprudence has not greatly aided the social scientist. Here and there a brilliant, flashing perception appears. Aristotle, Hegel, or Cardozo may be read for their wisdom or their style but not for their method. Except for the new school of experimental jurisprudents, such as Thomas Cowan (teacher of "Decision-Making Theory" at Rutgers Law School), there is little legal philosophy which is revelant for social scientists. Jurisprudence is fading as an intellectual activity. In its place we may expect to see an analysis of the legal system which surpasses the product of the legal realists —a view of the actual role of law in society.

The approach of the political scientist to legal materials was essentially traditional until World War II. Historical studies of the Supreme Court, such as the monumental work of Charles Warren, were in the accepted mode. Biographies of judges, such as Swisher's *Taney* and Beveridge's *Marshall*, were prevalent. More ambitious scholars, such as Edward Corwin and W. W. Crosskey, produced controversial reinterpretations of key clauses of the Constitution.

The tendency of traditional analysts has been to emphasize the institution of the Supreme Court and to glorify or castigate its role in American life. Robert Harris' *The Judicial Power of the United States* and Charles Black's *The People and the Court* exemplify the former, Fred Rodell's *Nine Men* and Thomas R. Powell's *Vagaries and Varieties in Constitutional Interpretation* the latter.

Among the best examples of traditional scholarship are Robert McCloskey's *The American Supreme Court* and Herman Pritchett's *The American Constitution*. These books attempt to summarize the historical development of legal doctrines by the Supreme Court. In brief compass they accomplish their limited goal of describing the ebb and flow of particular interpretations of the Constitution. This may be called the history of legal doctrines.

Today the traditional scholars are in the minority in the political science field. John W. Burgess, one of the first American political scientists, was a believer in the "science" which he learned in German universities in the 1880's. Writing in 1890, he separated political science from constitutional law and public law, and in his major work, *Political Science and Comparative Constitutional Law*, he attempted to create an evolutionary theory of politics. Burgess felt that in the comparative examination of political and legal institutions he had discovered a scientific method for understanding all societies. None of the traditional scholars of public law would make such claims today. The traditionally oriented writers intend to raise our understanding of the legal process by describing it historically. They do not claim to understand the total social environment of the legal system.

One of the leading traditional scholars began to move away from the earlier approach to constitutional law in 1941. C. Herman Pritchett attempted to produce a less legalistic and a more empirical explanation for Supreme Court decisions. Pritchett showed, in a series of articles and books, that Supreme Court judges tended to vote in blocs and that they jockeyed for support and bargained with each other like ordinary politicians. Although resisted at first, the Pritchett approach is now accepted by most experts as a valid starting point for understanding the judicial process.

After World War II, other analyses appeared. Some researchers attempted to combine forces with sociology and economics, borrowing some of their techniques and their data, while others turned to psychology or anthropology for assistance. The former cluster, which focuses primarily on groups, can be called "conventional" in approach; the latter, which emphasizes individual activity, can be called "behavioral."

Two of the leading conventional works are Herbert Jacob's *Justice in America* and Victor Rosenblum's *Law as a Political Instrument*. Both attempt to relate legal decisions to the social and economic environment in which courts make decisions. Both question the traditionalist assumptions regarding the role of precedent. Both are interested in the actual context of judicial policy making. Samuel Krislov, Martin Shapiro, Joel Grossman, and Kenneth Vines have each contributed valuable additions to conventional scholarship.

The impress of sociology upon political science is clearest in the area of small-group behavior. In 1958, Eloise Snyder suggested that the Supreme Court might be analyzed in the same manner in which sociologists studied small groups, clubs, and associations. Following this suggestion, David Danielski and Walter Murphy are interested in examining the personal interactions of judges, applying the methods of group dynamics to the Supreme Court. John Schmidhauser and Stuart Nagel have started on the still longer road of relating the judge's social, economic, and political background to his decision making.

The emphasis upon the personal attributes of the judges has marked the behavioral approach to legal analysis. Behavioralists are not unaware of legal, social, and political factors, but they prefer to stress the factors of judicial ideology, judicial attitudes, and judicial action. Behavioralists expect that the quantification, measurement, and prediction of judicial decision making will result from their efforts. Treating an outcome-decision as a "vote," they hope to scale and compare judicial decisions in different areas of substantive law according to modern statistical techniques. By this psychological-mathematical method, behavioralists believe that they can match the scientific accomplishments of other social sciences, and even of the natural scientists.

The behavioral approach tends to degrade the significance of legal texts and of legal reasoning. Beneath the surface of the case, they contend, lies the personal motivation of the judges. This motivation can be detected by measurement of their decisions, not merely by perusing their opinions. Glendon Schubert, Fred Kort, S. Sidney Ulmer, Harold Spaeth, Joseph Tanehaus, and Stuart Nagel are among the leading practitioners.

The sociology of law has a separate kind of development. Two of the pioneers of sociology, Max Weber and Émile Durkheim, did some of their major work in the area of law. The sociologists of law are primarily interested in the legal profession itself, its method of conceptualization, and the way in which it solves practical tasks. The uniqueness of the legal method of structuring social events is a matter of special interest.

Sociology of law and modern political science have begun to converge since World War II in their treatment of the empirical operation of law. Both are concerned with the process of judicial decision making and the role of lawyers. Content analysis of legal thinking, the growth of the legal profession, the social role of the profession, and the means of communication adopted within it are all of greater concern to sociology than to political science, but either field might study these phenomena. However, it must be admitted that sociology is much less culture-bound than political science. Cross-cultural comparisons, anthropological and historical comparisons, are much more likely to be made by sociologists.

The purpose of the scientific method is to produce transmissible knowledge. The scientist must collect data, develop hypotheses, evaluate the hypotheses, and integrate the find-

ings. The scientist must try to take the facts as he finds them
and intrude upon them as little as possible. In the study of
the legal system, several methods of fact-gathering have
proven useful. What divides the experts today is integration and explanation of the facts. Social scientists all agree
that a new approach is needed to collate their effort.

The systems analysis approach adopted in this book is not
new. But it can provide a common meeting ground for students and scholars interested in how the legal system works.
Like many analyses it is artificial and abstract, but by providing a common terminology it may prevent needless verbal disputes. The systems analysis approach has previously
been used by David Easton, Glendon Schubert, Walter Murphy, and Stuart Nagel, among others. It is expanded and
developed here.

The advantage of the systems analysis approach is that
it identifies and separates the important from the less important problems. For example, the compliance problem
treated in the last chapter is one which requires a great
deal more emphasis. All the existing studies deal with the
dramatic and sensational problems. Desegregation and
Bible-reading are interesting problems, but are they typical?
In what areas is noncompliance more likely to occur? When
does noncompliance produce feedback and a new input into
the legal system? These are fascinating and significant problems.

On a broader level, Americans should want to know how
other legal systems are joined to their social and political
systems. It appears that certain legal systems reflect the
culture of the society in which they are found, but in what
way? A comparative systems analysis approach would be a
vast improvement upon John W. Burgess' famous book. It
might achieve some of the goals he set.

The new nations provide an estimable laboratory for this
purpose. In Asia and Africa, new legal and social systems
are being formed under our eyes. Political independence has

led to a need for conscious creation of a framework for society and the law. Considerable experimentation is under way as these societies grope toward nationhood, and the search for a viable legal system is part of this quest.

Frontiers for students

The use of cybernetic terminology alerts us to many questions which are still unsolved, and which, in our present state of knowledge, appear insoluble. The unknown areas are like the dark side of the moon—we realize that they exist, but we have only a dim picture of them. But men shall one day land on the moon and know its geography as well as their home county's. In the same way, the legal system will be completely understood when social scientists and students explore it and map its contours.

The process of scientific discovery and verification is slow and laborious. Many students will have to spend their time, energies, and money to work out the details of some of the suggestions found here. Term papers and scholarly articles can fill out the missing spaces.

Among the problems which should be considered are:

1. *Compliance.* Empirical studies of compliance with state high court rulings or administrative decisions are very rare. It is suspected that compliance varies in different categories of substantive law, so that there may be greater compliance with property decisions than with criminal law decisions. Compliance may also be related to the prestige of a high court or the visibility to the public of a court decision.
2. *Direct causation related to external inputs.* It should be possible to examine specific extralegal material and relate it to decisions of courts in many jurisdictions. For example, one might examine references to popular books, such as Gunnar Myrdahl's *An American Dilemma* or Rachel Carson's *Silent Spring* or Michael Harrington's *The Other America.* Also, a count may be made of footnote references to such materials

for particular courts in particular areas and categories of law.

3. *The relationship of output to the race or social class of a party.* Some work has begun in this area, but an examination of sentencing in criminal law cases on a statistical basis needs to be done.

4. *The initiation of a civil case input.* How does an individual perceive that he has suffered an injury? Is this perception subject to regional variation? Who are the litigation-prone individuals? What psychological function is performed by bringing a suit?

5. *The initiation of a criminal case input.* How many arrests result in prosecution? What is the articulation between the police and the prosecutor? What category of crime is most and least litigated? What is the relationship between prosecutors, probation officers, and other social workers? How does class status or race effect the decision to prosecute?

6. *Feedback and evasion.* What category of law is most subject to feedback? How do legislatures "evade" court rulings by changing the common law? What are the time-spans of feedback reactions in different categories of law?

7. *Comparative studies.* Comparisons of different styles of output are uncommon. Cross-national comparisons are needed in areas such as compulsory arbitration or sentencing procedures. Great difficulties can arise, however, when one input or output element is taken out of the context of a whole legal system. Nonetheless, these comparisons are needed to discover common traits among different legal systems and to assist in reformist activity by learning from the experience of other nations. Gross comparisons between "the French legal system" and "the English legal system" cannot yet be made.

It should be obvious from this brief list that many techniques will have to be mastered to assemble the data. Students will have to familiarize themselves with documentary material, including cases, statutes, and administrative rules. Beyond this, individual interview work, such as meeting prosecutors, lawyers, judges, probation officers, and other public officials will be useful. Familiarity with sampling techniques will be needed if questionnaires or other opinion data are to be assembled. Statistical training will be needed for those concerned with demonstrating the existence or nonexistence of empirical causation. Mastery of the construction of scalograms may be required for studies of judicial attitudes.

Students cannot be satisfied with data obtained in a library if that material is not appropriate. In framing research the most important thing is to refine your question. The research should be an attempt to answer a specific question or to verify a particular hypothesis. Extraneous data must be pruned away, and the student must learn to narrow his topic and make it manageable in terms of the time and resources available. Your laboratory is the courtroom, the judge's chamber, and the attorney's office. A receptive inquirer can learn much if he knows what he is looking for.

On the whole, it is best to build on the work of another, rather than to strive for originality. A vast and growing body of literature is available on aspects of the legal system. It should be possible to find one or two which appeal to you and to extend upon or improve them. Studies made of federal agencies can be duplicated for state agencies and vice versa. Antiquated articles can be revised and, although cautiously, even refuted. Grandiose reinterpretations of legal history or of the meaning of legal phrases are usually unneeded. Similarly, judicial biography is usually available and requires little improvement. Above all, avoid novelty for its own sake, since your results must not only be valid, they must also be communicable.

Further on the horizon are studies of "lag" and "homeostasis." "Lag" is the difference in time between changes which occur within a whole system and the awareness within a part of the system of the change. The concept concerns the time period for correction within which a system reacts to its environment. Much more must be learned about problems of historical correction within the legal system before research into "lag" can advance. The homeostatic operation of the legal system is not clearly understood because the process of regularization and stabilization of society is not yet grasped by sociologists. Progress in both areas may await general advances in the social sciences.

Finally, the boundary line between the legal and the political systems is constantly shifting, as is the size of these systems within the social system. Matters like privacy are now legal issues, while many other once public matters are now private. Once it was possible for a jilted fiancée to sue her former betrothed for breach of promise. Today, such suits are not entertained in the courts. The expectations of society have changed. The limits of law are not fixed eternally, and we must remember that the law cannot solve all social problems. Americans in particular should recognize that legislation cannot make men good, nor repeal the physical laws of nature.

Index

A

Administrative agencies, regulation of, 206–8
Administrative Division, 78
Administrative Office of the U.S. Courts, 76
Administrative Procedure Act of 1946, 24, 206
Administrative process, 139–41
Admiralty and maritime jurisdiction, 215
Adversary system, 120–23
Advisory opinions, 166–69
Alien and Sedition Acts, 187
Amendments
　First, 202, 212, 224
　Fifth, 196, 209, 226
　Ninth, 211
　Tenth, 197–98
　Eleventh, 52
　Fourteenth, 26–27, 52, 170, 209, 211, 212, 226
　Sixteenth, 52
　Twenty-Third, 52
　Twenty-Fourth, 52
　Twenty-Fifth, 52
American Bar Association, 37, 84
　removal of judges, 103–4
　screening of judicial nominations, 97, 99–100
American Federation of Labor—Congress of Industrial Organizations, 62
American Law Institute, 37–38
American Medical Association, 62
Answer, 146
Antitrust Division of U.S. Justice Dept., 78
Appeals, 74, 141–43
　and clemency, homeostasis, 87–89
　courts of, 72, 74
Appellant, 142
Appellate court, 70, 71
Appointment, U.S. Supreme Court, 99–101
Aristotle, 229, 235
Arnold, Thurmond, 82

B

Baker v. *Carr,* 26–27
Bargaining for pleas, 131
Bible reading, 219–20
Bill of Rights, U.S., 209, 211, 213
Black, Hugo, 63, 196
Blackstone, Sir William, 230
Bloc analysis, 108
Board of Parole, U.S., 161
Brandeis, Louis, 39, 100, 195
Brief, 56
Brown v. *Board of Education of Topeka,* 137
Buffington, Joseph, 102
Bureau of Prisons, 161
Burgess, John W., 236, 239
Burr, Aaron, 189

C

Cardozo, Benjamin, 147, 234, 235
　quoted, 226–27
Case, 16
Case or controversy rule, 191
Cease and desist order, 164
Certification, 75
Certiorari
　defined, 75
　power to issue, 218
　in Supreme Court decisions, 192–93
Chandler incident, 103
Chase, Samuel, 189
Circuit Courts, 70
City solicitor, 83
Civil Aeronautics Board, 164
Civil judgments, 154–58
Civil law, 13–14
Civil Rights Act of 1964, 221
Civil Rights Division, 78
Civil Service Commission, 97
Civil suit, 127–29
Claims, U.S. Court of, 76
Clark, Ramsey, 97
Clark, Tom, 100
Clayton Act, 47
Code Civil, 14
Commission plan, 104